UNIVERSITY OF EVANSVILLE
HARLAXTON COLLEGE LIBRARY
HARL
G
HARL
ROO

27H.2/HIN

D0421516

GOD AND HISTORY

Aspects of British Theology, 1875–1914

UNIVERSITY OF EVANSVILLE
HARLAXTON COLLEGE LIBRARY
HARLAXTON MANOR
GRANTHAM, LINCS.

GOD AND HISTORY
Aspects of British Theology
1875–1914

———•———

PETER HINCHLIFF

UNIVERSITY OF EVANSVILLE
HARLAXTON COLLEGE LIBRARY
HARLAXTON MANOR
GRANTHAM, LINCS.

CLARENDON PRESS · OXFORD
1992

Oxford University Press, Walton Street, Oxford OX2 6DP
Oxford New York Toronto
Delhi Bombay Calcutta Madras Karachi
Petaling Jaya Singapore Hong Kong Tokyo
Nairobi Dar es Salaam Cape Town
Melbourne Auckland
and associated companies in
Berlin Ibadan

Oxford is a trade mark of Oxford University Press

Published in the United States
by Oxford University Press, New York

© Peter Hinchliff 1992

All rights reserved. No part of this publication may be reproduced,
stored in a retrieval system, or transmitted, in any form or by any means,
electronic, mechanical, photocopying, recording, or otherwise, without
the prior permission of Oxford University Press

British Library Cataloguing in Publication Data
(Data available)
ISBN 0–19–826333–3

Library of Congress Cataloging in Publication Data
Hinchliff, Peter Bingham.
God and history: aspects of British theology. 1875–1914/Peter
Hinchliff.
Includes bibliographical references and index.
1. Great Britain—Church history—19th century. 2. Great Britain—
Church history—20th century. 3. Theology, Doctrinal—Great
Britain—History—19th century. 4. Theology, Doctrinal—Great
Britain—History—20th century. I. Title.
BR759.H5G 1992
280'.0941—dc20
ISBN 0–19–826333–3

Typeset by Cambrian Typesetters, Frimley, Surrey
Printed in Great Britain by
Bookcraft (Bath) Ltd
Midsomer Norton, Bath

For Richard,
whose suggestions, criticisms, and encouragement
were a very great help.

Acknowledgements

THIS book would not have been written at all were it not for the generosity of my colleagues, the Master and Fellows of Balliol College, Oxford, who granted me leave for the Hilary and Trinity terms of 1989. During that time I spent some weeks in Glasgow as the Newlands Visitor to the University, doing research in the archives there. I am grateful to the Principal and Senate of the University for that opportunity and to the University Archivist, Mr Moss, for a great deal of kind and patient help. I was also fortunate enough to visit the Church Divinity School of the Pacific in Berkeley, California and the Episcopalian Theological Seminary in Alexandria, Virginia. Both these institutions provided me with the context and library resources in which it was possible to get a very considerable proportion of the actual writing done. I am extremely grateful to the acting Dean of CDSP (Professor Donn Morgan) and to Dean Reid of the Virginia Theological Seminary and their colleagues for much help and friendliness. I am also grateful to John Prest, Peter Ghosh, and David Nicholls for some extremely helpful criticisms and suggestions. Several graduate students working in nineteenth-century history under my supervision, Arthur Burns, Felicity Magowan, Paul Supple, and Alan Wilson, have helped me to understand a variety of issues or drawn my attention to valuable sources of information.

Contents

INTRODUCTION

THIS book is not, of course, a complete account of British theology at the end of the nineteenth century. Such works already exist, notably B. M. G. Reardon's *Religious Thought in the Victorian Age*. I have set myself a rather different task. One of the principal concerns, if not the principal concern, of many theologians in the period was the whole range of problems raised by new ways of understanding history and its relationship with faith. Concentrating on those who attempted to come to terms with these new ideas has enabled me to deal with the thought of the selected theologians in some detail. I have usually focused attention upon one particular work by each writer (except where—as happened surprisingly often—he changed his mind rather dramatically). This has enabled me to quote rather more lengthily than is usually possible and thus convey the real flavour of the style as well as the argument of the person quoted. I have also tried to sketch in the historical context by devoting some time and attention to the institutions within which the theologians worked, the universities as well as the churches of Britain.

Even as a survey of writings about the relationship between faith and history, what follows is not exhaustive. There were many who simply ignored the new ideas and continued to reassert conventional ones. I have not included them nor have I attempted to deal with those who believed that the new ideas could not be accommodated and who therefore abandoned belief. Indeed, I have not incorporated everyone who tried to grapple positively with the new understanding of history. Nor is this even a representative selection, in the sense that there is one person chosen from each school of thought: where ideas were particularly tenacious more than one exponent of them may be included. I cannot even claim that the thinkers who are dealt with were chosen because they were the most influential, most important, or most brilliant of all the possible candidates for inclusion. Indeed their thought was sometimes wrong-headed, untidy, or illogical; but they all seem to me, nevertheless, to have had interesting things to say.

This book, though it is about ideas, is not really a '*history* of ideas'. No serious or sustained attempt is made to demonstrate or explain the source of ideas or how the ideas of one thinker are related to those of another—unless there is clear evidence to rely on. For the same reason there has been no attempt to show whether the ideas of the British thinkers derived from or were influenced by Continental—and particularly German—scholars except when they themselves indicated that they were so indebted. This may give the false impression that each individual lived in a self-contained world of his own, but that has seemed preferable to a merely speculative attempt to say where a writer got his ideas from. There may be cases where he did not know where they came from. Even if he did know, he may not have acknowledged his sources, and sometimes his ideas may actually have been original.

Their world was, admittedly, a small one. They all knew each other and also knew nearly everyone else who was at all likely to be interested in the ideas they were expounding. They were all men, they were almost all middle class—and upper rather than lower middle class. They were preponderantly members of the established rather than the free Churches. Most of them were educated in the same institutions. The chief exception (the Scottish and working-class sectarian, A. M. Fairbairn) was someone who came to be regarded almost as if he were a middle-class, Oxford-and-therefore-Anglican Englishman. It is not, therefore, surprising that so many of them were concerned with the same issues.

BACKGROUND
Historical and Religious Understanding
in Nineteenth-Century Britain

In the late 1830s Thomas Arnold, headmaster of Rugby and formerly a fellow of Oriel, published his edition of Thucydides' *Peloponnesian War*, the first volume of which contained an appendix on the transition of nations 'from what I may call a state of childhood to manhood'.[1] In it he argued that there is a natural progress by which a country grows and develops, just as a human being does. This appendix was attached specifically to a sentence of Thucydides describing the transition from limited monarchy in the ancient Greek kingdoms to rule by despot. Using this as an example of the way in which government by aristocracy, based on birth, gives way to government by the wealthy, Arnold maintained that there was a natural process of development which, in the end, would lead all nations towards government by 'the commons'. England was, for Arnold, the obvious paradigm. Other factors such as geographical conditions, war, and outside interference, might distort this natural development but, left alone, that was the way the progression would go.

The analogy of nation with individual was not new. Arguments in favour of the establishment of religion had often maintained that, as a human being had a soul as well as a body, a nation needed a religion as well as a political structure. And throughout the nineteenth century the thought that societies, institutions, and even ideas developed in a manner analogous to that of individual human beings remained tremendously attractive. Herbert Spencer's conception of an evolutionary principle controlling and directing the history of the universe at every level, made the idea still more popular. In the second half of the century there were many theorists

---

[1] Thucydides, *The History of the Peloponnesian War*, with notes, chiefly historical and geographical, by Thomas Arnold, DD, 2nd edn. (Oxford, 1840), 503.

who believed that religion, too, always developed consistently and according to a natural progression as if it were an organism.

Arnold's concept, then, was in some ways very typical of the nineteenth century. Nor was it unsophisticated. He perceived very clearly that social 'sciences' were not sciences in the same sense as natural sciences. He said:

> even where the disturbing cause is certain in its interference, as in mechanics the resistance of the air always prevents a body from obeying the natural laws of motion, still the general principles are universally held to be essential to the attainment of a true knowledge of it. Much more does this hold good in political science, where disturbing causes need not of necessity come into action and what is true in principle may sometimes . . . be no less true in practice.[2]

The notion permitted Arnold to develop his idea of history as the biography of a nation and to distinguish between ancient and modern history. Both these ideas would reappear, in a modified version, in his inaugural lecture as professor of Modern History at Oxford.[3] But in his appendix to Thucydides, ancient history was the history of the 'childhood' of nations: modern history that of their more mature phases. The ancient history of one nation might coincide chronologically, therefore, with the modern history of another.

One of the advantages of the underlying analogy was that it allowed Arnold to account for the complex character of causation in history. For it is always a problem to know precisely how, or even whether, event A can be said to be *caused* by event B. Maintaining that there was a natural development or progression, which he thought could be proved or at least identified by examining certain periods of history as if they were controlling cases, he could then show how other factors modified, delayed, or hastened, that development. Not every historian perceived the question of causation quite so simply. Thomas Carlyle, a contemporary of Arnold, treated history as if it were, not so much the biography of a nation, as a series of biographies of the great. His history of the French Revolution begins with a lengthy sketch of the reign of Louis XV, padded out with arch allusions to, and apostrophizings of, his leading courtiers and courtesans. 'The

[2] Thucydides, *The History of the Peloponnesian War*, 514 f.
[3] Below, p. 11 f.

masses' receive no attention until the second chapter of Book II. Yet Carlyle saw causes as cohering in no single fundamental framework. He had said that actual events 'are no wise so simply related to each other as parent and offspring are; every single event is the offspring not of one, but of all other events, prior or contemporaneous, and will in turn combine with all others to give birth to new'.[4]

It is interesting to find that historians in the first half of the nineteenth century were very much aware that there were problems inherent in talking about causes in history as if they could be observed empirically. More than a century and a half later we are still commonly taught, as one of the first things we learn about history, that events have causes. We absorb the lesson quite unconsciously and, probably, those who teach it to us are as unconscious of teaching it as we are of learning it. 'What are the causes of the French Revolution?', we are asked. Without overmuch agonizing about the relationship between cause and effect, we answer that it happened *because* all wealth, all power, and all privilege belonged to an aristocracy, which also escaped the burden of responsibility which might have been expected to accompany those advantages. It simply seems to us fairly obvious that the one *caused* the other.

Further consideration, however, may suggest that we have jumped to an unjustified conclusion and that causation, in the normal sense in which we use the word, may not be applicable to history. There are two problems and both were touched on in Carlyle's remark. One is that the link between what we have labelled 'cause' and what we have labelled 'effect' is not simple or demonstrable. Carlyle pointed to the relationship of child and parent as an example of the direct and obvious cause and effect relationship. We might find a scientific experiment—in which the action of one element upon another produces a repeatable, testable result—a more natural example to use. The relationship between oppression and revolution is obviously much more tenuous than that. A revolution does not happen every time there is a certain degree of oppression. And, in that case, we are almost bound to ask

---

[4] T. Carlyle, 'On History', in *Critical and Miscellaneous Essays: Collected and Republished*, 7 vols. (London, 1872), i. 257. Carlyle was actually contrasting the 'solid' nature of history as experienced with the 'linear' character of history as narrated but what he said was directly related to the question of causation.

whether it is possible to talk—as many nineteenth-century historians thought it was—about 'scientific' history.

It was evidently a great temptation, a century and a half ago, to think that the study of the history of a particular nation or period would reveal certain truths, perhaps especially moral truths. One hoped that once one had recognized those truths, one could confirm them over and over again in other historical periods. Thomas Arnold, because of his conviction that history was national biography, maintained that a nation's outer life reflected its inner life, and its inner life, in turn, was controlled by its aim or purpose. One could distinguish clearly between those nations whose aims were 'unmoral', concerned only with wealth or power, and those which sought justice and humanity and were therefore moral. And, because the government of nations had the power to direct the actions of 'moral beings' they were capable of being classified as good or evil.[5]

And a nation's inner life consists in its action upon and within itself. Now in order to the perfecting of itself, it must follow certain principles, and acquire certain habits; in other words, it must have its laws and institutions adapted to the accomplishment of its great end. On these the characters of its people so mainly depend, that if these be faulty, the whole inner life is corrupted; if these be good, it is likely to go on healthfully.[6]

If one saw the history of nations in some such way as this, one might be encouraged to look for lessons in history. Arnold certainly believed that history held many treasures which might be won from it.

Whatever there is of variety and intense interest in human nature, in its elevation, whether proud as by nature or sanctified as by God's grace; in its suffering, whether blessed or unblessed, a martyrdom or a judgment; in its strange reverses, in its varied adventures, in its yet more varied powers, its courage and its patience, its genius and its wisdom, its justice and its love, that also is the measure of the interest and variety of history.[7]

It is not, however, always easy to believe that history proceeds with such regularity that lessons learnt from one period may be applied to another. Part of the problem lies precisely in the fact that it is difficult to apply *universal* laws of cause and effect to history.

[5] T. Arnold, *An Inaugural Lecture on the Study of Modern History* (Oxford, 1841), 15.   [6] Ibid. 20.   [7] Ibid. 29.

In modern times Karl Popper has tried to provide an example of a law which might have a universal application. He argues that 'if of two armies which are about equally armed and led, one has a tremendous superiority in men, then the other never wins'.[8] This may seem on the surface to be a fairly obvious instance of a universal causal law; but, in fact, history is littered with famous counter-examples which are the raw material of a variety of epic tales. The truth is that causal explanations in history are usually of a small-scale kind. For instance, W. H. C. Frend has argued that the Donatist schism flourished in those parts of fourth-century North Africa where the annual rainfall was less than twenty inches.[9] The argument is not at all an absurd one. Where there was less rain than that, there was extreme poverty. This poverty bred the kind of nationalism that encouraged Donatism. But this is not a *universal* law for it is applicable only in this one, limited context and even then one would hesitate to use it predictively. Yet common sense enables us still to think that there is some *explanatory* force in such a claim.

A further problem about causation in history is, however, hinted at in Carlyle's remark. Even if we accept that there is a causal connection between two facts, Occam's razor (the principle of economy) does not apply to historical explanation. One cannot assume that, because drought explains heresy, that particular explanation is complete and exclusive. There may be a great many other factors which also contributed to the existence of that same heresy. In other words the paucity of annual rainfall may be no more than a *part* of the explanation. If Carlyle is right and an event is the product 'of all other events, prior or contemporaneous, and will in turn combine with all others to give birth to new', other possibly contributing explanations do not immediately become otiose from the moment that we hit upon the relationship between heresy and drought.

There is a sense in which causality in history was the central issue for all the theologians to be considered in this book. If, as Carlyle thought, each historical event fits into a web of other events which together constitute both the source from which the event originates

[8] K. Popper, *The Open Society and Its Enemies* (Princeton, 1950), 448.

[9] W. H. C. Frend, *The Donatist Church: A Movement of Protest in Roman North Africa* (Oxford, reprint of 1971), 29. ff. Frend himself would be inclined to label Donatism a protest movement rather than a schism or a heresy.

and the destination in which it finds its place, then all historical events must belong together in a direct and obvious sense. Christian faith, and therefore Christian theology, possesses a historical dimension but the historical facts to which faith is related cannot be exempted from this web of interconnection without ceasing to be real facts of history. Nineteenth-century theologians came to realize this in a way in which their predecessors had not, on the whole, perceived it. Christians had always claimed that their religion was a historical religion, but this had usually been taken to mean that it was based on actual events and facts of history as opposed to the 'myths' which were said to be the stuff of other religions. It had not been perceived that to make such a claim meant that Christianity was lumbered with the problems as well as the advantages of historicity; and throughout the second half of the nineteenth century the problem of historicity, in one form or another, haunted the theologians.

As history itself became a more subtle, complex and sophisticated discipline, the problems of historicity became more obvious. If a religion was founded upon events in history, and the events possessed the particularity which all events must possess, how could they be of universal, redeeming significance? If a religion was historical, it must itself possess a history, all of which (and not merely the initial, founding event) existed within time and therefore within change. How could one be sure that contemporary Christianity was still the same religion as that which had been founded by Christ and his apostles? And if religious authority depended, in some sense, upon the continuity of the Church of the present age with the Church as originally constituted, how was authority related to history? Above all other problems, there was the most crucial question of all: how was a 'historical' religion to be related to God who could not be confined within time and space? In metaphysical terms, of course, that was no new question; but it was now being asked in terms of an understanding of history perceived as a real process. Because Christians claimed that their religion had been founded by a divine being, incarnate within a specific time and place, there was a sense in which they were compelled to regard God's actions as, in principle, observable in history and tied into the interconnected web of events, in precisely the same way as were human actions. That also created problems.

Perhaps the most painful question arose out of the development of the historical-critical method. Van Harvey has argued that there was a group of contemporary thinkers, and especially Ernst Troeltsch, whose ideas have had a peculiarly disconcerting effect on modern theology. He describes the discomforting impact of Troeltsch's thought as follows:

He discerned that the development of [the historical-critical] method constituted one of the great advances in human thought; indeed that it presupposed a revolution in the consciousness of Western man. To be sure, Western culture, in contrast to many others, has always been characterized by a sense of history. But only in the nineteenth century did this manifest itself in a sustained and critical attempt to recover the past by means of the patient analysis of evidence and the insistence on the impartiality and truthfulness of the historian. The distinctions between history and nature, fact and myth; expressions like the growth of language and the development of the state; the tendency to evaluate events in terms of their origins; the awareness of the relativity of one's own norms of thought and valuation; all these, Troeltsch saw, are but the by-products of a change so profound that our period deserves to be put alongside those of previous cultural epochs as a unique type.[10]

Most obviously of all, perhaps, this revolution involved the realization that the modern historian, possessing scientific knowledge about the way the universe and its components behave, cannot assume that things behaved differently in an earlier age when human beings did not possess that knowledge. The historian cannot simply report the explanation offered for events by his sources as if he shared the ignorance of the period he was writing about. Yet his sources would appear to offer evidence of things which the new scientific outlook did not encourage one to accept. The historian Lecky, for instance, pointed out in the 1860s that the *evidence* told heavily in favour of the existence of such things as witchcraft and miracles but that no nineteenth-century reader, at any rate if he were a Protestant, would believe that they had happened.[11]

There is a curious parallel here with the problem that seems to have afflicted many missionaries from quite early in the nineteenth century. If you found yourself living among people who believed in

[10] V. A. Harvey, *The Historian and the Believer: The Morality of Historical Knowledge and Christian Belief* (London, 1967), 3 f.

[11] W. E. H. Lecky, *History of the Rise and Influence of Rationalism in Europe*, 2 vols. (London, 1865), 155 ff.

witchcraft and practised the hunting out of witches, did you react by saying that witchcraft was a non-existent crime and no civilized man could believe in it for a moment?[12] And, if you took that line how could you make a clear and precise distinction between acts of witchcraft, which were nonsense, and the healing miracles recorded in the New Testament, which were acts of divine power which must be believed as a matter affecting one's salvation? For, in practice, the historian put aside the evidence in many of the parallel cases because it just seemed unreasonable not to do so. But he did not always do this consistently and it was difficult to say why he should choose to do so in some cases and not in others. He was, in fact, obeying one of the cardinal rules of modern historical scholarship—the importance of following the evidence—in some cases, and another cardinal rule—that the laws of nature do not change—in others. Because the nineteenth century was an era of radical change, not just in scientific knowledge but in scientific presuppositions and methodology, it was inevitable that, generally speaking, it was the second of these cardinal rules which prevailed in the long run.

But the changes described by Van Harvey as if they were instantaneous, radical, and revolutionary, actually took place, in both history and theology, slowly and unevenly. The nineteenth century saw the publication of a great many works which have become classics in the history of history. The hundred years that followed the publication of the first volume of Gibbons' *Decline and Fall of the Roman Empire* in 1776 produced such landmarks as Macaulay's *History of England from the Accession of James the Second*, Lecky's *History of England in the Eighteenth Century*, J. A. Froude's *History of England from the Fall of Wolsey to the Defeat of the Spanish Armada*, Freeman's *History of the Norman Conquest*, Stubbs's *Constitutional History of England*, and John Richard Green's *History of the English People*. The equally important contributions to the study of history made by Frederic Maitland, Lord Acton, and S. R. Gardiner occurred only just outside the limits of that hundred-year period. It was, in other words, a century that saw the emergence of modern British history.

Having said that, however, one has immediately to add that these historians stand in no straight line of developing thought. They do

---

[12] See P. Hinchliff (ed.), *The Journal of John Ayliff* (Cape Town, 1971), 43—an entry in a young missionary's diary for 10 Nov. 1825.

not all fall into the same general school or tradition nor did they all see English history in the same way. Just as it is always difficult to put nineteenth-century politicians into watertight compartments of political faction neatly defined by a set of principles, or to allocate nineteenth-century theologians to clearly identified ecclesiastical parties, so it would be unwise to say that some historians indubitably belong in this school of thought and others in that one. There are always fine shades of distinction, counter-influences, interconnections, and cross-fertilizations, personal links, and friendships, which blur the edges of each group. This is precisely the sort of case where, though one can only progress at all by making generalizations, every generalization is bound to be misleading.

It is possible to say that in the course of the century historians gradually came to concern themselves more with recovering the past by advancing this or that particular *interpretation* of events. Historical narrative, of course, always had concealed a particular interpretation within the narration itself; and earlier historians had written in order to extol the glories of their ancestors, to point a moral, or to prove the rightness of a cause. Even Gibbon, in his final analysis of the reasons for the collapse of Rome, had been concerned to identify the moral as well as the material causes of decay—and to see them as generally and universally applicable to human history. However, by the end of the nineteenth century the respected historian had become cooler and more detached, less anxious to make moral judgements. Lord Acton, who died in 1902, vigorously asserted that it was the function of an historian to maintain moral standards. By that date such views made him a controversial and somewhat eccentric figure.[13]

Claims that historians' understanding of their task changed during the course of the nineteenth century are, however, true only in a very general sense. Historians in the middle of the century were still drawing moral lessons from history as Thomas Arnold's writings demonstrate. By no means all the authors of the 'landmark' works listed above could reasonably be described as cool and detached. Some of them were very much concerned with history as the annals of their own ancestors. Dr Arnold thought that what marked modern history off most clearly from ancient history was that modern history was the biography of one's own

---

[13] Below, pp. 157 f.

nation and people. The Britons and Romans 'had lived in our country, but they are not our fathers'; 'the history of Caesar's invasions has no more to do with us, than the natural history of the animals which then inhabited our forests'.[14] Arnold's view of history as the biography of a nation was, at least in this respect, more restrictive than Carlyle's view of history as biography pure and simple, because Carlyle's heroes might serve as examples to people of every period and every race.

There was, therefore, no straight line of progressive development in historiography. Understanding of the nature of history developed erratically and a later writer might hold a view that seems to us less sophisticated than those of some of his predecessors. On the other hand, there *is* a sense in which the generalizations are true. Lord Acton may have been a throwback to an earlier age in his claim that a historian's function is to be a judge of morals, but his letter to the contributors to the *Cambridge Modern History*, which was the child of his mind and imagination, insisted that history must be written so that no one would be able to tell where Stubbs, the High Church Bishop of Oxford, had left off and Andrew Fairbairn, the Congregationalist principal of Mansfield College, had taken up the task.[15]

In the same generalized way it is possible to say that this was also a period when virtually every academic discipline was becoming more professional, more decidedly located in the universities, more a subject to be taught, studied, and examined than ever before.[16] History became a field in which the professional historian specialized rather than something in which the classically educated gentlemen-of-affairs (perhaps only very local affairs) might indulge. Incumbents of rural parishes began to find it difficult to write the serious, carefully researched, professional, and detailed studies that were now needed.

Thomas Arnold combined being headmaster of Rugby with holding the Regius chair of Modern History at Oxford for the last few months before his early death in 1842 at the age of 28. Father of the Broad Church party, creator of a powerful institution to

[14] Arnold, *Inaugural Lecture*, 32.

[15] The letter is printed in F. Stern (ed.), *The Varieties of History from Voltaire to the Present* (London, 1957), 247 ff. and NB p. 249.

[16] See e.g. A. J. Engel, *From Clergyman to Don: The Rise of the Academic Profession in Nineteenth Century Oxford* (Oxford, 1983), *passim*.

propagate liberal, undogmatic Christianity, influential as a proponent of a common-sense approach to New Testament scholarship, author of a history of Rome which was well regarded by later 'professional' historians like Freeman,[17] Arnold seems to epitomize the gentleman polymath, memorialized in so many early nineteenth-century Oxford and Cambridge inscriptions—tutor in one subject, professor in another, author of a seminal work in a third. For the truth is that, at Oxford in the 1840s, 'Greats', the general classical honours degree, was the only alternative to the simple pass degree. Everything else, even the sciences, were a spin-off from that great humanist tradition.

But in the second half of the century the situation was changing. By the time William Stubbs, the future bishop, came to occupy the same chair in 1866 the change was well on its way. Though he had been a rural clergyman he had become an outstanding specialist in a particular branch of history—medieval England. His expertise made him an authority in his field but once he had become professor he was much exercized about questions of syllabus, lecturing, and examination. His High Anglican theology led him to claim that papal decretals lacked the force of law in the English Church of the middle ages unless affirmed and promulgated by English synods. But when his own disciple, F. W. Maitland, demonstrated that the English Church, like the rest of the Christian West, had recognized and been bound by papal rulings, Stubbs accepted that it was historical evidence rather than theological presupposition which should determine the matter.[18] In this case, at least, history had become its own master.

One thing worth noting about the nineteenth-century historians who have been mentioned so far, is that so many of them were very directly linked with the theologians who wrote about faith and history and whose ideas are described in this book. J. A. Froude was the younger brother of Hurrell Froude, Newman's friend and

---

[17] J. W. Burrow, *A Liberal Descent: Victorian Historians and the English Past* (Cambridge, 1981), 174.

[18] For the debate between Stubbs and Maitland see *Report of the Commissioners on the Constitution and Working of the Ecclesiastical Courts* (1883); F. W. Maitland, *Roman Canon Law in the Church of England* (London, 1898) and the same author's contribution to the second volume of the *Cambridge Modern History*; W. Stubbs, *Seventeen Lectures on the Study of Medieval and Modern History* (Oxford, 1900). See also E. W. Kemp, *An Introduction to Canon Law in the Church of England* (Oxford, 1957), 11 ff.

protégé, and was embittered and disillusioned by the disastrous influence he believed the Tractarians to have had upon his sibling. Carlyle, a Scotsman with a profound belief in the divine, but impatient of creeds and ecclesiastical institutions, was an early influence upon Edward Caird. Thomas Arnold, as father of the Broad Church movement, played a very large part in forming the ideas of Benjamin Jowett. Stubbs belonged to much the same school of thought as Benson, Westcott, and Lightfoot, believing that history could demonstrate the truth of orthodoxy. Lord Acton may be conceived, as will be argued below, as a forerunner of some of the Catholic Modernists. Since there were these close links between leading figures in the history of history and those who played an important part in the developments and vicissitudes of Christian faith and theology in the nineteenth century, it is not surprising that the relationship of history to theology should have been an important issue in the period.

There is another reason, perhaps, why this particular issue should have come to the fore at the end of the nineteenth century. English historiography throughout the preceding hundred years had been haunted by one particular theme; and the theme itself explains why one has to talk, so often, of 'English' historiography, even when one is comparing it with 'British' theology. For the theme was that the peculiarly English genius for freedom, preference for gradualism over revolution, hatred of tyranny, and resistance to the arbitrary, all took their origin in the forests of Germany in the days of imperial Rome. From that source, in a continuity interrupted only occasionally by incursions from less reasonable and less freedom-loving cultures, there had come the rolling stream of English history.

Inevitably such a theory had a bearing on one's attitude to contemporary politics; and, because it was related to behaviour and beliefs, raised many of the same problems as were raised by the relationship of history to faith. The kind of English historian who looked back to German origins possessed, like the biblical scholars who sought the beginnings of Christianity in the gospels, an original story which was held to authenticate the tradition that developed from it. In each case the truth of the story could be—and was—challenged by historical evidence. In each case there was pressure to modify the ideological or theological claims to bring them into line with what seemed to be the demands of historicity.

The variety of ways in which the theme of German origins was used by historians was paralleled by the range of interpretations of the gospel narratives developed by critical theologians.

In general, by the end of the century, historians and biblical scholars would both be likely to claim a more detached, more professional approach than had existed earlier. Yet in neither case were the protagonists actually proposing to abandon their belief in the essential rightness of the tradition. They merely proposed a more intellectually respectable version of it, supported by more rational arguments. It was always possible to bend history to support the particular tradition—secular as well as religious—which one wished to defend or even create.[19]

The theory of German origins was not a simple one, for there was a sense in which imperial Rome was almost as important to the historians (particularly in the period when they were cultured gentlemen rather than professional academics) as their Teutonic past. For Rome, with Greece, stood for civilization. Gentlemen who had studied the classics at school and university, and wrote in Ciceronian periods, would be bound to think of the inhabitants of the German forests as barbarians. Ideas of law and empire made them the heirs of Rome. What they knew of aesthetics or of political philosophy made them the heirs of ancient Greece.

For the last eighteen hundred years, Greece has fed the human intellect; Rome, taught by Greece and improving upon her teacher, has been the source of law and government and social civilization; and what neither Greece nor Rome could furnish, the perfection of moral and spiritual truth, has been given by Christianity.[20]

Arnold's rhetoric enshrines an idea which a great many mid-century writers would have shared. Yet Arnold, as has been noted, did not really think of himself as having a stake in classical history, in spite of the fact that it was his history of Rome and his work on Thucydides, the Greek historian, which had probably obtained for him his chair at Oxford. For Arnold it was the Teutonic people who had created *modern* history, giving new impetus to the human race as classical civilization came to its end. 'We, this great English nation, whose race and language are now overcoming the earth from one end of it to the other—we were born when the white

---

[19] See E. Hobsbawm and T. Ranger (eds.), *The Invention of Tradition* (Cambridge, 1983). [20] Arnold, *Inaugural Lecture* 38 f.

horse of the Saxons had established his dominion from the Tweed to the Tamar.'[21] He thought, similarly, that France and Frenchmen began to exist when 'Clovis and his Germans' supplanted Roman and 'Keltic' Gaul.

There were many variations on this theme of Teutonic origins. J. R. Green's *History of the English People*, published in the 1870s, was not given that title accidentally. Nor was it intended to be synonymous with a 'History of England'. It was the English *people*, originating in the German forests, who as Teutonic immigrants brought the peculiarly *English* genius to the island. Green, therefore, opened his 'short' history with this account of the English in the fifth century when 'the one country which bore the name of England was what we now call Sleswick':

Of the temper and life of these English folk in this Old England we know little. But from the glimpses which we catch of them when conquest had brought these Englishmen to the shores of Britain, their political and social organization must have been that of the German race to which they belonged. The basis of their society was the free landholder. . . . Justice had to spring from each man's personal action and every freeman was his own avenger.[22]

Such a view of English history could obviously not accommodate, except in some very eccentric versions of the folk narrative, the British Celts. There were other (and Scottish) ways of understanding British history, which laid more emphasis on progress than on continuity. And progress (or lack of it) is the recurring theme of Lecky's writing about Ireland.[23] But, surprisingly, some of the non-English British were willing to accept the implicit arrogance of the dominant interpretation without demur. Thus a late nineteenth-century (normally resolutely, and aggressively, Scottish) clergyman argued for the establishment of a mission in East Africa in somewhat surprising terms. To create a Church of Scotland mission station would be to introduce an 'English' settlement which would (among other things) exhibit proper ideas of government and civilization.[24]

Some versions of the Teutonic theme had a very direct political

---

[21] Arnold, *Inaugural Lecture*, 32.

[22] J. R. Green, *A Short History of the English People* (London, 1874), 2.

[23] J. P. von Arx, *Progress and Pessimism: Religion, Politics and History in Late Nineteenth Century Britain* (Cambridge, Mass., 1985), 101 ff.

[24] The Revd Dr John Macrae writing in the Church of Scotland *Missionary Record* (Feb. 1875), 271.

bearing and were unashamedly designed to show how liberty—that is to say government by a House of Commons which represented all those sound men whose stability was guaranteed by the fact that they possessed a stake in the country—had derived from an almost primordial English tradition. In that story the Anglo-Saxon kingdoms were modern parliamentary England in embryo, with the *witenagemot* the forerunner of the House of Commons. The villains of this story were the Bastard of Normandy who imposed feudal tyranny upon the English, King John, and King Charles I: its heroes were vindicated by the Glorious Revolution; and the first Reform Act was, so to speak, the concluding 'recognition scene' in which what had always been true was manifested at last.

Unfortunately, there were difficulties with some aspects of this version of English history. There was no evidence, for instance, to support the continuity of early parliaments with the Saxon *witenagemot*. Nineteenth-century historians, to whom evidence was becoming more important, made modifications. For Macaulay (writing at about the same time as Arnold) it was Magna Carta, rather than the Teutonic forest, which was the true starting point for the history of English liberty. The High Church Tory, William Stubbs, took from German scholars, a decade or so later, the belief that the free village community was the ancient basis of all English society and had been introduced into Britain by the Anglo-Saxons. So Stubbs came to believe that history was the source of political wisdom as well as of political identity because centralized, codified law bred autocracy, and, conversely, because local precedent-based government guaranteed liberty.

These and other nineteenth-century historians were gradually tempering the tradition to make it conform more to the evidence and to judgement based on evidence. In spite of his suspicions of autocratic, centralized government, Stubbs was willing to recognize that William the Conqueror was not an unmitigated evil and that considerable advantages derived from his conquest. By the end of the century, S. R. Gardiner, though he exhibited some of the characteristics of earlier historians—particularly an anxiety not to burden immature minds with disturbing ideas—was still more sympathetic in his final assessment of the effects of the conquest.

Still more important was William's resolution to be the real head of the English nation. He had weakened it enough to fear it no longer, but he kept it strong enough to use it, if need be, against the Norman barons. He won Englishmen to his side by the knowledge that he was ready to do them justice whenever they were wronged, and he could therefore venture to summon the fyrd whenever he needed support, without having to fear that it would turn against him.[25]

Gardiner's account may gloss over some of the harshness of William's rule but he had clearly ceased to believe in anything like a 'Norman yoke', imposed tyrannically upon free Englishmen.

If one were to take Arnold's view of history seriously and assert that while Saxon history was part of the Englishman's own national biography, Celtic or Roman history was not, that left one with a problem. In his acknowledgement that the English owed much to Greece and Rome, Arnold added that 'what neither Greece nor Rome could furnish, the perfection of moral and spiritual truth, has been given by Christianity'. Since Arnold believed that Greece and Rome were not a real part of England's history, there was a risk in putting Christianity in the same category. It made Christianity, too, seem to be an outside influence rather than an integral component in the story of the nation's growth to maturity. Unless one could find some means of grafting the Christian story into the English story, Jesus would seem to be no more a part of one's own national history than the Greeks, the Romans, or the Celts.

This grafting process seems chiefly to have happened in two ways. The English Reformation, with its tales of heroism in times of persecution and of national triumph in times of foreign, papistical attack, provided one means of acquiring a vivid sense of having participated in a corporate biography of which Christianity was a natural part. The other was the belief that one's national history had been guided by 'providence' if not by God. J. A. Froude seems to have combined these two beliefs in his view of history. It is true that he was concerned to treat history scientifically in the sense of seeking to 'explain everything, whenever possible, by the instrumentality of causes which are now in operation'. 'The early records of all nations are full of portents and marvels; but we no longer believe those portents to have taken place in actual fact.'[26] We cannot, he thought, suppose that something could have happened

[25] S. R. Gardiner, *A Student's History of England from the Earliest times to the Death of King Edward VII*, 3 vols. (London, 1911), i. 106.

[26] J. A. Froude, *Short Studies in Great Subjects*, new edn., 3 vols. (London, 1877), ii. 567 f.

then which could not happen now. Those incredible tales must be regarded as being true, if they were true at all, in quite another sense.

Froude's Christianity was touched by doubt, was Low Church rather than Evangelical, common-sense and practical, non-sacerdotal and non-sacramental, the religion of the ordinary Englishman, embodied in a national Church, expressed in an austere morality. Throughout history, he thought, human beings tended naturally to become effeminate, effete, and ineffectual; seekers after happiness rather than virtue. Paganism and Catholicism were religious expressions of this natural tendency. True religion expressed itself as a protest against it, so that Islam was the noblest of non-Christian religions, Calvinism the best kind of Christianity.[27] The Reformation represented a fight for truth against the complexities of the spinners of doctrine.

This is to caricature Froude, though not very much. He clearly thought that British Christianity was expressive of the best of which human beings were capable. But he believed, of course, that all this was an achievement of the human spirit. In Evangelical or Anglo-Catholic hands the movement of history became very much more providential: God rather than the human spirit being responsible for the way in which things happened. Probably every nation has liked to feel that a particular providence has guided its development. The conviction that England had been awarded a very specially privileged place in the world was no new thing in the nineteenth century and had probably been widespread by, at any rate, the middle of the eighteenth. It was certainly powerful after 1815 in the general relief at the successful conclusion to the Napoleonic wars. Wellington's assertion after Waterloo that 'The hand of Almighty God has been upon me this day' easily became the nation's belief that the victory was no accident.

In the last quarter of the nineteenth century and the early years of the twentieth, national history became imbued with even greater significance. It was the period when imperialism acquired a new respectability, conventionally dated from Disraeli's becoming prime minister in 1874. The acquisition of the Suez Canal shares, rapid colonial expansion in the next two decades, the provision of an institutional form for the empire in the colonial conferences

---

[27] Ibid. 44 ff. and 52 ff.

from 1887 onwards, all contributed to a sense of English world power. The proclamation of Queen Victoria as empress of India in 1877, her golden jubilee in 1887, and diamond jubilee in 1897, gave it a symbolic force. All this contributed to the sense that history was something which was on the side of the English. The idea that providence had marked England out for especial responsibility became a persistent conviction that lasted well into the twentieth century. Quite late in his life, William Temple thought that there was a providential role for Britain in world history though it was not, in his case, a thinly disguised theological jingoism. He seems to have believed that the institution of the nation, like the institution of the family, was a special creation of God.[28] If someone of his theological and political sophistication could hold to this belief, it must all too often have been held by the theologically crude and naïve.

One of the most interesting figures in whose thought religion, scholarship, history, and politics came together was William Ewart Gladstone. He wrote a good deal about the works of Homer in the late 1850s and the 1860s and was, in a sense, both historian and literary critic; but his scholarship was always related to the political world in which he lived. Of it Colin Matthew says:

He believed that the neglect of Homer at Eton and Oxford during his years there was similar and parallel to the neglect of true religion. In Gladstone's mind the two were inseparably linked. The ideal of the Christian gentleman was in his view not the erastian pentameter-construing cynic of the late eighteenth century, but the churchman suffused with the civic qualities of the Homeric world.[29]

Gladstone was one of those, in other words, who believed that Greece and Rome, no less than Christianity, were part of 'our own' history and could shape society for the future; but his work on Homer set him in a curious position over against developing critical biblical scholarship. All his religious sympathies put him in the camp opposed to the critics. When Bishop Colenso's work on the Old Testament appeared in the middle of the period in which Gladstone was working on Homer, Gladstone disliked it intensely (as he disliked *Essays and Reviews*). He scribbled rude comments in

---

[28] W. Temple, *Christianity and the Social Order*, reprint (London, 1976), 64.
[29] H.C.G. Matthew, *Gladstone, 1809–1874* (Oxford, 1988), 153.

the margins of both works.[30] He wrote to Miss Burdett-Coutts in 1866, about her proposal to endow the see of Cape Town, in terms that make it quite plain that he abominated what Colenso stood for.[31] He and Jowett made each other very angry and Jowett thought that Gladstone's work on Homer revealed an essential near-insanity.[32] There was a sense, however, in which Gladstone understood, better than most, what the critics were doing. He was rather warmer in his reception of Seeley's life of Christ, *Ecce Homo*, than Jowett was.[33] He seems, in fact, to have believed that just as the traditional view of Homer could be defended by conscientious scholarship, so it was unnecessary for biblical criticism to be negative and destructive. He was a dispensationalist as well as something of a literalist: though he was quite orthodox on the doctrines of the fall and redemption, he believed that God had been, in some degree, revealed through the best traditions of Greek civilization.[34]

Gladstone was not alone, of course, in experiencing the explosive effects of the interaction between theology and historiography, though in Britain the pace of change was slower than in Germany, in spite of the fact that some of the rationalist ideas of English Deists had an effect on the Continent. In Germany the application of a secular and rationalist understanding of history to the study of the Bible advanced rapidly.[35] Because Christianity claimed to be a historical religion, it had been assumed that the account of its origins, recorded in the New Testament, purported to be history. The gospels seemed to be about things that actually happened in the external world, and some of them were miraculous. Historians no

[30] P. Hinchliff, *John William Colenso, Bishop of Natal* (London, 1964), 159 and P. Hinchliff, *Benjamin Jowett and the Christian Religion* (Oxford, 1987), 96.

[31] D. C. Lathbury (ed.), *Letters on Church and Religion of W. E. Gladstone*, 2 vols. (London, 1910), i. 131.

[32] Balliol College: Jowett to Florence Nightingale, 16 Nov. 1874.

[33] Hinchliff, *Jowett*, 109, and cf. Matthew, *Gladstone*, 154 f.

[34] F. M. Turner, *The Greek Heritage in Victorian Britain* (New Haven and London, 1981), 159 ff.

[35] There are a large number of books dealing with the development of biblical historiography in the nineteenth century, for example: H. W. Frei, *The Eclipse of the Biblical Narrative: A Study in Eighteenth and Nineteenth Century Hermeneutics* (New Haven and London, 1974); R. M. Grant, *A Short History of the Interpretation of the Bible*, rev. edn. (London, 1965); V. A. Harvey, *The Historian and the Believer* (London, 1967); R. Morgan with J. Barton, *Biblical Interpretation* (Oxford, 1988); J. Rogerson, C. Rowland, and B. Lindars, *The Study and Use of the Bible* (Basingstoke and Grand Rapids, 1988).

longer took such 'legendary' material seriously when they wrote about ancient people. Philosophers like Hume argued that an observer who had not encountered such events in his own experience, need not regard the accounts as good evidence. Through the influence of such men as Spinoza it began to be said that Scripture is not so much the actual 'Word of God' but rather bears witness to Christ, the real Word. Schleiermacher and others popularized the idea that to understand the Bible one should treat it as one would any other book. In that case it was essential to recognize that the books of the Bible have their own specific cultural, historical, and linguistic setting; a second sense, as it were, in which there was a historical aspect to the question. To understand them it was important to see them as they were written and not through the layers of dogmatic interpretation imposed upon them by later generations. So, by the end of the eighteenth century scholars like Semler and Ernesti could treat the Bible in a purely historical and rationalist manner, though neither of them was narrowly rationalist for its own sake. And in the nineteenth century exegesis came to be virtually identical with critical analysis of the text.

The question then became, in what sense do the books of the Bible, and the New Testament in particular, bear witness to Christ as the Word of God? In order to maintain the belief that there was a historically authentic revelation of God contained in the gospels, scholars might argue that they possessed a deeper spiritual or religious meaning, separate from the literal meaning of the passage. But, then, it might follow that the accounts of the life of Jesus (particularly of his miracles and, above all, of his resurrection) did not refer to concrete, objective, observable events in the external world. In that case, it was not clear precisely what their meaning was.[36]

It might be argued, as D. F. Strauss and others argued, that the stories were 'myths'. The term might mean no more than that these were the kind of legends that tend to grow up round any religious hero: but Strauss not only maintained that much of the gospels consisted of religious belief cast in narrative form, but also insisted that many of the tales were created because it was believed that Jesus, as the Messiah, *must* have fulfilled everything in the Old

---

[36] See Frei, *Eclipse of Biblical Narrative*, 268.

Testament which could be regarded as messianic expectation. Alternatively, it might be held that there were naturalistic explanations for the stories—that a supposed appearance of an angel, for instance, was actually caused by phosphorescence. The Heidelberg professor H. E. G. Paulus was famous for his enormously complicated naturalistic explanations of the gospel miracles. Again, it might be maintained that what were described as objective events had actually been subjective experiences—as in the case of the temptations of Jesus. A further possible approach was that of J. T. Beck (a professor at Tübingen in the third quarter of the nineteenth century, but not part of the Tübingen school) who argued that a spiritual interpretation of Scripture was necessary because it was *heilsgeschichte*—the history of God's saving acts—and therefore required a different treatment from that appropriate to ordinary history.

The existence of all these different responses, in turn, raised the question whether one ought to be consistent in one's interpretation of the material, or whether one could properly interpret some stories naturalistically, some as myth, and some as subjective experiences. If one were to invoke the idea of myth or of 'spiritual' history, the relationship between these interpretations and ordinary history would be a third level of historical problem. There was a fourth level of problem, raised, at least implicitly, by these questions, and that was whether modern Christians could understand the stories quite differently from the way in which they had been understood by earlier generations and remain committed to the same faith.

Precisely which episodes in the development of biblical historiography were supremely important, will be differently assessed by different scholars. The crucial moment may have come when Immanuel Kant drove a wedge between religion, on the one hand, and knowledge based on reason, on the other; or perhaps it came when Lessing produced persuasive arguments to show that historical facts, which are contingent, cannot prove necessary truths. In that case the crisis came in the eighteenth century. Hans Frei has also argued for an early date, maintaining that it was primarily the work of the pre-Hegelian rationalists, like Semler, which brought about the great change,[37] but Strauss's *Life of Jesus Critically Examined*

[37] Ibid. 247.

of 1835 is often cited as the decisive turning point, after which it was no longer possible to regard the gospels, simply, as super-natural history.[38] Though Karl Barth thought that the real epoch-maker was Schleiermacher, he placed Albrecht Ritschl last of all in his survey of *Protestant Theology in the Nineteenth Century*, as if to suggest that he represented the nadir of all Liberal Protestantism.

Nobody either before or since Ritschl . . . has expressed the view as clearly as he, that modern man wishes above all to live in the best sense according to reason, and that the significance of Christianity for him can only be a great confirmation and strengthening of this very endeavour.[39]

Since Ritschl, like Strauss, was in some sense a product of the Tübingen school of F. C. Baur, perhaps it was Hegelianism which was the really shattering force. Van Harvey, as we have seen, would make the decisive factor 'the shadow of Troeltsch', who lived well into the twentieth century and who insisted that 'Once the historical method is applied to biblical science and church history, it is a leaven that alters everything and, finally, bursts apart the entire structure of theological methods employed until the present'.[40] It was, moreover, Troeltsch's contemporary, von Harnack, who stated, most sharply of all, the problem of historical particularity for the theologian.

There are only two possibilities here: either the Gospel is in all respects identical with its earliest form, in which case it came with its time and has departed with it; or else it contains something which under differing historical forms is of permanent validity.[41]

It may be, however, that it is not important to be able to define the precise moment at which the whole shape of the problem changed. What matters is that it did change and that, even for religious believers in general, a great many issues related to history, and to historicity in particular, were raised by the critical study of the biblical texts. So long as the Scriptures could be treated simply as recorded fact, whose value for the student lay primarily in the immediate information they conveyed, even if that information required an esoteric expertise for its interpretation, questions

---

[38] e.g. Morgan, *Biblical Interpretation*, 62.

[39] K. Barth, *Protestant Theology in the Nineteenth Century* (London, 1972), 655.

[40] Harvey, *The Historian and the Believer*, 5.

[41] A. von Harnack, *What is Christianity* (London, 1901), 13 f.

relating to the philosophy of history could simply be ignored. And in Britain it was possible to do this for a surprisingly large part of the century.

A great many people continued to behave, until well into the last quarter of the nineteenth century, as if biblical scholarship was almost entirely a matter of knowing the *contents* of the Scriptures and the theological meaning which, over the centuries of Christian tradition, had come to be associated with certain books and passages.[42] Even the fact that textual criticism was often treated as if it were, somehow, less odious than other critical work, is itself significant. So long as one was concerned to establish the correct text, choosing between the variant readings in the manuscripts, one was implicitly doing a conservative thing. One was trying to *get back*, so to speak, to the original form. In textual criticism the assumption *had* to be that earliest was best, and even notorious liberals like Jowett quite happily worked on that assumption. This particular kind of enquiry, in other words, raised only one historical question, the straightforward one of how far back into antiquity it was possible to get.

It was very different with questions of what in Britain was called 'higher' criticism. The actual term seems first to have been used by William Robertson Smith in *The Old Testament in the Jewish Church* which was published in 1881. In that work he spoke of 'higher or historical criticism'. Though Robertson Smith, himself, was more often concerned with the *literary* methods and sources used by biblical authors, a critical approach to the content of the biblical books did raise historical problems in a number of ways; and *historical* criticism inevitably raised them in a peculiarly judgemental way.

The methods of historical criticism can be applied to any document; what they seek to determine is the value which the document possesses as a source for the reconstruction of history. Inevitably, therefore, the enquiry results in a pronouncement upon the value of the document. It is, willy nilly, a *value* judgement, which deals with the genuineness, unity, integrity, and trustworthiness of the document—*as a historical source*. The critic is asking questions about whether the document is as the original author first wrote it or whether it has become corrupted, distorted, or falsified

[42] Below, p. 101 ff., for the conservative approach to theology at Oxford in the 1860s and 1870s.

in the course of its history (for it is important always to remember that historical sources have their own history). He is asking whether the contents of a document are consonant with what is known of the supposed author and whether it reflects a situation appropriate to the time at which it is supposed to have been written. He can seldom check a biblical text against an account taken from a source external to the document being examined: he is dependent chiefly upon internal evidence which is seldom decisive.

In addition to these difficult issues raised by biblical historiography, there was a further complication. It was only too likely that the nature of the critical enquiry would be misunderstood. Historical criticism is properly concerned only with judging the worth of a document, *as a source for history*. But, when the document was part of the Bible, it was only too easy for it to seem that judgement was being passed upon its religious or spiritual worth. A decision that the Epistle to the Hebrews was not written by Paul and therefore could tell one nothing about the apostle, his theology, his acquaintance with rabbinic writings on the Day of Atonement or his life-style, could easily seem to be a declaration that the work was some kind of imposture and therefore not worth reading at all. Most of the critical scholars were believers who were attempting to devise a rationally justifiable approach to biblical scholarship and theology: they were widely regarded as wicked men deliberately seeking to undermine the faith.

In the Church of England, in the early nineteenth century, very little attention was paid to the work of German higher critical scholarship. This is not to say that it was entirely unknown. There is some information which indicates that German books and German ideas were more widely circulated than seems likely at first sight,[43] but most of the seminal works of German philosophy and biblical scholarship were not translated into English until late in the century: exposing oneself to their ideas required considerable effort. Works of religious history, notably H. H. Milman's *History of the Jews*, published in 1829, which attempted the detached, unbiased, rationalist approach, advocated by German historians like Niebuhr, were not well received.

[43] See e.g. K. Willis, 'The Introduction and Critical Reception of Hegelian Thought in Britain, 1830–1900', *Victorian Studies*, 32 (1988), 89 ff.; D. Nimmo, 'Learning against Religion, Learning as Religion: Mark Pattison and the Victorian Crisis of Faith', in K. Robbins (ed.), *Studies in Church History*, 17 (Oxford, 1981), 317 ff.; Hinchliff, *Jowett*, 79 ff.

Critical biblical scholarship itself was more or less abandoned after one or two preliminary attempts to engage with Germanic learning. At Oxford, Alexander Nicoll, Pusey's predecessor as professor of Hebrew from 1822 to 1828, was familiar with the latest opinions and theories of the German critics, disagreed with many of their conclusions, but was able to meet them on their own ground and remain on friendly terms with them.[44] Even Pusey himself had once been willing to argue that critical German scholarship, though only too often marred by infidelity and irreverence, was not wholly without redeeming features. This opinion involved him in controversy with Hugh James Rose, who had hitherto been regarded as one of the leading English experts on German theology, and in whose rectory at Hadleigh the famous meeting was to take place which some regard as the start of the Oxford Movement. Pusey said that he had expected to be misunderstood and attacked for what he had written; nevertheless he became more and more conservative after Rose's strictures upon his work.[45]

The poet, Samuel Taylor Coleridge, had begun to develop a new understanding of the authority of the Bible which might have saved the Church from a good deal of later agonizing. He believed that one's faith in Christ would lead one to an appreciation of the Scriptures as a whole and that this in turn, with the growth of spiritual discernment, would enable one to understand the truth and authority of particular passages. He was suspicious of all literalism and especially opposed to the literal rendering of passages which were clearly not intended to be understood literally. Foreshadowing Jowett's later attack on literalism he was, above all, critical of 'the practice of bringing together in logical dependency detached sentences from books composed at the distance of centuries, nay, sometimes a millennium, from each other, under different dispensations, and for different objects'.[46]

---

[44] J. L. Speller, 'Alexander Nicoll and the Study of German Biblical Criticism in Early Nineteenth Century Oxford', *Journal of Ecclesiastical History*, 30 (Oct. 1979), 451 ff.

[45] L. Frappell, ' "Science" in the Service of Orthodoxy: The Early Intellectual Development of E. B. Pusey', in P. Butler (ed.), *Pusey Rediscovered* (London, 1983), 1 ff.

[46] S. T. Coleridge, *Confessions of an Inquiring Spirit* (ed. H. StJ. Hart) (London, 1956), 38 and quoted in C. Welch, *Protestant Thought in the Nineteenth Century*, 2 vols. (New Haven and London, 1972 and 1985), i. 125 and cf. below, pp. 58.

There was little open engagement with critical scholarship within the established Church until the 1860s. Clearly there was a good deal of questioning going on. Not everyone was honestly convinced that every word in the Bible was quite literally true. When Bishop Colenso came under attack in the 1860s for his Old Testament work, one of the things that upset him most was that his leading critic among the English bishops, Samuel Wilberforce of Oxford, was quite happy to admit, in private conversation, that he did not believe that all the stories of the early chapters of Genesis were literally true. He was not, however, willing to allow anyone the freedom to say such things publicly *and* continue to hold office in the Church.[47] No doubt Wilberforce himself thought of this as something like 'not in front of the servants', but to the liberals it seemed like nothing more nor less than blatant hypocrisy. Certainly Jowett and his friends thought that, in producing *Essays and Reviews*, they were striking a blow for honesty as well as truth and liberty. They spoke quite openly of the way in which the champions of orthodoxy had terrorized the open-minded into keeping silent, and there is some evidence to support their claim.[48]

Connop Thirlwall in England (at any rate until he became a bishop) and John Tulloch in Scotland, though not themselves critical scholars, gave some support to the liberal cause. Thomas Arnold developed his 'common-sense' approach to the New Testament. But it was not until the late 1850s that there was any real attempt at genuinely critical scholarship in England and then it was exemplified by Samuel Davidson, the Congregationalist, in the second volume of Horne's *Introduction to the Holy Scriptures*, as much as by Stanley and Jowett's commentaries on the Pauline Epistles;[49] for it is not the case that English Nonconformity and Scottish Presbyterianism were the chief strongholds of narrow literalism. It could be argued, in fact, that theologians in Scotland were always more adventurous than their English counterparts; and that the theologians of the Free Church of Scotland were more adventurous than their contemporaries in the establishment.[50]

It was not, however, because they possessed a spirit of adventure that these men engaged in critical scholarship; nor were they

---

[47] G. W. Cox, *Life of John Williams Colenso D.D., Bishop of Natal*, 2 vols. (London, 1888), i. 470.

[48] I. Ellis, *Seven Against Christ* (Leiden, 1980), 49 and cf. p. 6.

[49] Ibid. 5.   [50] Below, pp. 180 ff.

deliberately determined to disturb the faith of the ordinary church-
goer. In the case of Bishop Colenso, for instance, it is patently clear
that his entire enterprise in critical biblical scholarship sprang from
passionate moral concern. One of the standard jokes about him
was that, having gone to Africa to convert the heathen, he had
allowed himself to be converted to higher criticism by a Zulu. There
was this much truth in the gibe, that Colenso was asked by one of
his converts whether some of the stories of the Old Testament were
in any sense morally superior to the rather bloodthirsty tales of the
Zulu people.

When Colenso finally published his *The Pentateuch and the
Book of Joshua critically examined* during the 1860s, the logic of
the argument behind the work as a whole went like this: (*a*) the Old
Testament contains too many inaccuracies and impossibilities for it
to be the direct dictation of God's words; (*b*) if it is not the words of
God but is, rather, the vehicle for the Word of God, then we are
liberated from having to believe every statement contained in the
Old Testament.

His concern was made very clear in a chapter entitled 'The War
on Midian' in Part I of *The Pentateuch and Joshua critically
examined.*

> . . . how thankful we must be, that we are no longer obliged to believe, as a
> matter of fact, of vital consequence to our eternal hope, the story related in
> N[umbers] xxxi, where we are told that a force of 12,000 Israelites slew all
> the males of Midian . . . and then, by command of Moses, butchered in
> cold blood all the women and children. The tragedy of Cawnpore, where
> 300 were butchered, would sink into nothing compared with such a
> massacre, if, indeed, we were required to believe it.[51]

The atrocities of the Indian mutiny of 1857 would still have been
very fresh in the memory of Colenso's readers. The bishop feared
that a sceptic might regard the story of the Midianites as evidence
that God was even more morally reprehensible than Nana Sahib,
who ordered his servants to massacre English women and children
at Cawnpore.

A fierce moral distaste Colenso also felt for those conservative
biblical scholars who, as he believed, evaded the obvious truth; for
the Germans were enlisted in support of conservative super-
naturalist orthodoxy as well as critical liberalism. Indeed, even the

---

[51] *Pentateuch and Joshua* (London, 1862), i. 143 f.

most radical of the English liberals tended to be less thorough-going than the Germans.[52] British conservatives were quite unable to come to terms with biblical criticism because the critical approach, almost by definition, ruled out any appeal to the supernatural. They were, nevertheless, able to invoke the prestige of carefully selected Teutonic scholars to shore up their conservative position. It is noteworthy that in the second half of the nineteenth century the Edinburgh publishers T. & T. Clark issued a string of translations of German biblical or theological works, most of which were conservative or adjudged harmless. Their series of over a hundred volumes, *The Foreign Theological Library*, included three of the works of E. W. Hengstenberg, who had been brought up a rationalist but had, by the time he was 40, become very conservative through the influence of Pietism.[53]

It was Hengstenberg who was the chief target of Colenso's scorn. The bishop believed that Hengstenberg attempted to 'force the Text of Scripture to say what it plainly does not say',[54] and he told F. D. Maurice that for the man himself he felt 'something like contempt, for his arguments are often dishonest—I can use no milder term—and that with a prodigious affectation of honesty and censure of others as suppressing the truth from interested motives'.[55] There were many others who, like Colenso, embraced critical biblical scholarship from a kind of moral fervour, a passion for honesty and truth.

[52] M. A. Crowther, *Church Embattled: Religious Controversy in Mid-Victorian England* (Newton Abbot, Devon, and Hamden, Connecticut, 1970), 66 ff.

[53] Ibid. 51 f. I am indebted to Professor Daniel Pals for drawing my attention to this fact.

[54] *Pentateuch and Joshua*, i. 24 f.

[55] Cox, *Colenso*, i. 196.

DEVELOPING BUT FAITHFUL:
Newman's Revised *Essay on Development*

VERY different from the liberals' passionate concern for honesty, but in its own way as passionate, was John Henry Newman's determination to obey his conscience in spite of the price which that exacted. Finding himself unable any longer to live honestly as an Anglican, he became a Roman Catholic. And his determination to maintain integrity was as much bound up with questions of history and truth as that of the liberal critics. As an Anglican he had been accustomed to arguing that Rome had added to, or altered, the truly Catholic faith. Becoming a Roman Catholic involved him— not in denying that claim—but in trying to explain how changes could be faithful to the original. Of all the issues raised by the new understanding of history, one of the most pressing was the perception that the ideas and values of any particular generation were unlikely to be of absolute and universal worth. This inevitably raised the question whether religious truth could grow and develop over the centuries and yet remain true. Newman's *Essay on the Development of Doctrine* is, therefore, one of the great landmarks in the history of nineteenth-century theology.

Newman is, for Anglicans at any rate, so inescapably a figure of the 1840s that it is difficult to remember that he was still active in the last quarter of the century. He was, indeed, still writing about the relationship between history and theology, producing an extensively revised version of his *Essay* in 1878 when he was not far off 80 years old. He belongs quite properly, therefore, in a survey of writers on religion and history in the last quarter of the century and for that reason deserves more than a mere mention here. Because the first edition of the *Essay* had been published in 1845, in the immediate context of his conversion to Roman Catholicism, his ideas will also serve as a useful way of introducing the survey itself; for these ideas were not entirely new to him even then but must have begun to be developed when he was, in appearance at least, still an Anglican. Among his published Oxford sermons is one on 'The theory of developments in religious doctrine', preached two years before the *Essay* first appeared.

At that stage Newman had spent most of his life in Oxford. He had become one of the brilliant constellation of fellows of Oriel when he was only 21 and was appointed vicar of the university church when he was 27. When, in 1843, he resigned the living on his way to becoming a Roman Catholic, he was in early middle age, with twenty years of what would have to be called, by the standards of the day, a moderately distinguished Anglican career behind him. He then began another career as a Roman Catholic which culminated in his appointment as a cardinal by Leo XIII in 1879. He did not die until August 1890. His life had spanned very nearly the whole of the century. He had lived longer than almost anyone of his generation. He had continued to think and to write throughout a period of more than sixty years.

For Newman, during all this time, the last enemy was always liberalism. In a speech which he made at the ceremony at which he was officially notified that the pope had raised him to the rank of cardinal, he defined liberalism as:

the doctrine that there is no positive truth in religion, but that one creed is as good as another, and this is the teaching which is gaining substance and force daily. It is inconsistent with any recognition of any religion as *true*. It teaches that all are to be tolerated, for all are matters of opinion. Revealed religion is not a truth, but a sentiment and a taste: not an objective fact, not miraculous: and it is the right of every individual to make it say just what strikes his fancy. Devotion is not necessarily founded upon faith. Men may go to Protestant Churches and to Catholic, may get good from both and belong to neither. They may fraternize together in spiritual thoughts and feelings without having any views at all of doctrines in common, or seeing the need of them. Since, then, religion is so personal a peculiarity and so private a possession, we must of necessity ignore it in the intercourse of man with man. If a man puts on a new religion every morning, what is that to you? It is as impertinent to think about a man's religion as about his sources of income or his management of his family. Religion is in no sense the bond of society.[1]

These words belong to a period only a few months after the publication of the revised *Essay* but, in a sense, he had rehearsed the same argument as early as 1841, in criticizing the remarks made

[1] W. Ward, *The Life of John Henry Cardinal Newman*, 2 vols. (London, 1912), ii. 460.

by Sir Robert Peel on opening a reading room at Tamworth.[2] Peel had said that the object of such an institution was to encourage education regardless of religious belief. In a reply, published in *The Times*, Newman had insisted that education could not replace faith since it could neither reform nor redeem fallen humanity. Christianity was important because it was true, not because it was either useful or entertaining.

The amusingly middle-class view of what constitutes the ultimate in legitimate privacy of opinion, with which Newman's 1879 speech ended, does not disguise the fact that the target of his attack had gradually shifted from the *rationalism* of the liberals to the relativism which he believed was implicit in their arguments for tolerance. Newman has proceeded by association of ideas rather than by strict logic.

The confusion was, in fact, probably created by the liberals themselves. They argued that truth in religion and theology were to be arrived at, like truth in any discipline, by a process of rational enquiry. In practice this was an anti-authoritarian, anti-dogmatic position.[3] It would be perfectly proper to accuse its proponents of lacking a desire to maintain the absolute truth of revealed religion. But the liberals went further. Perhaps they were influenced by Kant or perhaps they had learnt something of Locke's ideas about religious toleration from Thomas Arnold.[4]

In the best-known of his works, *The Principles of Church Reform*, Arnold had maintained:

Whoever is acquainted with Christianity must see that differences of opinion amongst Christians are absolutely unavoidable. First, because our religion being a thing of the deepest personal interest, we are keenly alive to all the great questions connected with it, which was not the case with heathenism. Secondly, these questions are exceedingly numerous, inasmuch as our religion affects our whole moral being, and must involve, therefore, a great variety of metaphysical, moral, and political points:— that is to say, those very points which, lying out of the reach of demonstrative science, are through the constitution of man's nature, peculiarly apt to be regarded by different minds differently.[5]

[2] See I. Ker, *John Henry Newman: A Biography* (Oxford, 1988), 721, who argues that Newman's *biglietto* speech echoes his criticism of Peel.
[3] See below, pp. 51.
[4] P. Hinchliff, *Benjamin Jowett and the Christian Religion* (Oxford, 1987), 48 ff.
[5] T. Arnold, *Principles of Church Reform, With an Introductory Essay by M. J. Jackson and J. Rogan* (London, 1962), 99.

The rationalism of the liberals thus came to be associated with the view that religious toleration was desirable because absolute agreement in matters of religion was impossible. Metaphysical truth could not, the liberals thought, be handled with the same kind of precision as empirical truth: the truth arrived at by human enquiry was not absolute but tentative. And so, finally, this very tentativeness of the liberals' conclusions created the impression that they were talking about feelings, 'sentiment', or 'taste', rather than about something which they believed to be objectively true.

In other words, the determination of the liberals to substitute rational enquiry for received dogma had brought them, paradoxically, to a position in which they seemed to be saying that it was all a matter of private taste. Whether or not Newman had perceived how that had happened, it is clear that for him religious truth must be absolute and given. Once committed to such a position, it was quite impossible for him to argue that truth was what lay at the end of a reasoned argument. Like most theologians he probably hankered after conclusive arguments for believing what appeared so reasonable: given free play, reason surely *must* come to the truth. More powerful still, however, was his feeling that to rely upon rationality was to risk the privatization of truth.

The controversy between the liberals and the Tractarians over the place of reason in establishing religious truth had been at its sharpest in the 1840s and 1850s. Yet, clearly, Newman was still deeply concerned about precisely the same issue in the 1870s. Indeed, it might almost be said that *everything* he wrote is about that issue, the relationship of faith and reason, and yet it does not seem that he had simply got stuck in the controversies and problems of his early middle age. The question seems to possess a personal intractability. Again and again, Newman seems to be striving to show that the truth can be established by clear, reasoned argument. Again and again, he seems to fail by the narrowest margin to achieve any such thing. He seems, in fact, to have had a genuine ambivalence about the capacity of the human mind to decide what was true. As a very old man he was accused by the Congregationalist, A. M. Fairbairn,[6] of a profound scepticism, of doubting reason's capacity to decide questions of truth at all. Fairbairn suggested that it was only to be expected that such a

---

[6] See below, p. 190 ff., for Fairbairn's theology.

profound sceptic should take refuge in the absolutism of Rome, where authority replaced the need to think and argue.

In part, as Newman pointed out, Fairbairn was simply misunderstanding what Newman meant by 'reason'. He maintained that Newman was using it to mean the faculty which distinguishes human beings from animals, in effect the mind itself. Newman insisted that he meant 'the dialectical faculty', 'the power by which man deduces one proposition from another, or proceeds from premisses to consequences'.[7] In other words, Newman insisted, his doubts about reason's capacity to decide what was true did not arise from a belief that the human mind was in its nature totally corrupt and unreliable, but that human beings were prevented from pursuing an argument to its proper conclusion because of the pressures brought to bear upon them by the world.

Newman's unwillingness to allow reason to be the ultimate arbiter of truth, born of his horror of liberalism, only partly explains why his arguments so often failed to come to a convincing conclusion; nor was it simply that religious questions are not capable of logical treatment. Again and again, his arguments—like his definition of liberalism itself—give the impression of not being *managed* quite properly. It is as though the last twist of a coil of hair escapes the hairpin and fails to fit completely into place. If the reader is frustrated by the result, one has the feeling that Newman was frustrated, too. Why else did so much of his writing consist of attempts to reorder what he had tried to say before?

Newman himself often invoked the idea of the moral to close the gap between reason and faith. He did this, for instance, when he had to accept the obvious impossibility of applying the canon of Vincent of Lerins as a simple, straightforward test of truth. There has probably never been any single article of faith believed everywhere, at all times and by all Christians. Newman, however, argued that the canon was, of course, to be applied morally not mathematically;[8] nor did he simply think this to be a convenient

---

[7] Ward, *Newman*, ii. 507 and H. M. de Achaval and J. D. Holmes, *The Theological Papers of John Henry Newman on Faith and Certainty* (Oxford, 1976), 140 ff.

[8] J. H. Newman, *Lectures on the Prophetical Office of the Church*, and quoted in the introduction to both versions of the *Essay on Development*. In the remainder of this chapter references are to J. H. Newman, *An Essay on the Development of Christian Doctrine* (London, 1845), cited simply as '1845', and J. H. Newman, *An Essay on the Development of Christian Doctrine*, new edn. (London, 1878), cited as '1878').

way out of a difficulty. He really did believe that faith and morals were organically related. His very argument that the capacity of human beings to reason logically was continually thwarted by the pressures of the world around them, demonstrates precisely why he believed that relationship to exist. In a university sermon of 1839 on the contrasting habits of mind associated with faith and reason he had argued that 'Faith is a principle of action, and action does not allow time for minute and finished investigations.'[9] Of course, that sentence would make equal and closely related sense if it read 'morality' instead of 'faith'. He thought that what marked faith off from reason, principally, was the fact that faith was willing to rely on 'antecedent considerations', 'previous notices, prepossessions, and (in a good sense) prejudices' while reason demanded 'direct and definite proof', 'actual evidence produced' in favour of a specified fact.

A little later, in the same sermon, Newman asserted that there was a sense in which 'Faith is a moral principle. It is created in the mind, not so much by facts as by probabilities; and since probabilities have no definite ascertained value, and are reducible to no scientific standard, what are such to each individual, depends on his moral temperament.'[10] How moral temperament enters into the question—and how moral temperament differs from the 'sentiment or taste' of liberal theology—was more fully explained in another of his university sermons, delivered in 1832. At the same time an analogy used on that occasion reveals the frustrations which the unmanageability of theological argument caused him.[11]

As a character in history, Newman is complex and paradoxical. He may be regarded as a prophetic figure who gave birth to a splendid range of ideas which have only come to be appreciated in all their brilliance in our own century. In that sense he is hailed as the forerunner of Vatican II—'always a herald of forgotten truths'.[12] But it is also possible still to regard him, as Faber regarded him, as one who was moved by feelings rather than reasonings. 'He was being impelled on that journey [to Rome] by something in himself which would not let him stand still. And this

[9] J. H. Newman, *A Reason for the Hope Within: Sermons on the Theory of Religious Belief* (Denville, New Jersey, reprint of 1985), 179.
[10] Ibid. 182.
[11] Ibid. 69 ff.
[12] C. S. Dessain, *John Henry Newman* (London, 1966), pp. xii and 168 f.

was not ambition nor a desire for intellectual consistency; it was the search for an absolute spiritual ruler.'[13]

Owen Chadwick's comment, that Newman's mental processes were all his own,[14] may come nearest explaining the paradox. Perhaps the truth is that Newman was always an originator of brilliant, fruitful ideas but not so effectively a constructor of watertight logical arguments. When one turns to the *Essay on Development*, the feeling that things are not quite being *managed* becomes acute in the most important section of it.

The actual problem faced in Newman's *Essay* had, perhaps, changed shape slightly over the course of the thirty years between the first and the last edition. In the 1840s the question was, 'Where is the true Church?', an issue which obsessed the Oxford men. Conventional Tractarian polemic maintained that the Church of England was undoubtedly part of the true Church (though it never went quite so far as to claim that it *was* the true Church without remainder) because it had neither added to, nor subtracted from, the ancient Faith of the earliest Christian Church. In one sense Newman was converted when he came to believe that maintaining the ancient Faith *unchanged* was not simply a matter of preserving dogmatic phrases and formularies in concrete. This is the point of his own claim that his work on the Monophysites and the Arians helped to bring about the Romeward move. Arians and Monophysites, alike, and with some justice, claimed to be preserving an older truth against later innovations, but perhaps the older past, in each case, had been overtaken by new situations, new needs, and new ways of saying things, and had become a dead past. Then the Tractarian appeal to the apostolic age (for which Newman himself had, after all, been partly responsible) began to seem like an appeal from a living Church to the dead past. There must be some *living* authority to determine truth *now*. So one finds Newman insisting that, whatever the differences between the Church of the fourth and the nineteenth centuries, the great saints and heroes of the early Church would feel more at home with post-Tridentine Roman Catholicism than with any other kind of Christianity.

By the 1870s these were no longer quite the questions but there were related issues of a more general kind to be faced by the

---

[13] G. Faber, *Oxford Apostles: A Character Study of the Oxford Movement*, 2nd edn. (London, 1936), 413.

[14] O. Chadwick, *Newman* (Oxford, 1981), 13.

Christian world as a whole: by his liberal opponents as much as by Newman himself. A year after the revised *Essay on Development* had appeared, Benjamin Jowett—though without overt reference to Newman—was pointing out, from the pulpit of Balliol chapel, that the Christian religion had not been static and unchanging through the centuries, so that 'if we could imagine a single individual living from the Christian era until now, he would have been, not of one religion but of several, and several times over would have anathematized and excommunicated himself'.[15] And if that is the case, Jowett asked his undergraduate audience, what is it that constitutes the essential or permanent element in Christianity?

The very way Jowett phrased the question would have seemed foreign to Newman. He was not looking for a core in the sense of a lowest common denominator between all the various Christianities of one period and another. (Nor, to do him justice, was Jowett— but his mind moved more nearly in that way than Newman's, because he tended to think that the original Christianity must have been simpler than the later versions and that, therefore, the essence was to be reached by pruning away the later elaboration.) Newman thought that Christianity was a living thing, always growing, always changing, always developing; but also that the *same* organism was always the subject of the growth and change and development. The fullness of the living thing could be present in its original, embryonic, apparently simpler manifestation as in a later, more explicit, and elaborate one.

So Newman's idea of development was of something much more analogous to the organic than the *minimal* persistent core sought for by those who believed in an 'essence of Christianity'; but it was also very much more difficult to define. Those who were looking for permanent elements in Christianity had at least set themselves a definable task. If they could demonstrate that something had not always been a part of Christian belief or practice, they could eliminate that element from the supposed core. If, however, one was thinking of something that could be compared with organic growth, one had to confront the question, 'What is it that grows?' If one is talking about a human individual it is difficult enough—

---

[15] The quotation is from a sermon of Jowett's entitled *The Permanent Elements of Religion*, preached in 1879 and published as a separate pamphlet. A copy is bound up with Jowett's *Sermons on Faith and Doctrine*, ed. W. H. Fremantle (London, 1901), in Balliol College Library.

especially if one is in a context where very little is known about genetics—to say what it is that is the subject of the verbs 'to grow' and 'to develop'. What is it, precisely, that develops from a tiny baby into a full grown, and then ageing adult? Is it a soul, an ego, a genetic fingerprint? What is it to whom the changes of life happen?

For a human individual there is at least a visible, tangible, physical body to provide an obvious continuity from cradle to grave. When one is dealing with the development of ideas rather than a living object, the problem is much more difficult, and when one is dealing with the development of Christian doctrine it is more difficult still, simply because there can be no parallels. There is only one Christianity. Therefore one cannot say that every Christianity will behave like this or like that as it develops, as one might say that every human being will become wrinkled as he becomes older.

It is true that one can, and Newman does, take individual doctrines or individual denominations (though he does not call them that) and use them as examples of development; but that is rather different. The very fact that he was anxious to establish tests which would distinguish between developments and corruptions (or, as he preferred to say in the 1878 edition, notes of genuine developments contrasted with corruptions) implied that he must be thinking of Christian doctrine as a single whole, growing and changing, sometimes properly and sometimes improperly. In that sense it must be the 'ideas' of Christianity as a whole which are the subject of development. Yet it is not quite the *idea* which behaves organically, like a living thing.

When Newman was attempting to define precisely how an idea develops he wrote:

This process, whether it be longer or shorter in point of time, by which the aspects of an idea are brought into consistency and form, I call its development, being the germination and maturation of some truth or apparent truth on a large mental field. On the other hand this process will not be a development, unless the assemblage of aspects, which constitute its ultimate shape, really belongs to the idea from which they start. A republic, for instance, is not a development from a pure monarchy, though it may follow upon it; whereas the Greek 'tyrant' may be considered as included in the idea of a democracy. Moreover a development will have this characteristic, that, its action being in the busy scene of human life, it cannot progress at all without cutting across, and thereby destroying or modifying and incorporating with itself existing modes of thinking and operating. The development then of an idea is not like an investigation worked out on paper, in which each successive advance is a pure evolution from a foregoing, but it is carried through and by means of communities of men and their leaders and guides; and it employs their minds as its instruments, and depends upon them, while it uses them. And so, as regards existing opinions, principles, measures and institutions of the community which it has invaded; it develops by establishing relations between itself and them; it employs itself in giving them a new meaning and direction, in creating what may be called a jurisdiction over them, in throwing off whatever in them it cannot assimilate. It grows when it incorporates, and its identity is found, not in isolation, but in continuity and sovereignty. This it is that imparts to the history of both states and of religions, its specially turbulent and polemical character. Such is the explanation of the wranglings, whether of schools or parliaments. It is the warfare of ideas under their various aspects striving for the mastery, each of them enterprising, engrossing, imperious, more or less incompatible with the rest, and rallying followers or rousing foes, according as it acts upon the faith, the prejudices, or the interest of parties or classes.

Moreover an idea not only modifies, but is modified, or at least influenced, by the state of things in which it is carried out, and is dependent in various ways on the circumstances which surround it. Its development proceeds quickly or slowly, as it may be; the order of succession in its separate stages is variable; it shows differently in a small sphere of action and in an extended; it may be interrupted, retarded, mutilated, distorted by external violence; it may be enfeebled by the effort of ridding itself of domestic foes; it may be impeded and swayed or even absorbed by counter energetic ideas; it may be coloured by the received tone of thought into which it comes, or depraved by the intrusion of foreign principles, or at length shattered by the development of some original fault within it.[16]

Ever the enthusiastic employer of the semicolon, Newman here seems to have lost his way somewhat in the mounting climax of each sentence. The version of this passage which appears in the first edition, though not very different, seems at first sight both shorter and cooler,[17] but in neither version is it very easy to keep one's head—or perhaps it is one's feet—in the midst of the number of times the word 'develop' is used. The subject of the passage is supposed to be the *development-of-an-idea* but sometimes it seems to be about the development of developments, and sometimes about the development of societies and institutions. When one analyses it carefully the earlier version is, in fact, more confusing

[16] 1878, pp. 38 f.   [17] 1845, pp. 37 f.

than the later. The opening sentence is about a 'process', which is the 'development of an idea'; but then the second sentence asserts that 'it', which must—grammatically—be the development of an idea, has 'the necessary characteristic' that it cannot 'develop' except in certain ways. The third sentence begins 'Its development' and that must mean the development of the development of an idea; and, finally, that development may in the end be destroyed by the 'development of some original fault within it'.

It is equally difficult to remember that the 'warfare' of ideas is a metaphor only. Both passages actually say that the development of ideas is 'carried on through individuals and bodies of men' or 'through communities of men and their leaders and guides', and both say that it 'employs their minds as instruments, and depends upon them while it uses them'. But in both versions Newman seems sometimes to write as if the ideas themselves were actually locked in some direct titanic struggle, as though they possessed wills and ambitions of their own. One may hazard a guess that the explanation for both these difficulties, apart from the sheer pleasure Newman derived from literary extravagance, is that in his own mind the real subject of the passage in each case is actually the Church. It is the Church which is the community within which the ideas develop. It is the Church whose leaders and guides provide the means by which it is carried on. It is the Church itself, rather than the idea, which 'may be enfeebled by the effort of ridding itself of domestic foes' or 'be depraved by the intrusion of foreign principles'. It is even, perhaps, the Church itself which develops rather than the doctrine. It is really the Church which behaves organically, as a living thing.

Yet there is a sense in which such analysis of Newman's argument misses the point. There is an instructive parallel in Matthew Arnold's *Dover Beach*, perhaps the most haunting and the most beautiful of all Victorian poems. Arnold's metaphors melt into one another so that the 'sea of faith', itself a metaphor for an earlier universal Christianity, is said to lie 'like the folds of a bright girdle furl'd' round 'earth's shore': the metaphor of the sea has suggested the further metaphor of girdle round dry land. Though Arnold himself may not have been fully aware of what it was that he was doing, the metaphor seems to have provided him with a magnificent way of conjuring up the flux, as well as the depth, of an idea like faith. In the end, however, it will not bear too close a scrutiny if one analyses the passage as if it were a logical argument.

Perhaps one ought to regard Newman as poet rather than as a constructor of arguments. That would explain why he sometimes proceeds by conflation of images or by association of ideas; it would explain why he is irritated by the unmanageable nature of theological reasoning; it would explain why, in spite of the flaws in his arguments, one is so often left with the feeling that the ideas convey something beautiful, moving and true.

This is particularly the case when one tries to assess the value of the 'notes' for recognizing legitimate developments in doctrine (as they are called in the 1878 version: in the earlier version they were called 'tests'). The seven notes are as follows (when the 'tests' of the first edition were differently labelled, the fact is noted in square brackets):

1. the preservation of type [preservation of idea or preservation of type *or* idea]; 'the adult animal has the same make, as it had on its birth; young birds do not grow into fishes, nor does the child degenerate into the brute, wild or domestic'; and Newman cites as an example the way in which the command to Peter to eat unclean animals, though a great shock to the apostle, was actually implied 'in that faith which he held and taught':[18]

2. continuity of principles; 'A development, to be faithful, must retain both the doctrine and the principle with which it started';[19] plainly a difficult point to define with precision, because Newman has several attempts at it, but perhaps it became clearest when he noted that a belief in the transitoriness of worldly goods will lead an Epicurean, with his principles, in one direction and an ascetic, with his, in another: every belief has to be applied in terms of certain principles which exist alongside it; any true development of it must be applied in terms of the same principles:

3. power to assimilate ideas from outside [power of assimilation]; this is a reversion to Newman's concept of the idea's existence 'in the busy scene of human life'; a 'capacity of expansion, without disarrangement or dissolution';[20] the point is made that ideas behave quite differently from 'mathematical and other abstract creations'; this seems to mean that an idea may be able to take in others and provide them with a new and cogent organization, without itself being destroyed in the process:

---

[18] 1878, p. 176.   [19] Ibid. 181.   [20] Ibid. 186.

4. logical sequence [in the first edition the order of (4) and (5) is reversed]; 'Logic is the organization of thought and, as being such, is a security for the faithfulness of intellectual developments'; 'this logical character which the whole wears becomes a test that the process has been a true development, not a perversion or corruption';[21] this seems to mean internal coherence, in other words, but more than that since the early fathers 'might be without any digested ideas of Purgatory or Original Sin, yet have an intense feeling, which they had not defined or located, both of the fault of our first nature and the responsibilities of our nature regenerate':

5. anticipation of its future [early anticipation]; the analogy is with the way individuals and institutions sometimes foreshadow, early in their history, things which will become their most distinctive and important characteristics, for example Pachomius's instructing his fourth-century embryonic monasteries to establish libraries, though manual labour was thought to be a much more proper activity for monks than study until comparatively late in monastic history:

6. conservative action upon its past [preservative additions]; a true development 'may be described as one which is conservative of antecedent developments, being really those antecedents and something besides them'; as the *cultus* of the Virgin and the saints 'subserves, illustrates, protects the doctrine of our Lord's condescension [the incarnation] and mediation [the atonement]':[22]

7. chronic vigour [chronic continuance]; because development is an essential characteristic of ideas, they will *not* stand still; corruptions, therefore, cannot last, they will quickly reach the point of total dissolution; an idea that persists over a long period must be a *true* development.

It has to be said that not all Newman's illustrations or analogies are well chosen. The section on 'conservative action', for instance, contains a long passage which deals with the way that, in nature, things grow, mature, and then decay; but the point that he intends to make is that there *is* a true, preservative development which actually contradicts the impression that has been carefully built up in his reader's mind that all growth leads to corruption. All too often Newman finds it easier to provide analogies which are the opposite of the characteristic he is talking about, so that one grasps

---

[21] Ibid. 189 and 190 f.   [22] Ibid. 200 and 202.

the point through his assertion that it is *not* like this or that; and then one may find it difficult to hit upon a precise example of the positive, other than those which Newman himself provides, which sometimes smack a little of special pleading. The examples he gives of 'corruptions' are not always self-evidently such, nor are his examples of 'true' development manifestly more faithful to primitive Christianity. Sometimes one simply feels that he has written nonsense, as in the seventh point when he says that heresies are necessarily short-lived.

The 'unmanaged' nature of the argument is fairly obvious and the author never seems to have been satisfied with it. Not only is the 1878 version a radical reordering of the 1845 edition, but that had itself been 'rewritten and rewritten again'.[23] Perhaps the greatest weakness of all is that the 'notes' themselves are not, by their very nature, of such a kind as to enable one to tell true from false developments *as they happen*: they could really only be applied in retrospect, and then somewhat uncertainly.

The two versions of the *Essay* are chiefly different from each other in *arrangement*, and the rearrangement involved was so drastic and complex that, as Owen Chadwick sardonically remarks, it is surprising that only one sentence of the 1845 edition has found its way into two different places in that of 1878.[24] There is general agreement, however, that, in spite of the rearrangement, the argument has not really been altered;[25] and yet this very fact is bound to give one pause. If so much of the argument could be drastically cut up and moved about and stuck together again, without having any effect other than possibly to shift an emphasis, then one is entitled to ask whether the constituent bits and pieces are really an *argument* at all, and whether they come to a conclusion. A conclusion, after all, is meant to be the end of an argument.

Yet, perhaps, Newman is simply following respectable theological precedents. Aquinas's 'five ways' are not in any strict sense *proofs*

[23] Faber, *Oxford Apostles*, 448.
[24] O. Chadwick, *From Bossuet to Newman*, 2nd edn. (Cambridge, 1987), 190.
[25] Dessain, who had an expert's knowledge of Newman's writings, hardly mentions the 1878 version, having discussed the 1845 one in a manner which he thought would cover both. See Dessain, *John Henry Newman*, 80 ff. and 164, and cf. Chadwick, *From Bossuet to Newman*, 191, and N. Lash, *Newman on Development: The Search for an Explanation in History* (London, 1975), 103.

that God exists: they are indicators which will encourage someone who believes in God to think himself rationally justified in doing so. Indeed the whole natural theology/natural law tradition which relies upon the concept of 'a man of good will' is virtually declaring that its arguments are not intended to convince anyone other than those already predisposed to accept the conclusion. There is something to be said for the view that religious beliefs are adopted for reasons that have little to do with rational argument. The reasoning comes later as the believer attempts to test the validity of the beliefs he or she has adopted.

To say, then, that it is something like this which Newman is doing is not really to complain about his technique. He is behaving exactly as other great theologians have behaved. In fact, the view that religious reasoning follows conviction rather than precedes it accords well with Newman's own attitude and cast of mind in a number of different ways. His objections to theological liberalism make it clear that to him faith was prior, in importance, if not in time, to intellectual enquiry. Many commentators on his work have supposed that Newman attached this priority to faith because of the religious attitudes he had initially acquired as an Evangelical in his youth.[26]

Evangelicals, however, would not have found Newman's concept of development congenial, and not simply because Newman used it in defence of post-Tridentine Roman Catholicism. Almost every 'orthodox' Christian in the earlier part of the nineteenth century thought that, if truth was true, then truth did not change. Newman's great achievement was to liberate himself from such a fear of change. In comparison with that, it may be less important that he was unable to provide a workable test to distinguish between true and false changes, or that he found it impossible to define precisely how doctrinal ideas do evolve.

Interestingly, it has been suggested that the thought of the *Essay* was actually developed from Newman's one really serious venture into the writing of history. His *The Arians of the Fourth Century*, published in 1833, was concerned with dogmatic history and argued that what was defined at Nicaea was something new, something which had only existed in embryo in the ante-Nicene

---

[26] Dessain, *Newman*, 5.

period.[27] At that stage, perhaps, Newman even thought of himself as a historian, though not in any sense which excluded his being a theologian as well. In the 1845 edition of the *Essay* he claimed to be following the strictly historical methods of someone like Gibbon and he devoted some twenty pages to a discussion of historical method.[28] All this was omitted from the 1878 edition, not at all surprisingly, considering how far historiography had developed by that time. Gibbon would have seemed very old-fashioned by then.

At the heart of Newman's treatment of the Arian controversy, as Ian Ker asserts, was 'his understanding of the early Church principle of "economy" ',[29] which meant that even the doctrine of the Trinity could be seen as only 'the shadow, projected for the contemplation of the intellect, of the Object of scripturally-informed piety; a representation, economical; necessarily imperfect as being exhibited in a foreign medium, and therefore involving apparent inconsistencies or mysteries'.[30] It was a concept of which Newman seems to have been proud. In 1859 he wrote that his own word to describe the 'indirect vision' that human beings have of God, through a glass darkly, 'from first to last has been *economical*, as I have explained it especially in my work on the Arians'.[31] 'Economy' was a principle, in other words, which was designed as much to explain why dogmatic definition was necessary at all, given the intractability of true knowledge of God, as to account for development in doctrine. It went some way to defend the necessity of doctrinal formulations which, because they are framed in propositions, belong to history, and are contingent, but attempt to convey something of the nature of the eternal and absolute.

It was no accident that Newman saw these questions emerging from his study of Arianism. The Arians, like Catholic-minded members of the Church of England, appealed to the past in defence of a doctrinal position which Newman had come to regard as isolating and undeveloped. They had not moved with the demands

---

[27] R. Williams, 'Newman's *Arians* and the Question of Method in Doctrinal History', in I. Ker and A. G. Hill (eds.), *Newman after a Hundred Years* (Oxford, 1990), 263 ff. Of all the mass of material published to mark the centenary of Newman's death, this article was the only one which appeared to attempt a serious consideration of Newman's ideas about history.

[28] 1845, pp. 182–202 and cf. Williams, 'Newman's *Arians*', 265.

[29] Ker, *John Henry Newman*, 49.

[30] Ibid. 50, quoting from Newman's *Apologia*.

[31] De Achaval and Holmes (eds.), *Theological Papers of Newman*, 160.

which the passage of history made upon them. They could not move because they lacked living authority: they could only appeal to the dead past. The Arians were also, in Newman's eyes, like the liberals of the nineteenth century. They were sceptics, raising clever philosophical objections to the traditional belief that the Son existed eternally with the Father; they attempted to make human reason the judge of the mysteries of revelation; they refused to concede that there might be valid reasons for doctrinal definitions which went beyond what was said in Scripture. This parallel had seemed clear to Newman in the 1840s, and thirty years later, when he was again thinking and writing about Arianism, he once more saw modern secularism and liberalism as the opponents of truly developed doctrine.[32]

Newman talked about the nature of history, in a way that showed that he was aware of some of the problems it raised, at various points in his life. About six months before he resigned his living in Oxford, he was planning to edit a series of lives of the saints of the British Isles. It seemed to him to raise considerable historiographical problems. He recognized the difficulties of interpretation. Opinion, he thought, inevitably intruded into history, but he seems to have believed that, in principle, it need not do so but for the fact that the result would be so boring and thus commercially unattractive.[33] Fifteen years later, at about the same time as his assertion that he had always used the term 'economical' to describe the indirect vision and when he was involved in much controversy over *The Rambler*, he argued—curiously, also in connection with the life of a saint—that if 'history is to mirror the actual course of time, it must also be a course itself'.[34]

If, however, Newman recognized the existence of the problem of interpretation and if his concept of development was in part an admission of the contingent character of what takes shape in history, he does not seem to have found the miraculous to be historically problematical. In the 1840s he had thought that one of the problems in writing about saints was that one would either want to concentrate on miracles, monkery, and popery, or one would not.[35] As a historian, at that time, Newman thought that miracles were simply a matter of taste or opinion like monks and

[32] Ker, *John Henry Newman*, 48 f. and 667 ff.   [33] Ibid. 281.
[34] Ibid. 484.   [35] Ibid. 281.

popes. One might like them or not: they were facts like any other. In the 1870s, in the aftermath of the Vatican Council and as he moved toward the revised edition of the *Essay*, he recognized the sharpening contradiction between science and history, on the one hand, and Scripture and dogma, on the other.[36] But the pairs, history and science: Scripture and dogma, are significant. Just as Newman simply ignored the problems raised by the biblical critics as signs of infidelity and rationalism, so he also ignored the historians' problems with the miraculous. Indeed, as Anthony Kenny points out, Newman was quite content to dignify somewhat unconvincing historical coincidences with miraculous status so that 'the fact of Napoleon's defeat in Russia within two years of his being excommunicated by the Pope' is an indication 'to the illative sense of those who believe in a Moral Governor, of his immediate presence'.[37]

The great achievement of the *Essay* lies quite simply in Newman's grasping the idea that the precise form truth takes can change, depending on its context and the implications of its own structure, without being disloyal to its original, embryonic source. One has only to compare the flexibility of Newman's thought with the dogged, obstinate way in which Pusey, for instance, refused to admit of any development in theology lest he seem to deny that the faith had been once delivered to the saints,[38] to perceive how far Newman had moved since the days when he and Pusey had been allies. The importance of the concept which lies behind the *Essay* may be measured by the difference between the attitudes of the two men.

It is perhaps surprising that Newman made so little overt use of Darwin's ideas in the 1878 edition, though one may think him wise in view of the nonsensical uses to which the hypothesis was put by some of his contemporaries.[39] But Newman was not shocked by Darwin. He understood that evolution was a natural process, whether in the physical world or in thought. His claim that it was natural in theology was the more remarkable because he first made

---

[36] Ker, *John Henry Newman*, 669.

[37] A. Kenny, 'Newman as a Philosopher of Religion', in D. Brown (ed.), *Newman: A Man for Our Time* (London, 1990), 115.   [38] Below, p. 100.

[39] *The Transactions of the Ethnological Society* are full of references to these absurdities. See e.g. J. Crawfurd, 'On Language as a Test of the Races of Man', New Series, 3 (1865), 1 ff.

it more than twenty years before Darwin. It was an adventurous stroke of genius and most modern Christians instinctively react to the notion with a feeling that *of course* it must be something like that. The pity of it was that the brilliance of the idea was not matched by the way in which it was worked out and applied, and it is at this point that what was said earlier about the importance of treating Newman as poet, rather than as constructor of arguments, is relevant. It is the nature of effective poetry that it makes the reader respond with a sense of acceptance; that this is what *must* be true. But that acceptance is at a level entirely different from the analytical: it may be almost impossible to explain to anyone else what one has learnt from a poem or how one intends to apply it to one's own thinking.

It has to be said, of course, that for most Anglicans and Free Churchmen, the idea of development in doctrine would be so firmly associated with Newman's Roman Catholicism that they could not easily have borrowed it.[40] Roman Catholics themselves, in this period, were primarily concerned to assert the absolutely immutable character of dogmatic truth. All this, no doubt, partly explains why Newman's concept of development died with him. He was not entirely without disciples in later generations of Roman Catholics and Anglicans, and yet none of those of who wrestled with the problem of relating history to faith took up his attempt to define development in philosophical terms. It does seem to have been the case that there was little in his argument, or in the examples which illustrated it, or in the ways it could be used, to attract anyone else to take up where he had left off. Because his explanation and argument were less convincing than the fundamental conception, it was never pursued.

[40] Leonard Prestige, Gore's biographer, for instance, was repeating Gore's view that Newman was a 'false prophet' as late as the middle of the twentieth century. This is surprisingly late for vigorously anti-Newman feeling from within the Anglo-Catholic tradition. G. L. Prestige, *The Soul of a Prophet* (London, 1948), 25 f.

3

A HISTORICAL CUL-DE-SAC
Jowett's Liberal Protestantism

BROAD CHURCHMEN in the Church of England were not a party as High Churchmen or Evangelicals were. At the moment it is fashionable to say that none of the ecclesiastical parties is easy to define in terms of beliefs: there were too many cross-currents, interconnections, and mavericks. But it is nevertheless possible to generalize about some groupings. It is not wholly meaningless to say that the Evangelicals regarded justification by faith, penal substitution, and the literal inspiration of the Scriptures as essential doctrines. It is not remotely possible to define Broad Churchmen in such a way. Tait, Hampden, Jowett, Stanley, Arnold, Maurice, Colenso, and Frederick Temple are all usually reckoned to be Broad Churchmen, yet there is little that is common to all their theologies. There were some sharp differences among them, so that Jowett could describe Hampden as 'a Janus' and Mrs Tait labelled Jowett 'Latitudinarian'.[1] Above all else, they were individualists who tended to go each his own way.

In fact the English Broad Church stream tended to divide into two. One arm went from Coleridge to people like Maurice and Colenso: the other went from Arnold to Stanley, Jowett, and Frederick Temple. It would be an over-simplification to say that one was Cambridge and the other Oxford, but perhaps that had something to do with it. Between the two there was very little contact. This was not because of any apparent animosity. One can find evidence of the occasional approving comment about a member of one group by someone in the other.[2] They made

[1] Balliol College: MS 410, an undated, and incomplete, letter from Jowett to Stanley; and Lambeth Palace Library: Tait Papers: Personal Letters, vol. 79, fos. 25 ff. 'Churchmen', 'Churchmanship' and related terms are almost impossible to render into non-sexist language without tiresome and verbose circumlocution. Since the people described were almost all men, anyhow, I have retained the terminology.
[2] For F. D. Maurice's assessment of Jowett, see F. D. Maurice, *What is Revelation* (London, 1859), 213, and for Jowett's of Colenso see E. Abbott and L. Campbell, *The Life and Letters of Benjamin Jowett*, 2 vols. (London, 1897), ii. 65.

common cause in practical affairs quite often. Both Jowett and Colenso were present, for instance, at a meeting in 1864 in support of a bill to abolish all religious tests for Oxford degrees,[3] but there simply seems to have been very little contact and little or no exchange of ideas in spite of the fact that both groups were much influenced by Platonism.

What the Broad Churchmen did have in common was a belief that all truth originated in God and had a divine character. This explains their attitude to the discoveries of the natural sciences. Jowett thought that these discoveries simply did not compare in significance with the beauty of Plato's metaphysics.[4] But a scientific truth was a truth, even if it turned out to be a rather unimportant one. It was something established by divine creative activity. One must not, therefore, deny it, even if one were to find that it appeared to conflict with some traditional dogma of the Church.

One of the ways in which Arnold influenced other Broad Churchmen, and Jowett in particular, related to this very point. He made them see that an important difference between empirical and metaphysical truth is that empirical truth can be established with a far greater degree of clarity and precision. Theological truth, because it lay outside 'the reach of demonstrative science', would inevitably be 'regarded by different minds differently'.[5] This did not mean that theological truth was less important or even less certain, only that it could not be stated with a precision which would win agreement from everyone.

Conservatives believed that theological and metaphysical truth *could* be stated with precision and *ought* to be assented to by everyone; for truth was that which was guaranteed by authority, and the most important authority was God's. Statements about God, guaranteed by God's own authority, could be made with at least as much certainty and precision as statements about empirical truths. The conservative position was, therefore, very different from that of the liberals for whom all truth was the result of human enquiry. It was perceived, formulated, and expressed by human minds. Therefore it was felt to have a tentative, provisional nature, as well as an imprecise and speculative one. This partly explains why liberals like Jowett were inclined to press the claims of

---

[3] L. Campbell, *On the Nationalization of the Old English Universities* (London, 1901), appendix containing a list of all those present at the meeting.

[4] Abbott and Campbell, *Jowett*, ii. 431.   [5] Above, pp. 33 f.

'*common* sense'. He was using the term in its strict and original meaning, 'the sense *commonly* attributed to something', 'the sense it would normally be given by the *generality* of people'.

For this very reason Arnold's ideas about interpreting the New Testament also had a very considerable influence upon the young Benjamin Jowett. Arnold believed that common sense was the most important instrument in trying to understand the text of Scripture. One should treat a book of the Bible as one would treat a classical author, should try to get at what the author originally meant, and then try, as best one could, to put it into modern thought forms. But this—which Arnold called the 'scientific understanding'—was to be distinguished from the 'devotional understanding' in which 'God spoke to the reader'.[6]

Arnold's influence reached Jowett through A. P. Stanley, son of the bishop of Norwich and formerly one of Arnold's star pupils at Rugby. As undergraduates together at Balliol College, in the University of Oxford, and for several years thereafter, Jowett and Stanley were very close friends. Through Stanley, Jowett came to take up many of Arnold's ideas. What Arnold had done in turning Rugby into a centre for Broad Church Christianity, to which—nevertheless—the rising middle classes delighted to send their sons, Jowett was to try to do after he became master of Balliol in 1870.[7]

Jowett himself is chiefly remembered in that role, as a great master of the college, one of those who made modern Oxford what it is, and as a successful picker and groomer of undergraduates for high office. After the publication of *Essays and Reviews* in 1860 and the subsequent furore, he wrote no more theology; but that was because he had come to believe that he could spread his ideas much more effectively by gaining control of Balliol. Long afterwards he was to explain to Florence Nightingale, so often his confidante, that behind-the-scenes influence was always much more effective than the drama of controversy. 'The only way', he told her, 'is to work through the press—newspapers, Magazines, Books—especially through private and carefully written letters to distinguished persons. There is no means more efficacious than this.'[8] The equivalent behind-the-scenes strategy for the propaga-

---

[6] A. P. Stanley, *The Life and Correspondence of Thomas Arnold*, 6th edn. (London, 1846), 164 ff.

[7] P. Hinchliff, *Benjamin Jowett and the Christian Religion* (Oxford 1987), 27 ff.

[8] Balliol College: Jowett to Florence Nightingale, 6 July 1883.

tion of liberal theology was to preach it to the undergraduates in the college—the influential and distinguished persons of the future. Given the Oxford system and the autonomy of colleges, he would be beyond the reach of his opponents, provided he had an unshakeable control of the college and provided that the college continued to attract good undergraduates in sufficient numbers. In a much earlier letter written not long before he became master he told Miss Nightingale that he would concentrate on preaching, 'putting off the more heterodox aspect of things until I have gained (if I can) some hold'.[9]

Jowett's situation in 1875 was anomalous. In the university, as a whole, the theological conservatives, led by Pusey, were very definitely in the ascendant. In spite of Jowett's opposition, an honour school of theology had been created because Pusey and his allies believed that liberalism was a spent force, and that sound orthodox churchmen would always be able to control the teaching and examining for the school.[10] But Jowett, who was probably perceived as the leader of Oxford theological liberals,[11] was safely ensconced as master of Balliol. This had been the culmination of a long, and sometimes very unpleasant, campaign in which he had been defeated once, in an earlier mastership election of 1854, and had thereafter played David to his successful rival's Saul.[12] As a fellow of the college and virtually leader of the opposition to the master, he really controlled Balliol from about 1864,[13] and, of course, he continued to do so after his own election as master.

He built very successfully upon the sound foundations laid by some of his predecessors, which had made the college, as the report of the royal commission of 1852 had said, one of the most distinguished in Oxford at least as regards its fellows and scholars.[14] So the college continued to attract extremely able young men and, because Jowett was willing to widen the social class from

---

[9] Ibid.: Jowett to Florence Nightingale, 31 Aug. 1865.

[10] Below, pp. 102 f.

[11] See an article, probably by J. H. Millar, in *Blackwood's Magazine*, No. 161, entitled 'Mr Jowett and Oxford Liberalism', 723.

[12] Hinchliff, *Jowett*, 39 ff. and 95 ff.

[13] H. W. C. Davis, *History of Balliol College*, revised by R. H. C. Davis and R. Hunt (Oxford, 1963), 193.

[14] J. H. Jones, 'Sound Religion and Useful Learning: The Rise of Balliol under John Parsons and Richard Jenkyns, 1798–1854', in J. Prest (ed.), *Balliol Studies* (London, 1982), 89 ff.

which his undergraduates were drawn, recruited them also from strata of British society hitherto untapped as far as Oxford was concerned. Jowett also had an extraordinary ability to generate an enthusiastic loyalty among the undergraduates (as among his colleagues).[15] Even as a very old man he was capable of being almost hero-worshipped by the young, perhaps because he had the gift of being interested in current concerns. It is not surprising, then, that in his heyday—preaching regularly in the college chapel in an era when attendance at the services was still an essential part of college life—he should have been a successful popularizer of liberal theology.

To say this must be to make Jowett sound like a devious and scheming propagandist and there was, indeed, an element of the devious in his character. This is not to say that he was insincere or shallow in his religious beliefs. He had begun life, like so many of the leading religious thinkers of his generation, as an Evangelical from a family of pious Evangelicals. In a biographical sketch of Jowett, Edward Caird, his successor as master of Balliol, maintained that even after he became a theological liberal, his idea of what religion was, remained essentially Evangelical.[16] He retained, at any rate for most of his life, the Evangelical's warm personal devotion to Jesus Christ. 'Friendship with Christ' was one of his favourite ways of speaking about religion. And at a more theological level the same reconstructed Evangelicalism can be seen in his contribution to *Essays and Reviews*. Though he came out very firmly against the belief that the Scriptures were to be taken literally, his view was surprisingly 'biblicist'. As a classical scholar, his primary interest lay in establishing the *text* of Scripture and he was not much concerned to advocate an historico-critical approach to the Bible. Historical enquiry, he believed, could play an important part in arriving at the text itself, behind the centuries of comment and interpretation which had come to be inextricably associated with it; but once one had got back to the text, historical enquiry had done its work. One simply then read what the authors had written. He even believed that understanding the Scriptures required 'a vision and faculty divine'.[17] Where he differed from the

[15] Hinchliff, *Jowett*, 152 ff.

[16] E. Caird, 'Professor Jowett', *International Journal of Ethics*, Oct. 1897, p. 43.

[17] B. Jowett, 'On the Interpretation of Scripture', *Essays and Reviews*, (London, 1860), p. 337.

literalists was in what he thought the books meant and in the nature of the inspiration which he believed to lie behind them.[18]

He was passionately critical of the old orthodoxy just because it seemed to him that it involved shutting one's eyes to the truth and this, he believed, was a terrible thing. He once said of Tait, who had been his tutor and became a close friend, that he would have been a very great man if only he had thought that the truth mattered more than 'keeping the Church together'.[19] But when Seeley's *Ecce Homo* appeared, though Jowett thought it useful because it did not content itself with reproducing orthodox ideas, he was also highly critical of it for treating Christ as purely human and not as a 'sacred individual'.[20] His liberal theology was, in fact, a good deal more conservative than was often supposed.

It seems clear that Jowett's determination to capture Balliol was, at least partly, a result of the very fact that religious feeling and moral behaviour were immensely important to him. Oxford claimed—or pretended—to be a religious institution. Its members had formally to accept the official articles of religion of the Church of England. Its teachers had, by and large, to be ordained clergymen of the Church. Many of its ceremonies had a religious form and everyone had to attend divine service regularly. Yet the truth was that Oxford was far from being a deeply religious place. The religious observances were all too often merely observances. Jowett felt caught in a trap. He was forced to accept formal religious tests and exercises which encouraged neither real religious feeling nor genuine intellectual enquiry. And so it became his ambition to create an educational institution where one would not be forced to conform to a dead ecclesiasticism; where there would be an ethos which would actively encourage the spiritual as well as the intellectual development of the undergraduates.

Before he became master, Jowett had begun to attract attention, mostly adverse, as a liberal theologian. In 1855 he had published two volumes of commentaries, the first on Thessalonians and Galatians and the second on Romans, as part of a projected series on the Pauline epistles with A. P. Stanley (who contributed a volume on Corinthians). Though the commentaries made very little use indeed of critical biblical scholarship—and where they did, Jowett's position was mostly a fairly conservative one—he made it

[18] Hinchliff, *Jowett*, 74 ff.   [19] Abbott and Campbell, *Jowett*, ii. 394 f.
[20] Ibid. i. 425 f.

perfectly plain that he did not believe that the Scriptures were always literally true. He also insisted that such a belief was retrograde and dishonest.[21]

The real controversy was caused by a number of essays scattered in Jowett's volumes and focused chiefly on his theology of the atonement. The commonly held penal substitutionary theory he described as immoral, and his attacks were also levelled at the satisfaction theology of Anselm.[22] Both the Evangelicals and the High Churchmen were therefore outraged by what he had to say. Jowett's rejection of the prevailing belief that the atonement was to be understood as a sacrifice in which Christ bore the *punishment* due to human sin led to his being accused of teaching contrary to the Thirty-nine Articles. The vice-chancellor summoned him to his study and required him to subscribe the articles again. In this the vice-chancellor (who was Pusey's brother-in-law and devised a number of tactics for attacking Jowett) seems somewhat to have exceeded his authority, but Jowett, nevertheless, submitted. He was accused then,[23] and has often been accused since, of being unprincipled and unscrupulous for doing so.[24]

Jowett's attitude was, in fact, quite clear and difficult to fault. There were only three phrases in the articles which he could possibly be accused of contravening. Article VI says that 'Holy Scripture containeth all things necessary to salvation: so that whatsoever is not read therein, nor may be proved thereby, is not to be required of any man that it should be believed as an article of faith'. But there is nothing there to say that it has to be understood literally. On the atonement, Article II says that Christ 'truly suffered . . . to reconcile his Father to us and to be a sacrifice, not only for original guilt but also for all actual sins of men', and Article XV says, 'He came to be the Lamb without spot, who, by sacrifice of himself once made, should take away the sins of the world.' In neither case is anything said about *penal* substitution and there have been many theories of the atonement, throughout Christian history, which have said nothing about punishment and have yet been regarded as perfectly orthodox. Jowett seems to have

[21] On the commentaries and the controversy they generated, see Hinchliff, *Jowett*, 45 ff.   [22] Ibid. 62.
[23] See instances given in J. M. Prest, *Robert Scott and Benjamin Jowett* (Supplement to the *Balliol College Record*), 1966, pp. 10 ff.
[24] See e.g. A. M. Ramsey, *From Gore to Temple* (London, 1960), 60.

been wholly justified in arguing that he was not contravening the articles but only departing from the interpretation often put upon them.

In this view he was perfectly consistent. In the 1840s, when A. C. Tait was leading the attack on Newman and other Tractarians, alleging that they were disloyal to the Church of England in their interpretation of the Thirty-nine Articles, Jowett had refused to support Tait. His objection to Tait's campaign was that it surrendered the right to interpret the articles (not to the Church or to the State, who between them had originally authorized the articles, but) to the Hebdomadal Board of the University. In the 1850s Jowett was, once again, opposing the Board's attempt to insist that the articles must be interpreted in a particular and narrow way.[25] He believed, in an Arnoldian sense, that any theological statement must, in the nature of the case, be open to a variety of interpretations. One could be called upon to say, for instance, that Christ had done for man's sins, one could not be compelled to accept that that statement could be true in one sense only, particularly when that sense itself was not specified in the original. He saw no reason why he should not sign the articles, humiliating though it might be. It was 'the meaner part', he told Stanley.[26]

Jowett's other venture into theological writing was, of course, his notorious contribution to *Essays and Reviews*, where the chief damage was done by an incautious phrase. Jowett insisted that the Scriptures should be read 'like other books'. This was not the first time he had used the phrase, though it does not seem to have attracted attention earlier. Twelve years before *Essays and Reviews*, Jowett and Stanley had published a pamphlet on university reform in which they asked—among other things—for the creation of a theological school, in which the Bible would be studied along the lines advocated by Arnold. Jowett, describing the desired approach, had used virtually the same phrase, urging that the Bible should be regarded as having a clear, objective, and fixed meaning such as would be attributed 'to any other book'.[27]

So the notorious phrase was, in fact, a sort of shorthand for the

---

[25] Prest, *Scott and Jowett*, 7.
[26] G. Faber, *Jowett, A Portrait with Background* (London, 1957), 226.
[27] The pamphlet was published anonymously as *Suggestions for an Improvement of the Examination Statutes* but its authorship seems to have been an open secret.

Arnoldian approach to Scripture described earlier.[28] Jowett did *not* mean, as he was sometimes accused of meaning, that the value of the Bible was no greater than that of other books, nor that what one derived from it, or the way in which it was derived, was the same as with other books. He meant that, in order to understand what the author intended, one had to read a book of the Bible as one would read anything else, concentrating on what was actually being said on the page before one. It was essentially a plea for a common-sense approach.

Jowett's essay, the last in the book, was a long one, almost double the length of the other contributions. He insisted that it was essential that the results of scientific enquiry and critical scholarship be taken seriously, but he did not himself make much use of critical methods in the essay any more than he had done in his commentaries. A book of the Bible, he maintained, ought to be treated in its context and as expressing the mind of a particular author, an era, and a cultural setting. It had to be interpreted as one would interpret—for instance—a classical text. One's job was to discover what the author had meant, not some curious mumbo jumbo which divine inspiration was thought somehow to have imposed upon it. So Jowett wanted to get rid of the complex patterns of symbolic, traditional, and allegorical interpretation which, he asserted, had been read into, rather than out of, the actual text. He thought that trying to 'prove' doctrinal positions from Scripture was an ill-conceived and impossible task.

He was really concerned to make a very simple point; that the way to interpret Scripture is to discover the meaning which it had for those who first wrote, or read, it. The only way to avoid fanciful or idiosyncratic exegesis was to place each writer in his proper place on the continuum that makes up the Bible as a whole. And for this reason he accepted a version of the theory of progressive revelation. The controlling continuity in the Bible lay in the unfolding knowledge of God, which reached its climax in Christ. Legitimate Christian teaching from the apostles onwards looks back to Christ.[29]

The actual phrase is quoted from the pamphlet, but without any recognition that it was the phrase which was to cause so much trouble later, in Abbott and Campbell, *Jowett*, i. 175.

[28] Above, pp. 52.

[29] For a detailed discussion of this and other points made in Jowett's essay, see Hinchliff, *Jowett*, 69 ff.

Jowett was always an eclectic rather than a systematic thinker. One of his admirers once claimed that he believed that adopting a system 'closes the eyes of the mind'.[30] By the time he came to write his contribution for *Essays and Reviews*, he had developed a scheme of theological ideas which, because of his hatred of systems, he would not have called a system; and, of course, a proclaimed dislike of systems left him free to indulge his own tendency to eclecticism. He seems to have developed a passionate interest in Kant, Hegel, and Schleiermacher in turn, borrowing ideas from each and sometimes misusing them, then coming to the conclusion that the temporary hero did not, after all, possess the final answers to every question, and so moving on to the next enthusiasm.

From the closing section of Kant's *Critique of Practical Reason* he borrowed the idea that there are two things which excite awe—'the starry heaven above and the moral law within'[31]—and made of it one of his central theological concepts. God, he thought, should be understood as 'personality clothed in law'; for he came to believe that it was possible to hold together religion and the external world precisely by means of a belief in God as law-giver, responsible for both the moral and the physical laws. He found Hegel attractive just because he seemed to be bringing together again what Kant had sharply separated—religious and empirical knowledge. Hegel had made an attempt, too, to provide an explanation of how God acts in history, though Jowett disliked the dialectical form in which Hegel framed that explanation.[32] So the process of borrowing and redesigning ideas went on, with Schleiermacher also falling prey to it. Jowett, though he thought Schleiermacher too subjective and too inclined to emphasize the importance of the Church, took up Schleiermacher's concept of 'God-consciousness' (though he did not use that term) and made it the basis of his theory of the atonement.[33]

The ideas which seem to constitute Jowett's theology may be summarized as follows. Like the older German rationalists, he treated morality as the touchstone for the authentically religious: religion manifests itself in the individual as morality and everything moral is attributable to God. All reality, he often maintained and

---

[30] Davis, *Balliol College*, 190.

[31] Jowett's own translation of Kant, quoted in *The Epistles of St. Paul to the Thessalonians, Galatians and Romans*, 2 vols. (London, 1855), ii. 413.

[32] Abbott and Campbell, *Jowett*, i. 130.   [33] Hinchliff, *Jowett*, 83.

even more often implied, is spiritual in nature. This thought, which
he took from Hegel, doubtless explains why he so often argued that
the true and demonstrable facts of history and science (a favourite
phrase) are neither to be feared nor ignored. The laws by which the
world of nature operates are the workings of the divine mind, and
God is to be recognized in history, though as a continuum or
process rather than, as Hegel had maintained, as a dialectic of self-
realization.

God is to be found most immediately in Jesus, with whom it is
possible—because he is human—to have something which could be
described as 'friendship'; but a friendship which is also a
relationship with divine power. Indeed, his personal devotion to the
Christ of the gospels was a powerful emotional feeling, one of the
surviving influences of his early Evangelical upbringing and
perhaps always the most important part of his religious belief. But
because he refused to follow Schleiermacher in conceiving of the
Church as the means by which Christ is communicated to the
believer, he had to propose an alternative locus for discovering the
Jesus Christ through whose friendship the moral life becomes
possible for the believer. For Jowett, of course, this locus was the
Bible—understood, as Arnold had wished to understand it, in a
common-sense, straightforward way. What one would arrive at
would be, not an ecclesiastically preserved set of dogmas, but a
rationally justifiable belief distilled out of the historical form taken
by revealed truth. Revelation had its climax, its fullest moment, in
Christ: what went before him, led up to him: what followed,
looked back to him. And that Christ, Jowett believed, was available
to everyone.

Though it is clear that Jowett's 'borrowing' of ideas from the
German Protestant theologians was as much a process of distortion
as of simple borrowing, it is equally clear that he shared a great
many of their presuppositions. He was more familiar with German
theological writings than most of his English contemporaries.[34] His
lectures in Oxford, in the 1850s, were almost the only place where
one could learn about Hegel's thought, unless one was able to read
the original German. He was pre-eminently an individualist. He
believed that the mind, set free to make its own enquiry, would
arrive at the conclusion that religion was rationally justifiable and

[34] Hinchliff, *Jowett*, 78 ff.

that Christianity (as it really is, rather than in the form in which the dogmaticians had understood it) was the highest form of religion. The test for truth in religion, Jowett believed, was whether it would be found to fit with experience. He was probably, in other words, as near to a German Liberal Protestant as any religious thinker England produced in the nineteenth century. His was essentially an optimistic position. It placed great trust in the progressive power of the human mind, or at least of the élite human mind.

As master of Balliol it was, of course, to the élite of the future that Jowett believed himself to be preaching in the years between 1870 and 1893. The liberal gospel which he expounded from the pulpit of the college chapel twice a term,[35] was—at any rate up to about five years before his death—a reflection of the theological scheme set out above. On the whole, at least in his heyday, he handled the preacher's job rather well. There were those who complained about the effects his radical views had upon the young.[36] There were those, including even some undergraduates, who complained that he emasculated the gospel of much of its strength and passion.[37] But his style was lucid, simple, and direct. He made use of critical biblical scholarship and of ideas taken from the great German theologians, but presented them in a form which the average undergraduate would not find too indigestible. The occasional character of the sermon, itself, meant that it suited his eclectic mind. He did not need to be expounding a coherent system. He could deal with one idea at a time. If the idea expounded in the next sermon did not quite fit with the subject matter of this one, the audience would probably not notice; and, on the whole, his audience was impressed with what he had to say. They thought he dealt with 'real' subjects, rather than with remote and abstract doctrinal themes.[38] Those who criticized his theology as simplistic were nevertheless captivated by his style.[39]

Even to the twentieth-century reader what Jowett's sermons seem to convey is not the Jowett as described in most of the ecclesiastical histories which deal with the period. There he is presented as a

[35] Balliol College chapel, unlike most Oxford chapels, actually possesses a pulpit.
[36] Lambeth Palace: Tait papers: Personal Letters, vol. 90, fos. 199 f. and cf. W. H. Mallock, *Memoirs of Life and Literature* (London, 1920), 30.
[37] S. Paget, *Henry Scott Holland: Memoir and Letters* (London, 1921), 27 and 34.
[38] E. Caird, 'Professor Jowett', 47, and W. H. Fremantle (ed.), in B. Jowett, *College Sermons* (London, 1895), p. ix.   [39] Paget, *Scott Holland*, 33 f.

hypocritical, arid, faithless person. It is a clear case of the historians having taken over the kind of things that contemporary critics said about Jowett, without asking themselves whether, viewed from a different standpoint, the criticisms would still be valid. The sermons, in fact, are clearly the work of a man with a very obvious, even emotional, devotion to Jesus of Nazareth and a deep affection for the young men sitting at his feet. The echoes of Kant, Hegel and Schleiermacher which the sophisticated reader may detect, would not, of course, have been perceptible to most of the undergraduates in chapel. Perhaps, most apparent to them would have been the strong note of moral endeavour, of doing one's duty, which runs through every sermon and with which almost all of them end.

In fact it is fairly obvious that Jowett was not entirely conscious of this aspect of his preaching. He used to warn his disciples against moralizing in sermons by quoting to them the words of a butler whose employer's son was a clergyman and a former pupil of Jowett. When Jowett enquired one day how the young man was doing, the butler replied, 'He offends the people by reproving them for drunkenness. 'E should 'a stuck to the doctrine, sir, that could do no harm.' And Jowett would add, 'There must be more to your discourse than mere morality. If you give them a moral essay, not a poor woman in the congregation but will feel there is something wrong.'[40]

Jowett had set out in black and white in his contribution to *Essays and Reviews* what he thought the preacher's aim should be. 'If we would only be natural,' he had said, 'and speak of things as they truly are, with a real interest and not merely a conventional one!' One ought to 'avoid the form of argument from Scripture, and catch the feeling and spirit'. Scripture is itself a kind of poetry, when not overlaid with rhetoric; and so one ought not to deal with 'questions of Jewish law, or controversies about the sacraments, or exaggerated statements of doctrine which seem at variance with morality'.

The life of Christ, regarded quite naturally as of one 'who was in all points tempted like as we are, yet without sin', is also the life and centre of Christian teaching. There is no higher aim which the preacher can propose to himself than to awaken what may be termed the feeling of the presence of God and the mind of Christ in Scripture.[41]

[40] Abbott and Campbell, *Jowett*, ii. 272.
[41] *Essays and Reviews*, London, 1860, p. 429.

Had Jowett managed to live up to his own prescriptions, he would, no doubt, have left less of an impression of burdensome moralizing. He avoided well enough those pitfalls which he urged preachers to steer clear of. It was the positive rules which he laid down which he was less able to observe himself. Preaching the life of Christ came to have less to do with hope, love, and forgiveness than with the necessity of living the moral life, and a repetitive stress upon morality could create despair as well as endeavour.

In fact, the emphasis on moral striving seems to have derived from a combination of two things in Jowett's religious thought. On the one hand there was his strongly emotional personal devotion to Jesus. On the other, there was his insistence upon taking critical scholarship seriously, while refusing to give any systematic consideration to its bearing upon what the gospels actually said. The two acted sharply against each other and created a curious gap in Jowett's theology. He used morality as an apologetic device to get out of any problems created by that gap; and the more obvious the gap became, the heavier also became the emphasis he placed upon the need for moral living.

After he became master, one of the favourite themes of the sermons he preached in the college chapel was 'following Christ'. The central thrust of what he had to say in the years between 1870 and 1890 is very well represented by a sermon on 'The Permanent Elements of Religion' preached in 1879.[42]

The sermon was concerned with the problem, already referred to in the previous chapter, that Christianity has changed and developed a great deal over the centuries. If that is the case, what constitutes the essence, or continuing central core, of the faith? Jowett's immediate answer, in keeping with everything he had said about the holiness, love, and beauty of Jesus of Nazareth, was clear and direct. The essential Christianity lay in the simplicity of Christ himself who went about doing good.

But he was clearly aware that it would be naïve to leave the matter like that. He went on to examine some other possible answers to the question, all of which he believed to be false. In keeping with his usual technique he did not burden his hearers with specific references to the writings (or even the names) of theologians

---

[42] The sermon was separately printed as a pamphlet. A copy is bound up with the copy of Jowett's *Sermons on Faith and Doctrine* in the Balliol College library.

who had advocated the various points of view; but he discarded the theory that the heart of Christianity was to be found in specific institutional forms, because these would be 'relative to the age and state of society which gives birth to them'. Nor is it to be found in the 'internal certainty which good men have of the truth which has been vouchsafed to them', because the same intensity of conviction can be found among people with very different ideas of what truth in religion really is. Nor can it be found in supposedly historical, but miraculous, facts, because all historical facts are subject to historical enquiry and must be judged by the rules of historical evidence. 'If we saw them with our own eyes and in the full light of day, we should have a difficulty in verifying them or appreciating their import; how can we see them more clearly when they are far away in the distance?'

Jowett argued, instead, that the true, essential Christianity possessed three characteristics. (And it is important to remember that it was implicit in his argument that one ought to get back to this true, essential form of the Christian religion.) The first point was the perfection of the nature of God. Everyone, Jowett thought, would agree that God was perfect holiness, love, and truth; and everyone would also agree on what those qualities were and that one could never have too much of them. Therefore, Christians ought to stop arguing about metaphysical issues such as the being of God or the origin of evil, and content themselves with an essentially moral definition of what God is.

His second fixed point is worth quoting in the form in which Jowett himself put it:

Secondly, among the fixed points of religion is the life of Christ Himself, in whose person the Divine justice, and wisdom, and love are embodied to us. It may be true that the record contained in the Gospels is fragmentary; and that the life of Christ itself far surpassed the memorials of it which remain to us. But there is enough in the words which have come down to us to be the rule of our lives; and they would not be the less true if we knew not whence they came, or who was the author of them.

Jowett's third fixed point in the essence of Christianity ought to have forced his hearers and himself to face the crucial question which, in fact, he continued to refuse to tackle; for his third point is 'that we must admit all well-ascertained facts of history, or science. For these, too, are the revelation of God to us, and they seem to be gaining and accumulating every day.'[43] Coming immediately after his assertion that the first two essential points of Christianity are the perfect nature of God and the embodiment of that divine perfection in Christ, it ought to have forced him to attempt a reconciliation between the categorical nature of those assertions and the problematic character of the New Testament evidence.

In one sense, of course, he was simply reiterating in a sharper and clearer way a point he had been concerned to make over and over again for almost forty years. That the facts of science, if true, must not be denied, he had been asserting since the 1840s. In the commentaries he had insisted that there cannot be two kinds of truth, one for religion and another for the real world. And, along with that refrain, he had also been saying that true faith cannot be assailed by other aspects of truth. Previously, when the 'well-ascertained' facts of science or history had actually seemed to assail the truth of faith, he had always taken refuge in an appeal to morality—how one actually lived the Christian life was what mattered, not the intellectual problems. Every time he had felt obliged, in his early days as master, to remind the undergraduates that the gospel evidence was fragmentary or uncertain, he had gone on to say that that was really unimportant because there was no uncertainty about how Christians ought to live. Moreover, he was also accustomed to insist that it did not matter if the Bible seemed sometimes to convey a picture of God which conflicted with our own ideas of what was best and highest. We were entitled to maintain the highest possible concept of God and to believe that it was *this* God which had been revealed in Christ. That was precisely what he did again in 1879, in spite of having stated the problem in what appears at first sight to be an inescapable form. This is the force of his insistence that 'there is enough in the words that have come down to us to be the rule of our lives; and they would not be the less true if we knew not whence they came, or who was the author of them'.

In fact Jowett went on to summarize the whole argument of the sermon in one telling sentence. 'This, then, is what we believe to be the sum of religion: To be like God—to be like Christ—to live in every true idea and fact.' In essence this was what he had been

---

[43] Cf. H. F. G. Swanston, *Ideas of Order: Anglicans and the Renewal of Theological Method in the Middle Years of the 19th Century* (Assen, 1974), 151 ff.

trying to say all along but had never enunciated quite so clearly, comprehensively, and without obfuscation. The very fact that he thought he could put the whole thing in this one sentence suggests that he was not aware of the problem he was creating—or, perhaps, he did not think it was a problem. He hated and feared systems and he did not believe that logic could overrule common sense. He seems here to have reached the point of almost saying that one could invent one's own idea of Christ, read it back into the Gospels, and still claim to be living 'in every true idea and fact'.

This sermon really restated all Jowett's favourite themes; asserted them more precisely and clearly than usual; and put them bluntly side by side even when they appeared to contradict one another. He was firmly rejecting, as never before, the idea that religious truth was founded upon authority, whether of Bible, Church, tradition or orthodox dogma. The whole edifice of faith had become the achievement of the individual's rationality.

In effect, moreover, Jowett was declaring the truths of science and history to be part of the essence of Christianity, like the nature of God. They had become *de fide*, the third essential element in religion because it was in them that one had to live. But he seemed to display a much more sceptical attitude than he had shown, before, towards the narrative material of the gospels. He was no longer simply saying that the record was uncertain: he was asserting that a great deal of it cannot be true. Yet this did not alter his appeal to Christ. 'And if anybody asks', he said, 'Where, after all these assaults of criticism and science, and the concessions made to them, is our religion to be found now? We answer, Where it always was—in the imitation of Christ.' He gave no hint of being aware that it might be difficult to imitate a Christ about whom one could learn little: or, worse still, that it might be far too easy to imitate a Christ whom one had virtually invented for oneself.

Jowett probably failed to see the problem because, having started with a firm Evangelical attitude towards Christianity, it was possible for him to reinterpret his faith in terms of the new facts of science and history which he encountered and still cling to his previous understanding of the God revealed in Christ. It is not so clear that he was able to expound it to a new generation, which did not share those assumptions, to whom he was not prepared to teach the old certainties, and to whom he was yet looking to solve the problems.

Amid all the changes to which, during centuries to come, the Christian faith may be exposed, either from the influence of opinion or from political causes, the image of Christ going about doing good, of Christ suffering for man, of Christ praying for His enemies—this, and this alone, will never pass away.

Obviously he believed that, in spite of any detailed criticism which the gospel narratives might suffer, there would survive an unassailable sense of a *person* which could be conveyed to future generations. He might not be able to justify his methodology or expound precisely how the desired object was to be achieved; nor would he even have wanted to systematize it. To him it was just a matter of common sense that it was so.

Perhaps, then, it is not surprising that the sermon ended with what sounds like a reductionism which Jowett had, up to this point, managed to avoid:

To have a firm conviction of a few things is better than to have a feeble faith in many, and to live in a belief is the strongest witness of its truth.

For he is not a Christian who is one outwardly; neither is that Christianity which is in the letter only.

But he is a Christian who is one inwardly, and walks, as far as human error and infirmity will allow, in the footsteps of Christ.

Faced with an insoluble problem, Jowett seems to be saying that one would just have to give up believing a few more things while continuing to live as though one were certain of everything. Even to say that is to impose a kind of neatness—a conclusion—upon Jowett's position. In fact, it was rare for him to strike this kind of despairing, minimalist note. Far more often he would assert with blithe confidence his curiously contradictory conviction that one could live like the Christ about whom one could have little certain knowledge.

Jowett had embarked on his free enquiry with enormous confidence. He was certain that it would provide as secure a foundation for belief as could be provided by any dogmatic authority, but he lacked the rigour to be critical about his own ideas. His eclecticism and the gaps in his theological scheme created the curiously flawed gospel which he preached throughout most of his years as master of Balliol. Influential though he was, very few were able to follow his essentially simplistic approach to the problem of Christ and history. His was not, in fact, really a tenable position at all. Leslie Stephen's outline sketch for a life of Jowett reveals very clearly why so many members of the younger generation found Jowett's brand of the Liberal Protestant approach impossible to accept. It is true that Stephen was not a Balliol man; nor did he really understand what Jowett was attempting to achieve through the college. But while, for many, the problems created by this liberal gospel were quite simply obscured by their admiration for Jowett, Stephen was able to assess it more objectively. Finding Jowett's position quite unconvincing, he—and others like him—moved on and adopted an openly agnostic position.[44]

Even those Balliol men whom he influenced most, rejected his approach in the end. This means that Jowett stands in a very unusual position in the history of religious thought in Britain. His influence is almost entirely a *personal* one. It was the way the next generation of thinkers—mostly his own pupils—regarded him personally, rather than the preservation and propagation of his ideas, which was important. His influence may be traced through three groups in particular.[45] Most obviously, perhaps, some of his ideas survived through the work of the British Idealists. Jowett has, rather implausibly, even been called the John Henry Newman of the Idealist movement.[46] The implication of this title is presumably that Jowett was the person who initiated the movement, became critical of it, and moved away from it, yet would defend it against its enemies—as Newman had been in relation to the Oxford movement. But he also had a surprising influence upon the young Charles Gore, which has very largely been ignored by historians because Gore's biographer regarded Jowett as the embodiment of a liberal Christianity which was not worth believing.[47] Through Gore—and also more indirectly through William Temple—some of Jowett's liberal emphases found their way back into the more orthodox streams of Anglican thought. Finally, within Balliol itself, he established a tradition of open-minded, rational, but genuinely devoted Christianity which was expressed in terms of service to

[44] Cf. L. Stephen, *Studies of a Biographer*, 2nd edn., 2 vols. (London, 1910), 123 ff. and 131 ff. and, for a recent reconsideration of Stephen's loss of faith, J. P. von Arx, 'The Victorian Crisis of Faith as a Crisis of Vocation', in R. J. Helmstadter and B. Lightman, *Victorian Faith in Crisis* (London, 1990), 262 ff.

[45] See Hinchliff, *Jowett*, 152–81 and 209–32.

[46] H. Jones and J. H. Muirhead, *The Life and Philosophy of Edward Caird* (Glasgow, 1921), 126.

[47] For the evidence of Gore's relationship with Jowett, see Hinchliff, *Jowett*, 170 ff.

society, and to the casualties of society in particular. To this tradition belonged R. H. Tawney and William Temple, Arnold Toynbee and W. H. Fremantle, and all those who devoted themselves to movements like the Workers' Educational Association and the East End settlements.

None of these would have expressed their Christianity in terms precisely like Jowett's, but all, in some degree or another, were influenced by his insistence that it was perfectly possible to be an intelligent, rational believer. Yet they all had important reasons for finding his Liberal Protestant approach seriously deficient. T. H. Green and Edward Caird—the first of the British Idealists—found him too unsystematic and too wedded to history.[48] Bishop Gore, on the other hand, though he much admired Jowett's passion for truth, found him too cavalier in his attitude to Christian tradition. There are passages in Gore's essay in *Lux Mundi* which read almost like a debate with Jowett, to whom Gore owed a great deal but whom he could not follow. Even those Christian Socialists who belonged to the tradition founded by Jowett in Balliol, came to find his ideas far too Platonic and élitist. His was, in fact, too individualistic an approach, too subject to his own prejudices, to be satisfying even to those most exposed to his teaching. In this he was, perhaps, more Liberal Protestant than the Liberal Protestants. The mainspring of the Liberal Protestant attempt to find a rationally defensible version of Christianity was the individual's ability to pursue a critical enquiry and to come to a conclusion for himself. All too often, and certainly in Jowett's case, this carried with it a tendency to reject the corporate and the traditional. One's religion was one's *own* synthesis of ideas.

For this reason Jowett would not have been upset that his own particular understanding of Christianity was not taken up by any of his pupils. His hatred of systems, his dislike of teachers who tried to 'make disciples',[49] and his conviction that everyone ought to make up their own minds, all led in the same direction. Admittedly there were times when he behaved as though what he really wanted was for all his pupils to come to a full acceptance of *his* ideas by the free exercise of their own enquiring minds; but the fact that there never was a school of Jowettian theology was a great triumph for his own concept of freedom for truth.

---

[48] Below, pp. 124.   [49] Hinchliff, *Jowett*, 152 ff.

In the end, Jowett's optimistic confidence in liberalism was undermined. There is some evidence that, at some point in the last decade of his life, his earlier sense of a warm, vivid, personal 'friendship' with Christ began to fade. His sermons in this period are also rather different from his earlier preaching. Many of the later ones are 'biographical'—talks about a bewildering array of people such as Wycliffe, Loyola, Bunyan, Spinoza, and Tait. Others were little humane addresses about courage and sympathy and the right use of time, money, and conversation.[50] It is difficult to avoid the feeling that something had gone out of his own personal religion, and this is confirmed by a story told of the very last year of his life. It appears that he invited Cosmo Gordon Lang, the future archbishop of Canterbury, to come back to Balliol as chaplain. When Lang demurred, on the ground that he did not agree with Jowett's theological position, the master insisted that that was why he wanted him. His own liberal school, he said, had 'the truth . . . but we have no fire'.[51]

If there was a loss of faith or enthusiasm in the last years, it may have been a consequence of the incoherent, and therefore untenable, position he had taken up on the Jesus of history. It may also have been a consequence of an unusual friendship which grew up between T. H. Huxley and Jowett at the very end of the latter's life and which culminated in Huxley's Romanes Lecture delivered shortly before Jowett's death in 1893. The very subject of the lecture—'Evolution and Ethics'—seems to have been suggested by Jowett.[52]

Jowett had believed, all his life, that morality proved the truth of Christianity. If he had put it into words the argument would have gone something like this: morality is man's highest achievement and marks him off from the animals; it is the product of religion and is sanctioned by it; Christian morality is the highest morality, and so the Christian religion which has produced it must be the highest form of religion. Huxley's lecture[53] was principally directed against the followers of Herbert Spencer and argued that every human advance in morality and civilized behaviour has involved a

[50] Hinchliff, *Jowett*, 194 f.

[51] J. G. Lockhart, *Cosmo Gordon Lang* (London, 1949), 101.

[52] Imperial College London: Huxley Papers: Scientific and General Correspondence, vii. fos. 88 f., Jowett to Huxley, Feb. 1892.

[53] T. H. Huxley, *Evolution and Ethics and Other Essays* (London, 1894), 80 ff.

deliberate going against what he called the 'cosmic process', the biological mechanisms on which the Darwinian hypothesis depended. The lecture also advanced a defence of morality which made it wholly independent of religion. It was, in that sense, a ruthless attack on Jowett's belief that religion was the source of morality and therefore man's highest achievement. He and Huxley were in frequent contact in this last year of his life. Jowett was too ill when the lecture was delivered, and died too soon afterwards, for us to have evidence of his actual reaction to it. But, unless he was able to devise an answer to Huxley's argument, of which no trace survives, he is bound to have felt that one of his great axioms was axiomatic no longer.

Jowett's individualism, which made him so typically a Liberal Protestant, also made him very much an embodiment of the age in which he lived. Prevalent attitudes affected the very meaning of the word 'belief'. Even for those who were not particularly Protestant it had come to have an individualistic rather than a corporate meaning. It was what you worked out for yourself. For Jowett, 'belief' was primarily a passionate sense that the world was not simply a material and mechanistic system. It was a vehicle for the spiritual and the divine. The rest was an attempt—in his case an unsystematic and incomplete attempt—to discover what that spiritual dimension was like, to which Christ was the clue. For him, as for many others, belief was no longer a matter of accepting a set of propositional statements as if they were straightforward truths. They were mere hints, or indications, to be explored. His was almost the direct opposite of the position adopted by Newman's *Essay on Development*.

However, if he had not reflected the attitude of the age, Jowett's influence could hardly have been as great as it was. The immense change in his standing between 1860, when *Essays and Reviews* appeared, and the 1870s, when he had become master, is otherwise inexplicable. His election to that office, in itself, probably partly explains the change, but heads of Oxford colleges were not always automatically regarded as respectable and worthy persons. Jowett's radical religious position did not in any way prevent his becoming someone who was influential in the corridors of power and to whom important people would willingly entrust the education of their sons.

The change in religious attitudes may best be seen in the different attitude towards doubt. At the beginning of the century, doubt was almost universally regarded as a temptation, something to be stifled, resisted, and put away. By the end of the century, it had almost become an indicator of real religious feeling. For people like Jowett, doubt told one what questions to ask, what areas to explore. It was no longer an evil: it might be a staging post towards the truth. And, in the smallish world of Victorian intellectual society there were others who shared his views. Lord Tennyson, so much admired by the Queen, was a friend of Jowett and Jowett expounded the significance of *Lux Mundi* to the Poet Laureate when staying at his home on the Isle of Wight. It was all very respectable. And the opening stanzas of *In Memoriam* express a religious attitude which Jowett would have shared wholeheartedly (even if he preferred Browning's rather turgid and prolix poems, *Christmas Eve* and *Easter Day*).[54]

> Strong Son of God, immortal Love,
> Whom we, that have not seen thy face,
> By faith, and faith alone, embrace,
> Believing where we cannot prove;
>
> Thine are these orbs of light and shade;
> Thou madest Life in man and brute;
> Thou madest Death; and lo, thy foot
> Is on the skull which thou hast made.
>
> Thou wilt not leave us in the dust:
> Thou madest man, he knows not why;
> He thinks he was not made to die;
> And thou hast made him: thou art just.
>
> Thou seemest human and divine,
> The highest, holiest manhood thou:
> Our wills are ours, we know not how;
> Our wills are ours, to make them thine.
>
> Our little systems have their day;
> They have their day and cease to be;
> They are but broken lights of thee,
> And thou, O Lord, art more than they.

[54] Abbott and Campbell, *Jowett*, ii. 355.

4

THE OLDER THE BETTER:
Benson (and Lightfoot and Westcott)

A GOOD liberal, like Jowett, believed that truth was indivisible and that there could not, therefore, be any real danger in following where one's reason took one. In the end, one would come to truth about God. A mirror image of that conviction could also, all too easily, fasten itself upon another kind of mind. There were good, serious, devout scholars who were so convinced of the indivisibility of truth that it seemed to them that all scholarship must reflect what one knew to be religious truth. It was not dishonest to look for evidence to support traditional Christian truth: if it was true, the evidence must be there to prove it. Moreover, if the liberals got into difficulties because they sat too lightly to tradition, most people who took history seriously were likely to be, almost by definition, those who regarded tradition with immense veneration. And, perhaps, Cambridge, rather than Oxford, was the place where most such scholars were to be found in the later nineteenth century. There seems to be about Cambridge, as one looks back on it, a quiet, conservative, theological solidity, based on an interest in history and tradition, which is very different from Oxford's divisions and controversy. Cambridge was, after all, the home of the Camden Society (founded 1839), which concerned itself with the historical, liturgical, architectural, and ceremonial aspects of the High Church tradition, rather than the more deeply controversial theological ones.

This is not to say that nothing in Cambridge was theologically disturbing or disturbed. Herbert Marsh had there disseminated ideas of a critical kind about the Bible, in a particularly abrasive manner, in the very early part of the century. Seeley, whose *Ecce Homo* disturbed even Jowett,[1] was Regius professor of History at Cambridge from 1869. But *Ecce Homo* had been published four

---

[1] Above, p. 55.

years earlier, when he was a professor in University College,
London, and most of his later writings were purely historical. No
doubt undergraduates and even dons were unsettled by new ideas,
just as they were in Oxford. Leslie Stephen resigned his fellowship
and eventually his orders because of his doubts (and became the
founder of the *Dictionary of National Biography*). J. B. Lightfoot
told a select committee of the House of Lords that:

It is impossible to shut one's eyes to the fact that a flood of new ideas has
been poured in upon the world, and that at present they have not found
their proper level; minds are unsettled in consequence, and young men do
not like to pledge themselves to a very distinct form of religious belief.[2]

But Cambridge had never been as overwhelmingly clerical as
Oxford and, in the days before university reform, was perhaps less
deplorable. It seems, also, to have been strong on history. The first
Dixie professor of Ecclesiastical History was Mandell Creighton in
1884, who had founded the *English Historical Review* with Lord
Acton in 1866. Seeley, as Regius professor, had seen history
primarily as a school for future diplomats and statesmen and, for
that very reason, as an important and practical discipline. The same
sensible and practical approach to history seems to have marked
Cambridge theology.

Most accounts of nineteenth-century critical scholarship in
Britain, give the 'Cambridge Triumvirate' (Lightfoot, Westcott, and
Hort) pride of place in this respect. It is always stressed that they
possessed precisely this kind of good, sensible, faithful learning
which took what was best from the critical approach but avoided
the exaggerations of the more radical. Their contemporaries took
this view of them, too. Westcott, Lightfoot, and Hort all served on
the New Testament panel for the translation of the Revised Version
of the Bible, published between 1881 and 1885, while Jowett
always bitterly resented the fact that he had been—though
professor of Greek—omitted from the committee. Lord Acton once
asserted that in England it was ecclesiastical historians who first

---

[2] Quoted in V. H. H. Green, *Religion at Oxford and Cambridge* (London, 1964),
303. A. M. C. Waterman, 'A Cambridge "Via Media" in Late Georgian Anglicanism', *Journal of Ecclesiastical History*, 42 (July 1991), 419 ff., has assembled
evidence for a view of Cambridge theology in the late eighteenth and early
nineteenth centuries which makes it appear much more vigorous than anything
Oxford produced in the same period.

developed modern critical methods for the study of history, and that Lightfoot and Hort were amongst the greatest of them. And Hastings Rashdall was to say that the three Cambridge scholars raised English biblical scholarship 'from a condition of intellectual nullity up to the level of the best German work, while they infused into it a characteristic English spirit of caution and sobriety'.[3]

The trouble is that language of this kind is relative. What appeared dangerous and extreme in the 1880s will seem modest in the 1980s. Twentieth-century commentators, who complain about the radical and negative character of some nineteenth-century critics, sometimes hold views, themselves, which those same critics would have thought horrifying in the extreme. In a comparative sense, no doubt, the so-called triumvirate possessed that most English of all virtues, a concern not to rock the boat, but what probably marked them off from other critical scholars most of all was their obvious concern that their scholarship should serve the immediate needs of the Church—and of the Church of England in particular. One need not doubt their scholarship. They were historically learned men who believed that their learning could determine truth; and there was temptation implicit in that fact for non-rockers of boats. Quite without intending to do so, they might make historical enquiry serve a preconceived theological truth.

It is not clear, moreover, that the usual triumvirate is the right one to examine. Westcott, Lightfoot, and Hort seem to have become associated with each other in the collective, historical memory for reasons which are much more than fortuitous but ought not to be wholly determinative. Westcott and Hort worked together to produce a definitive Greek text of the New Testament. Their names are for *that* reason inextricably linked. Westcott succeeded Lightfoot as Bishop of Durham (though he was by three years the older man) and that fact joins their names together. In addition, of course, the three men *were* close friends. They were all associated with Trinity College, Cambridge. They had many interests in common. In that triumvirate, however, Hort is the odd man out. He was a product of Rugby under Arnold and Tait. He spent a considerable part of his life as incumbent of a parish outside Cambridge—and did not enjoy the work of a parish priest. He

---

[3] J. E. E. Dalberg-Acton, 'The Study of History', in J. N. Figgis and R. V. Laurence (eds.), *Lectures on Modern History* (London, 1912), 6 and 44, and H. Rashdall, *Principles and Precepts* (Oxford, 1927), 164.

never possessed quite the same established position in Cambridge enjoyed by the other two, though he was, in the last twelve years of his life, Hulsean professor and then Lady Margaret professor of Divinity.

On the other hand, Hort was ready to face very much more radical questions than either Westcott or Lightfoot, as was shown in the posthumously published *The Way, the Truth, the Life*, which revealed a determined faith nevertheless willing to be open to a wide range of critical questions. He was interested in a great many important issues—through the influence of F. D. Maurice and others he was concerned about social problems; he took a keen interest in the relationship between Christianity and the new natural sciences; he planned to write commentaries on the gospels; but he was prevented from properly pursuing any of these interests by the pressure of his textual critical work. Moreover, he was someone whose personal history was almost entirely intellectual: any biographical study of Hort, which focused entirely on his *actions*, would inevitably be very slight.[4] Lightfoot and Westcott, academics though they undoubtedly were, were also involved in the life of the Church in a way in which Hort never was. If one were to look for a more natural 'third' to associate with them, it would not be Hort but Edward White Benson, Archbishop of Canterbury from 1883 to 1896.

Benson shared with Lightfoot and Westcott a common education at the King Edward VI School in Birmingham and at Trinity College, Cambridge. It is true that Westcott was four years older than Benson and that those years would have mattered a great deal to schoolboys, but Lightfoot was only a year older than Benson and therefore, much more an inhabitant of the same world. The two were very close friends throughout their school days. Though Benson was elected a fellow of Trinity he never actually took up the fellowship and, therefore, was not an academic as Westcott and Lightfoot were. He also appears not to have shared their political views. They were, like Hort, interested in ideas which could be described as 'Christian Socialist'. At Harrow, where he was an assistant master, Westcott introduced Charles Gore to 'the spiritual

---

[4] There is a recent brief study of Hort—G. A. Patrick, *F. J. A. Hort: Eminent Victorian* (Sheffield, 1987). It should be noted, however, that the work transposes the publication dates of *Essays and Reviews* and Darwin's *The Origin of Species*.

glories of simple living; and a love of the poor'.[5] Benson, in spite of his friendship with Gladstone, to whom indeed he owed his appointment as archbishop, seems to have remained all his life a Tory in politics. Like Westcott, he became a schoolmaster—but at Rugby where he overlapped for a very brief time with Frederick Temple, who came to be headmaster there shortly before Benson himself left to take charge of the newly founded Wellington College in 1859.

Benson seems to have made up his mind that there was to be no more schoolmastering for him after Wellington and that he would move into some appointment which would enable him to play a fuller part in the life of the Church.[6] In this decision Westcott (who had become a canon of Peterborough in 1869, retaining the canonry after his appointment as Regius professor of Divinity at Cambridge in 1870) seems to have played a part. Rather to everyone's surprise, because it was thought to be something of a step down after Wellington, Benson became chancellor of Lincoln Cathedral until he was consecrated first Bishop of Truro in 1877. He was to succeed Tait as archbishop in 1883.

Meanwhile Lightfoot, having been a private pupil of Westcott's, became, himself, a tutor at Trinity in 1852 and then Hulsean professor in 1861, a canon of St Paul's a decade later, and Lady Margaret professor of Divinity at Cambridge in 1875. Four years later he was made Bishop of Durham, until his death in 1890, when he was succeeded by Westcott. At a crucial point in Benson's archiepiscopate the presence of Westcott at Durham, to act as a close adviser and also as a kind of unofficial spokesman and interpreter of his thoughts to others, was of immense importance.

It is extremely difficult to allocate any of them to the main ecclesiastical parties of the day. When he was at Wellington, Benson was once accused of arranging offensively Tractarian services in the chapel. His reply was to say:

I am myself neither High, nor Low, nor Broad Church, though I hear myself consigned by turns to all—as often to one as to another.

But I find too much to do in bringing before boys the weightier matters of honour, truthfulness, industry, obedience, mutual kindness, ever to

---

[5] G. L. Prestige, *Life of Charles Gore* (London, 1935), 9.

[6] I am indebted for much of my understanding of Benson to Felicity Magowan, a graduate student doing research on Benson and his influence on cathedrals in particular.

trouble myself, or them either, with party views, party questions, or party practices.[7]

That is a reply which the great Dr Arnold himself might have made. He also would have brushed aside party observances in favour of teaching the boys the real moral values; but Arnold's Broad Church sympathies were very different from Benson's. Whatever the latter may have *said* about the relative unimportance of ceremonial practices, it is perfectly clear that ordered and beautiful worship mattered to him a very great deal. The services at Wellington were actually planned in minute detail. The movements and positions of those participating, as well as the broader outline of the liturgy, were rigorously controlled,[8] though the ceremonial was not quite in the mould of the contemporary followers of the Tractarians. It is easy, of course, to claim not to belong to any party even when one is, in fact, deeply committed to opinions almost indistinguishable from the slogans of one of them, but Benson may have been more honest than most who make such a claim. His son was to say of him:

It is curious to note how difficult it is at this date to define exactly his ecclesiastical views. We find him devoted to Christian art and tradition, using ancient forms of devotion and hymns from Breviary and Missal. Yet he permits Evening Communions and simultaneously shocks a master by calling it a Mass; he is at the same time a devoted friend of both Kingsley and Temple.[9]

These last words are perhaps the most important part of that quotation. It was the influence of very un-High Church friends which prevented Benson from throwing in his lot entirely with that tradition. He was a great friend and admirer of Frederick Temple who actually visited Wellington to help the new master get the school started. This friendship made Benson, if not sympathetic to, at least not narrowly bigoted against, liberal ideas. Yet to someone who complained that he was not sufficiently critical of *Essays and Reviews*, he replied:

I will, if I have a chance, bring out more still my dislike—my horror—not my *dread*, for I will not fear it—of *Essays and Reviews*. But I did say,

---

[7] A. C. Benson, *The Life of Edward White Benson, sometime Archbishop of Canterbury*, 2 vols. (London, 1899), ii. 179.   [8] Ibid. ii. 175.
[9] Ibid. ii. 178.

(1) 'That the whole conception of the book was *wrong*.' (2) 'That it went *infinitely* farther than even that wrong conception.'[10]

He was also, when he had become archbishop, very much influenced by Randall Davidson, perhaps because of his gifts as an ecclesiastical politician and diplomat; and Davidson embodied and represented the tradition inherited from Tait, who was neither Evangelical nor Broad Churchman, but a sort of Anglicized Scottish Moderate who believed in holding the Church together.[11] Lightfoot, too, was very much an admirer of Tait and a friend of both Stanley and Jowett among the liberals. Moreover, since they had been educated at King Edward VI School in Birmingham, Benson, Westcott, and Lightfoot, were all influenced by the headmaster, Prince Lee, the future bishop of Manchester, though Benson perhaps least of the three.

None of these influences, different though they each were, could be thought of as remotely within the Tractarian tradition. It is, in fact, particularly difficult to say precisely what the Churchmanship of Benson, Lightfoot, Westcott, or Hort was. Some authorities describe Westcott and Lightfoot as 'Liberal Evangelical'.[12] Hort was a self-confessed 'sacerdotalist', a 'life long High Churchman'.[13] Lightfoot, whatever his Churchmanship, is remembered as the man who beautified the interior of the chapel at Auckland Castle, the home of the bishops of Durham.[14] The interest which they all had in history gave them a sense of the Church as a body which extended much farther than the England of the nineteenth century. It seemed to them important to recognize that the Church of England was only a fragment of a Christian world which had existed for very little short of two millennia. It also seemed important to establish what could be known of Christian history so as to judge the Christian present—though they did not wish to condemn it to remain unchanged. Such an attitude to Christian history made them feel that they shared a very great deal with the heirs to the Tractarians. Like them, they valued the rich inheritance from earlier history, but none of them possessed the Tractarian

[10] Ibid. i. 303.
[11] P. Hinchliff, *Benjamin Jowett and the Christian Religion* (Oxford, 1987) 18 ff. and 98.
[12] L. E. Elliott-Binns, *English Thought, 1860–1900: The Theological Aspect* (London, 1956), 123.   [13] Patrick, *Hort*, 97.
[14] G. R. Eden and F. C. Macdonald (eds.), *Lightfoot of Durham: Memories and Appreciations* (Cambridge, 1932), 72 f.

concern for establishing precisely in what sense the Church of England was the 'true' Church.

It was not at all that they doubted that the Church of England was both true Church and Catholic Church. It was, rather, that they simply took it for granted, both as an existent, and as part of the Church universal. They were perfectly happy to argue about what the position *was*, and what the position *ought* to be, in the Church of England, without asking questions about whether, in terms of the ideal and true 'Catholic' Church, the English Church had a right to exist at all. In the 'Church crisis', at the end of the century, this issue was to come to a head, splitting even the Anglo-Catholics between those who regarded the Church of England as an automotive institution and those who regarded it as two provinces of the Catholic Church.[15] It would hardly have occurred to men such as Benson, Lightfoot, and Westcott that there could be any doubt about the answer to that question. For them the Church of England was an institution which determined its own shape and had every right to do so.

They also possessed a Protestant conscience, in the sense that they all tended to require Protestant reasons for doing or authorizing High Church things, and they were anxious to insist that things should not be done for which there was no specifically Church of England authority.[16] Benson and his allies are probably best understood, in fact, regardless of what formal labels may or may not be attached to them, as continuing the attitudes and sympathies of the old pre-Tractarian High Church tradition. *Serious* Christians, in every sense of the term, (and seriousness was undoubtedly a characteristic of Benson, Westcott, and Lightfoot alike) these older High Churchmen are now often represented by historians as the 'orthodoxy' of the Church of England at the beginning of the nineteenth century. So far from accepting the Tractarian assessment of those who belonged in this tradition as high and dry, without vigour or enthusiasm—'Zs' in Hurrell Froude's estimation—

[15] I am indebted for my understanding of this issue to the Revd Alan Wilson who has recently completed a D.Phil. thesis in the University of Oxford on the Anglo-Catholic party and the Church crisis.

[16] e.g. A. Westcott, *Life and Letters of Brooke Foss Westcott, sometime Bishop of Durham*, abridged edn. (London, 1905), 478 ff. On the King case, to be discussed below, Westcott maintained 'that the Church Association *has* a case: that the aggrieved feelings are unconsidered of persons conscientiously afraid of Rome'. A. C. Benson, *Edward White Benson*, ii. 329.

historians will now argue that much pastoral and diocesan reform and reinvigoration was begun long before the Tracts started to appear and that, by creating party divisions, the Tractarians actually hampered the revival of the pastoral episcopate which they claimed to be promoting.[17]

In Benson's own archiepiscopate many of these very issues were raised in the trial of Bishop King of Lincoln in 1889 and 1890, which also very clearly demonstrated Benson's own attitude to the role to be played by history in the theological life of the Church. Bishop King was a saintly and much-loved Tractarian, with a pastoral reputation second to none. He was not an extreme man. He had been appointed chaplain of Cuddesdon to counteract the inflexible attitudes of H. P. Liddon. The Roman Catholic scholars he admired were 'liberals' like Döllinger and Sailer. He was, in fact, a moderate High Churchman of the early Tractarian kind, not over concerned about matters of ceremonial.[18] He was also pre-eminently a pastor. Not many Victorian bishops ministered to condemned murderers in prison or desired to be accessible to the ordinary working people in their dioceses. King was known for both these things.

The charges were brought against him by the Church Association, a vigorously Protestant body which had already prosecuted several High Church clergymen for 'ritualism'. The Association's enthusiasm for litigation to maintain the reformed character of the Church of England had waned somewhat by the end of the 1880s. Its funds had been depleted, paradoxically, by its earlier successes which had turned out to be curiously self-defeating. High Churchmen had been willing to go to prison rather than accept the decisions of courts which they regarded as secular and Erastian; the public could not believe that it was right to imprison respectable clergymen. The Association decided, nevertheless, to prosecute King for certain ceremonial practices. This required a courage that is not always recognized. It must have been perfectly clear that popular sympathy would, in any case, be on the side of such a bishop. Moreover, the Association decided to prosecute King in a

---

[17] This is one of the themes argued in R. A. Burns, 'Diocesan Revival in the Church of England, 1825–1865' (Oxford University D.Phil. thesis, 1990).

[18] J. A. Newton, *Search for a Saint: Edward King* (London, 1977), 58–64: as its title suggests, a somewhat hagiographical work, which makes out a very plausible case for regarding King as an early 'liberal' Anglo-Catholic.

court which was outside the normal judicial structures. High Churchmen had refused to recognize the decisions of those secular courts which had been empowered by law to judge ecclesiastical matters. The Association hoped that, since the archbishop's court of special jurisdiction was undoubtedly a court which possessed no secular authority, there would be no excuse for evading its decisions.

With hindsight, it is possible to feel that the scales were weighted in King's favour. The Church Association seemed to have chosen to fight the battle on the most unfavourable ground possible. And the archbishop might, in any case, be expected to favour the bishop's cause. Whatever his Churchmanship, Benson was certainly not a belligerent Protestant. His temperament and office would both make him disinclined to action which would divide the Church. He had been a canon of Lincoln Cathedral during the episcopate of King's predecessor Christopher Wordsworth (another moderate High Churchman whom both Benson and King admired). He had already turned down an appeal from the Church Association against King's veto upon a prosecution of a clergyman in the diocese. But the bishop plainly did not think the outcome a foregone conclusion. He seems to have found the case a great ordeal which made it extremely difficult for him to continue with his normal episcopal functions. All his friends talked about the way in which it was almost breaking his heart.

An entry in the archbishop's diary—written during the preliminary manœuvrings—draws attention to the difference of attitude between Benson and King. Benson thought King was ambivalent about the independent authority of the Church of England. He appeared to believe that he had a duty to maintain obedience to a notional 'Catholic' tradition, if not an actual 'Catholic' authority, outside the national Church. The archbishop wrote, 'The Bishop of Lincoln's point apparently is that he extends liberty by breaking the law—very sad! I wish he would lay to heart, holy man that he is, what the Prayer Book says "of ceremonies".'[19] The reference is to the prefatory declaration entitled 'Concerning Ceremonies, why some be abolished and some retained' in the Book of Common Prayer of 1662. It contains the words, 'And although the keeping or omitting of a Ceremony, in itself considered, is but a

[19] A. C. Benson, *Edward White Benson*, ii. 325.

small thing; yet the wilful and contemptuous transgression and breaking of a common order and discipline is no small offence before God.' Benson then went on to note down a series of points which he thought that those who sympathized with the Bishop of Lincoln would do well to consider. They included the following:

1. That our Church of England was free to make her own orders as to rites and ceremonies, and that she had made them; that they commanded our obedience and were not to be altered into conformity with the usages of another Church; that her dignity and our loyalty were engaged; that we are free to use other means, argument, preaching, and writing, to get the law altered; that this freedom was especially English, but the liberty to break the law was not real liberty, nor an English habit.[20]

King's very different understanding of the matter appears in a letter which he sent to every incumbent in his diocese, together with a copy of his formal protest against the constitution of the archbishop's court:

. . . it is not, and it has never been, my desire to enforce any unaccustomed observance on an unwilling congregation; but my hope now is that this prosecution may, in God's providence, be so overruled as ultimately to promote the peace of the Church by leading to some authoritative declaration of tolerance for certain details of ritual observance, in regard to which I believe that they are either in direct accordance with the letter of the Prayer Book, or at least in loyal and perfect harmony with the mind of the Church of England.[21]

The archbishop's appeal to 'Englishness' now has a somewhat comic sound to it. It would not, even at the time, have had much effect on the Anglo-Catholic party, but it reflects the essentially pragmatic approach of Benson and his friends. The Church of England existed. It had its own history, which was as real and as valid as any other part of Christian history. What the archbishop had to deal with was that Church—not some Church of England as it existed in the imaginations of either the Low Church or the High Church parties, but the Church of England as it actually was. That Church of England included people whose imaginings were of both kinds. Some of them imagined the Church of England as simply a product of the Reformation, a pure and Protestant institution.

---

[20] Loc. cit.
[21] G. W. E. Russell, *Edward King, Sixtieth Bishop of Lincoln* (London, 1912), 166 f.

Others imagined it as two provinces of the One, Holy, Catholic, and Apostolic Church, temporarily separated from the other provinces in appearance but not in essence. To pragmatic Anglicans, each of these imaginings seemed as impractical as the other. If the Church of England was to survive in any shape remotely like that which, by the late nineteenth century, it had come to possess, these two imaginings had each to be persuaded to acknowledge the validity of the other. The archbishop and his friends hoped that, by taking up with energy the proposal that he should exercise the jurisdiction of a metropolitan over his suffragans, history could be used to bring a more pragmatic note into the apparently irreconcilable controversy about principles.

In one sense Benson was ideally fitted to do this. He knew a very great deal about ancient liturgy, more perhaps than many of those who claimed to stand in the 'Catholic' tradition. He also knew something of ancient canon law, and acquired more knowledge of it while the case proceeded. He was interested in the history of the Church. His work on St Cyprian was done during his archiepiscopate, which meant that he was steeped in the thought of the early Christian centuries. He had attempted at Lincoln—now King's own see city—to revive and modernize the educational work of a great cathedral and he had been determined at Truro to create a modern diocese whose cathedral would embody, in the nineteenth century, the ideals for which its medieval predecessors had stood. These things meant that he also knew something of the Middle Ages. In terms of the scholarship of his day, the archbishop was historically educated. He would not make obviously silly mistakes in his handling of the issues.

He was, however, setting himself a formidable task. First of all, he had to sit in person. That was the essence of the whole matter. Just because the High Churchmen refused to recognize the authority of secular courts, they had to be persuaded that the archbishop as metropolitan could exercise a purely ecclesiastical and spiritual jurisdiction over the bishops of the province. To allow any of his law officers to appear on his behalf would not only be interpreted as undermining the dignity of the bishop who was being tried. It would also be interpreted as making the court not the archbishop's court, but the court of an official who was part of the hated secular and Erastian system. Because he had to try the matter himself, Benson had to be able to move easily and with competence in the legal minefield created by the earlier prosecutions for 'ritualism'.[22] His first historical task was quite simply to acquaint himself with as much as possible of the whole history of canon law, both before and after the Reformation.

This was particularly important because of the uncertain character of the very court itself. The archbishops of Canterbury had only once since the Reformation sat in judgement on any of their suffragans. That case had been very different, because then the bishop had, in effect, been tried for immoral behaviour. It was far from clear, therefore, that it constituted any precedent for Benson's proposed action. Moreover King claimed that the very form of the court was invalid. He argued that *all* the bishops of the province should sit together to try one of their number whereas Benson proposed to be the only judge. He would sit with five of the bishops of the province acting, at his own invitation, as assessors.

Because the constitution of the court was challenged, Benson had to be prepared to deliver a public and judicial decision on the matter, which would come under a great deal of learned scrutiny. He also had to do a great deal of arguing behind the scenes to convince the various parties that it was better to constitute the court, in spite of the dubious nature of the precedent, rather than exercise any supposed archiepiscopal 'discretion' to avoid hearing the case, however tiresome the prosecutors might seem to be.

There was, next, the actual substance of the case itself. King was accused of performing certain actions during the celebration of the Holy Communion which were unlawful in terms of the directions of the Prayer Book. They were:

1. Mixing water with the wine in the chalice *during the service* and then consecrating the mixed cup;

2. Facing east during the first part of the service, with his back to the congregation;

3. Standing on the west side of the altar during the consecration prayer in such a way that the congregation could not see the manual acts being performed;

4. Causing the hymn *Agnus Dei* to be sung after the consecration prayer;

[22] Since 'rite' refers to the actual words of a service, this term is strictly a misnomer. What the 'ritualists' were accused of was the performance of certain *ceremonial* acts; but to insist on calling them 'ceremonialists' would be to court confusion.

5. Performing the ablutions of the chalice and paten at the end of the service and in the presence of the congregation;

6. Using lighted candles—which were not needed for the purpose of giving light—on the altar, or on the retable behind it, during the service;

7. Making the sign of the cross with an upraised hand, facing the congregation, during the absolution and the blessing.

Weighing these actual charges involved two kinds of consideration of liturgical history. There was first of all the consideration of general issues, such as the authority of a bishop to allow or perform liturgical actions, or the nature of rubrics themselves—whether they were legally enforceable requirements or general directions as to the kind of action which was appropriate. Moreover, since liturgical and canonical tradition tended to the latter view, while the judicial committee of the Privy Council in earlier 'ritualist' cases had taken the other opinion, there had to be a somewhat delicate examination of very recent history in the Church of England. Pragmatic considerations, of the kind that Benson favoured himself, also meant that he had to analyse both ancient and medieval ecclesiastical traditions as well as the Reformation history and the intentions of the reformers. All this had to be done in such a way as to ensure that the historical enquiry itself, if not the specific conclusions to which the archbishop came, would be recognized by all the parties as relevant to the issue. This last point was, perhaps, the most important of all. The High Church party had to be persuaded to recognize that the post-Reformation history of the Church of England had a bearing on the way nineteenth-century 'Catholic' priests and bishops ought to behave. The Low Church party had to be persuaded that the liturgical and canon law traditions of the pre-Reformation Church were relevant to what happened in the Church of England in their own day.

In the event the archbishop's judgement was a very scholarly performance. How far it was influenced by considerations of ecclesiastical politics, it is now impossible to say. As far as one can tell from the actual arguments, it seems to be a genuinely unbiased piece of reasoning, honestly set out. Its general conclusions, however, were so exactly what was needed in the circumstances that one is bound to wonder whether they were arrived at by pure scholarship.

The judgement went against the Bishop of Lincoln on the matter of the mixing of the chalice and the use of the sign of the cross at the blessing and absolution. He was told that it was not enough that he did not intend to hide the manual acts at the consecration: he must intend that they should be visible. And there were various *obiter dicta* unpalatable to the High Churchmen, such as Benson's expressed belief that anything that gave the ablutions the appearance of being part of the service—which, as he pointed out, was not in question in the case—would be illegal. There was general agreement among the learned that the judgement displayed considerable and accurate scholarship.

In fact, however, it was not really the degree of historical learning displayed in the judgement which really mattered. The vital issue was whether it would be accepted by both parties and especially by the High Churchmen. His son's biography of the archbishop claimed that there was never any doubt about the acceptability of the judgement to the High Churchmen,[23] but the very material contained in the volume suggests that this was not really the case. What was clear was that the High Churchmen were pleased that an archbishop of Canterbury had come down on their side on a number of important points like the eastward position. But no one can seriously imagine for a moment that they were willing to abandon practices like making the sign of the cross at the blessing or mixing water with the wine in the chalice.

Benson himself plainly thought that he had succeeded in his enterprise. His own assessment of his judgement, contained in a letter written to the archdeacons and rural deans of his diocese, was:

Looking now at the conclusions of the Court, the accurate limits of those conclusions, and that which emerges from them, I would ask the clergy primarily to observe that each conclusion relies on the whole claim of the history of each observance, and on the fact that the English Church is a true faithful branch of the Church Catholic, enjoying the right of every branch to order its own rites and ceremonies within the limits of Scripture, and of the 'edification whereunto all things done in the Church ought to be referred'; and that our Church asserted in its Reformation and made use of this its authority, and specially by the restoration of the primitive order and tone in the Holy Communion.[24]

---

[23] A. C. Benson, *Edward White Benson*, ii. 366 ff.
[24] Ibid. 372.

The whole tone of this passage suggests that the archbishop thought that he had achieved what he had set out to do. He had gone into the *history* of each practice and come to historical conclusions about it. But he had done so in a manner which made two cardinal assumptions, that the Church of England was a true and faithful branch of the Catholic Church and that in the Reformation it had asserted its independent right to order its own ceremonies. Randall Davidson's biographer, commenting on the case, wrote that 'On two points in particular Benson set an especial value. The first was that history had been proved admissible in the interpretation of the substance of rubrics. The second was that the judgement of the Privy Council could be reversed.'[25] That 'history had been proved admissible' would have seemed the most important thing of all.

In an age when differences of Churchmanship had become a very serious problem for the Church of England it must have seemed that historical investigations and historical conclusions were one of the very few ways in which some sort of solution could be found. Benson was, in fact, facing a particularly acute case of the general problem outlined at the beginning of this chapter. History had become a formidable tool for reconstructing the past. It was capable of providing answers to a great many doubtful questions. Establishing with certainty precisely what had happened seemed to be the crux of historical scholarship. If it could provide objective answers to theological questions it might transcend the biased opinions of the quarrelling parties.

Underlying this new [historical] science was an almost Promethean will-to-truth. The aim of the historian, it was declared, was to 'tell what really happened'. The magic noun was 'fact' and the honorific adjective was 'scientific'. Description, impartiality, and objectivity were the ideals, and the rhetorical phrase and the value judgement were looked upon with disdain.[26]

Moreover, if there was a will-to-truth, there was also a sense that the truth was accessible as it had never been before. In such a climate of thought it must have seemed particularly desirable to discover an objective test which would determine what was and what was not permissible within the Church of England and so

[25] G. K. A. Bell, *Randall Davidson Archbishop of Canterbury*, 2nd edn. (London, 1938), 149.
[26] V. A. Harvey, *The Historian and the Believer* (London, 1967), 4.

bring party disputes and divisions to an end. But there were two difficulties about this programme. One was that it contained an implicit confusion between history and theology. History was to be used to answer theological questions, which it was hardly competent to do. The other was that it required an almost superhuman absence of bias on the part of the adjudicator.

It has to be remembered, of course, that Benson would not have assumed that what was determined by history would then be unchangeable for all time. He had insisted, before the Lincoln case began, that 'we are free to use . . . argument, preaching and writing, to get the law altered' and that 'this freedom was especially English'.[27] He must have believed, then, that there was a proper process—though he might not have liked to call it a democratic process—for changing what history revealed. What he objected to was the determination to change the situation by simply refusing to be bound by it. And, perhaps, what he would have found most sad about the situation after the judgement was the way in which all parties proceeded to do just that. They behaved as they thought fit, without any regard for what the archbishop would have seen as the proper demands of the Church. Toleration came to the Church of England not because everyone knew which traditions had been part of its history and decided to permit those traditions to continue or to add new ones. Toleration came simply because people who did not accept the historically determined situation went on breaking the law until a blind eye had to be turned towards their activities.

No primate could really be happy about such a situation. As archbishop, Benson was responsible for seeing that bishops and clergy in his province obeyed the law of the Church. A great part of the problem was that no one knew precisely what the law required. It was all very well for people to say with gratitude that the Church of England, as by law established, was part of the English constitution. There was no English constitution in the sense in which there was an American constitution, a written document which every citizen could consult. The 'English constitution' was a mass of legislative acts, custom, precedent, convention. Ten years before the King case Lewis Dibdin, who was to become one of the most eminent ecclesiastical lawyers, had said:

The whole system of ecclesiastical courts is to most people an unfathomable mystery. Their origin, their functions, their procedure are equally

[27] Above, p. 83.

obscure, and the only thing which repeated experiment has made clear about the Church judicature is that it will not work. The machinery is either so complicated as to be beyond the manipulation of modern craftsmen, or so rusty and worn out as to be practically useless.[28]

In other words, the only way to discover what the legal position of the Church was, was to go to law about specific points and even then the answer might be disputed. And this was the cause of many of the lawsuits of the nineteenth century—and the pretext for even more.

Benson's situation was not particularly different from that of his immediate predecessors. Tait had also felt the burden of the task of holding the Church together and had been despised by some of his friends because he seemed to place unity above truth.[29] But Tait had tried to find the solution to the problem in the Public Worship Regulation Act of 1874. He had thought that the clergy could be compelled to accept a redefined set of rules and regulations to govern the use of the Prayer Book and to set limits upon permissible modifications of it. But those rules had been made and imposed by Parliament. Anglo-Catholics would not obey them, and Benson was sufficiently sensitive to scruples of that kind to refrain from falling into a similar error. The very language he used in his letter to his archdeacons and rural deans shows that he was aware of the way in which High Church clergymen thought and spoke. Tait had had no interest in history, certainly not in the kind of history which fascinated Benson. Benson's interest in the past may have been decidedly romantic, but he was determined to make history useful to the Church.

The Victorian belief that it was possible to determine, objectively, what had happened in the past was often expressed in the idea that the facts could speak for themselves. We should now be much more hesitant about making such claims. Modern historians recognize that their function *is* to interpret the facts, perhaps, even, that their function is to *be* subjective, and it is frequently argued that it is precisely when the historian thinks that he is not being subjective that his work becomes most distorted by unconscious bias. In this respect Benson and his friends may have been unsophisticated, though they were plainly aware of the polemical uses to which

---

[28] Quoted in S. C. Carpenter, *Church and People, 1789–1959* (London, 1959), 226 n.   [29] Hinchliff, *Jowett*, 98.

history could be put. Perhaps they were too easily convinced that they had established the truth, when what they had really done was no more than to set out the arguments for the conclusion that they wished to arrive at.

The same combination of thorough historical scholarship and a modicum of wishful thinking, which seems to be manifested in the King judgement, is also to be found in Benson's treatment of the variant readings in St Cyprian's *De Unitate*. There can be no doubt of the worth of his life of Cyprian which was published post-humously. It is an astonishing achievement for someone as busy as a late nineteenth-century archbishop of Canterbury. It is still, a century after its publication, regarded as a serious contribution to historical scholarship. It would be dangerous for anyone writing about Cyprian now to ignore altogether what Benson had to say, but the work is not without its weaknesses. There are times when the thoughts and ideas attributed to Cyprian seem more appropriate to a nineteenth-century English headmaster than to a Carthaginian bishop at the time of the Decian persecution. Sometimes the author assumed that canon law had become much more elaborate and fixed by the middle of the third century than seems entirely likely. But the most worrying feature of the work is really the way in which the picture of second-century episcopacy which emerges turns out to be so convenient for the nineteenth-century Church of England.

What is true of the book as a whole is particularly true of the chapter which deals with the variant readings in *De Unitate*. There is much greater agreement now about how those variants may have come to exist than there was in Benson's day. It would probably be fairly widely agreed that Cyprian may actually have written both versions, adapting his argument to fit changed circumstances.[30] A good deal of the heat has also gone out of the argument in other ways. It is recognized that Cyprian might well have changed his mind about the primacy of Rome, without this necessarily implying a major theological revolution. Moreover, it does not necessarily follow that whatever view Cyprian can be shown to have held is binding upon the Church for all time. In the much more polemical situation of a hundred years ago, however, it seemed to Benson

---

[30] P. Hinchliff, *Cyprian of Carthage and the Unity of the Christian Church* (London, 1974), 109 f.

extremely important to establish that Cyprian had not written the version which appears to attribute to Rome, as the see of Peter, a primacy over all other bishops, and to make communion with the see of Peter a condition of being part of the universal Church.

The archbishop's final judgement in the matter is well known for its acerbic character. 'The words [in the Petrine text] are spurious,' Benson wrote. 'The history of their interpolation may be distinctly traced even now, and it is as singular as their controversial importance has been unmeasured. It is a history which will make it the most interesting of literary forgeries. But the Ultramontane is still unconvinced, and as he may long remain so, we lay the evidence before others.' Having done that to his own satisfaction, he concluded, 'Thus if there never was a viler fraud than the inventor's, there never was a worse nemesis than the honest obtuseness of his instrument.'[31] For the archbishop believed that those anxious to strengthen the Ultramontane case had tried to suppress the so-called *textus receptus* and bring copies of it into line with the Petrine text and had done so in such a clumsy fashion as to leave plain traces of what they had been up to.

In surveying the evidence Benson demonstrated how thorough was his grasp not only of the events of Cyprian's own lifetime and of the content of his writings (and of those sometimes falsely attributed to him), but also of the history of the manuscripts and of the printed editions, of the principles for establishing the preferred reading in disputed texts, and of the general history of papal theory. It is a real *tour de force*. And yet, precisely as with the Lincoln judgement, one cannot help wondering whether the conclusion is not just too neatly and exactly the conclusion which would have suited Benson best. He was able to imply that the case for papal supremacy was rather dishonest, that the evidence in its favour was weak, that Cyprian was clearly against it, and that, therefore, the earliest available evidence showed that the doctrine was foreign to the early Church. The conclusion seems to be that any honest person looking at the arguments for and against would abandon the Ultramontane position forthwith.

The case was, of course, less straightforward than that. Benson was, no doubt, correct in arguing that the third century knew no

---

[31] E. W. Benson, *Cyprian: His Life, His Times, His Work* (London, 1897), 201 and 209.

developed doctrine of papal authority such as that held by Roman Catholics in the last two decades of the nineteenth. He was probably correct in concluding that Cyprian did not intend to advance the bishop of Rome's claim to exercise an authority over other bishops. It would run contrary to everything we know of Cyprian's character to suppose that he had done so. But whether Cyprian was the author of the Petrine text of *De Unitate* is another question, and, in fact, none of these matters has very much bearing upon the *theological* issue of papal authority and jurisdiction. That was a matter to be determined on wholly other grounds than the historical points involved in establishing the correct text of Cyprian's treatise.

Late nineteenth-century thinkers, however, seem to have been haunted by the assumption that historical enquiry could somehow determine theological orthodoxy, that theological questions could be settled by an appeal to history. This assumption may have originated, partly, in the relationship between critical, historical study and textual criticism,[32] for in establishing the correct reading in a text there is a very good reason for saying that the earliest version is the best. It is, after all, nearest to the original. In settling doctrinal issues, however, it is not always the case that what was 'first believed' was 'believed rightly'.

It was, perhaps, no coincidence that all the Cambridge men, including Benson, were so concerned with textual criticism. The great contribution to scholarship of Westcott and Hort lay in their establishing the text of the Greek New Testament and Hort's statement of the principles and methods to be used in textual criticism 'is now regarded as the definitive statement on the subject. It was the first attempt in any language to summarize the theory and science of textual criticism, and its conclusions still stand. . . . Indeed it has been acknowledged that it lays down the criteria which are valid for the interpretation of any kind of writing—historical documents, for instance—and not solely for ancient biblical manuscripts.'[33] Lightfoot's work on the Apostolic Fathers is, in its way, just as much of a watershed in the history of patristic texts.[34] His consideration of the Ignatian epistles and his conclusion, contrary to his initial assumption, that all seven letters

---

[32] Above, p. 25.   [33] Patrick, *Hort*, 77.
[34] J. B. Lightfoot, *The Apostolic Fathers, with Introduction, Notes, Dissertations and Translations*, 2nd edn., 3 vols. (London, 1890).

were substantially genuine is a masterly piece of scholarship,[35] but is, again, primarily concerned with establishing which were earliest and best. Even Benson, as we have seen, was very much concerned with matters of textual criticism in his study of Cyprian.

It is unlikely, however, that an interest in textual criticism entirely explains the attitude to history adopted by Benson and his friends. They were, after all, extremely able in their historical scholarship. One has only to compare the kind of work they were doing with the work of the previous generation of ecclesiastical historians, like Stanley, to realize what a very considerable advance in scholarship they represent. A. P. Stanley had been professor of Ecclesiastical History at Oxford from 1856 to 1864. He did not die till 1881, but his contribution to the subject was of a kind which would not now be regarded as very significant. Bernard Reardon's assessment of his scholarship is almost a perfect example of damning with faint praise.

. . . like Milman he possessed a lively imagination, even if accuracy was apt to elude him. . . . He was better at popular history, as in his lectures on the history of the Eastern Church (1861)—still worth perusal—or on that of the Jewish Church (1863–65), or historical travelogues such as *Sinai and Palestine* (1856). All these works have a certain charm, 'period' though it now is. Their chief fault is an excess of colour, a too florid eloquence.[36]

The work of Lightfoot, Westcott, Hort, and Benson, on the other hand, is recognizably of value in the whole story of the development of their discipline. There is a good deal of truth in the often repeated opinion that the work done by these *ecclesiastical* historians not only brought the history of the Church into line with the work being done by the most eminent of secular historians but actually helped to set the standards for critical and scientific history in general. In addition to Acton, whose opinion was cited at the beginning of this chapter, there were many others who, like Mandell Creighton in his inaugural lecture as Dixie professor at Cambridge in 1884, were prepared to assert that it was among the theologians rather than the professional secular historians that the best examples of the new historical scholarship were to be found.[37]

[35] J. B. Lightfoot, *The Apostolic Fathers*, pt. II, vol. i. pp. 328 ff.
[36] B. M. G. Reardon, *Religious Thought in the Victorian Age: A Survey from Coleridge to Gore*, rev. edn. (London, 1980); 246.
[37] M. Creighton, *Historical Lectures and Addresses*, ed. L. Creighton (London, 1903), 2.

It may be, therefore, that one of the reasons why this group of scholars seems to have been so anxious to establish the *earliest* form of things was, simply, that they wanted to get at the actual historical facts. The techniques to which they were themselves contributing placed a considerable emphasis on determining precisely what had happened in the period one was investigating. Accurately determining the value of one's sources and taking account of the credibility of those sources in the light of contemporary scientific knowledge, was of the essence of the historian's discipline. It might seem thoroughly sensible to assume that—in a situation where historical events appeared to be germane to a theological controversy—the doctrinal issue might be settled by one's ability to prove that it went back a long way.

They all, however, seem sometimes to have taken refuge in the facts of history, to evade the difficult theological problems. Or, perhaps, it was rather that they recognized that there were *some* theological issues in which the facts of history were not going to prove very helpful. Both Westcott and Lightfoot preferred to use popular lectures or sermons as the vehicle for their theological ideas. It may be unkind to suggest they chose this way of presenting their ideas because they could not then be expected to present their argument rigorously and in detail, but it does seem, sometimes, that they deliberately avoided engaging in discussion of historically difficult theological issues. Thus Westcott's *Characteristics of the Gospel Miracles*, first published in 1859 and still being reissued as late as 1913, does not deal at all with the question whether the miracles actually happened. That is assumed. The sermons which comprise the book are devoted to the theological interpretation of the miracles. The only place at which the question of historicity is faced is in an appendix on the three accounts of the conversion of St Paul contained in Acts.[38] By implication Westcott's detailed and meticulous examination of the precise shades of meaning of each word in the Greek is a defence of the truth and coherence of the three narratives.[39]

There is a somewhat similar case in Lightfoot's commentary on Galatians. This was first published in 1865, appeared in a great many new editions until well into the present century, and has been

[38] Acts 9: 1–9; 22: 5–11; 26: 12–18.
[39] B. F. Westcott, *Characteristics of the Gospel Miracles: Sermons preached before the University of Cambridge*, first cheap edn. (London, 1913), 72 ff.

widely regarded as the volume which really set the pattern for all modern commentaries.[40] This, also, is curiously patchy in matters of historicity. Lightfoot devoted thirty-five pages of the introduction to questions relating to the people and churches of Galatia and a further appendix of a dozen pages to the question whether the Galatians were Celtic or Teutonic people. No doubt, general interest in the comparative value of Celtic and Teutonic civilization had something to do with the space given to this question.[41] Lightfoot argued against there having been any significant Teutonic settlement in Galatia with a vast armoury of historical learning, enabling him to conclude, 'Thus in the age when St Paul preached, a native of Galatia spoke a language essentially the same with that which was current in the southern part of Britain.'[42] One suspects that he did not share Dr Arnold's preference for the Teutonic history of the English.

The real issue, however, was one of historicity. 'Galatia' could conceivably mean the Roman province of that name or it could mean, more popularly, the smaller area, dominated and inhabited by Gauls from the third century before Christ, which was in the interior of Asia Minor. The trouble was that Acts has no reference to St Paul's having visited that Galatia; Gaulish Galatia. The only bit of the Roman province of Galatia that is mentioned in Acts is the southern part of the province, Iconium, Pisidian Antioch, Derbe, Lystra, and other such cities. Lightfoot preferred the Galatia of the Gauls and a large part of the introduction to the volume was devoted to this question. The extraordinary thing is that a much more pressing matter relating to historicity was dismissed without any real discussion. It is very difficult indeed to make the chronologies of Paul's life, as given in Acts and in Galatians, conform to each other at all. Lightfoot blandly remarked that the two accounts are not contradictory but that 'the impression left by St Luke's narrative needs correcting by the more precise and authentic statement of St Paul'.[43] What is even more striking is that Lightfoot used precisely the same technique to produce agreement as Westcott had done with the varying accounts of Paul's conversion, insisting that a very pedantic interpretation of particular

---

[40] Elliott-Binns, *English Thought*, 167.   [41] Above, pp. 14 ff.
[42] J. B. Lightfoot, *Saint Paul's Epistle to the Galatians; a Revised Text with Introduction, Notes and Dissertations*, 7th edn. (London 1881), 251.
[43] Ibid. 92.

verbal and grammatical forms enabled one to reconcile the apparently irreconcilable.

It would be somewhat unfair to accuse these very orthodox Anglican Churchmen of appealing from the living Church of the nineteenth century to the dead Church of the past. They were not, simply, inflexible antiquarians intent on compelling all moderns to live under the rule of what once had been; and their true position seems to have been known and recognized. One of Westcott's 'disciples' wrote of him that he was powerfully attracted by the *beginnings* of the Church's life, 'the total force that makes the movement exist'; but he also acknowledged that Westcott believed that the truth was not unchanging because the divine life manifested in each age through the divine society 'will find a fresh and corresponding expression'.[44] The whole tenor of Benson's judgement in the King case was that the history of the Church of England was a *process* and that the whole of the process had to be taken into account—the earliest life of the Church in the sub-apostolic age and the life of the Church of England after the Reformation alike. In the course of that process changes had occurred. The archbishop felt himself compelled to examine each of the disputed practices, for instance, and see whether these had ever been deliberately discontinued. Changes of that kind had to be taken into account when assessing what should be done in the contemporary Church.

Consciously or unconsciously, Benson seemed to assume that history will have developed its own rules for deciding when changes are legitimate. He was, therefore, very anxious to discover the proper traditional rules for determining when liturgical customs should be judged to have fallen into desuetude, or to have been modified by a genuinely and continuously developing usage. This would have been very much in the tradition of old-fashioned High Church orthodoxy, for it is extremely likely that the early leaders of the Oxford Movement inherited their tendency to appeal to the Church of the first few centuries from the older High Churchmen, along with so much else which they were afterwards to disparage. It was only later that Newman began to think of it as an appeal from the living Church to a dead one.

The new kind of orthodox High Churchmen—like Benson,

---

[44] *Westcott's Fear*, by A Disciple (Cambridge, 1930), 98 and 18.

Westcott, and Lightfoot—were, on this reading of events, reviving an older form of the appeal to the past history of the Church to determine truth. It was a much more sophisticated, much more critical and scientific, much more scholarly approach to the study of history itself than the older version, even if, sometimes, the human being conducting the enquiry could not bring himself to face the answer that seemed to be emerging. Behind the enquiry lay the old assumption that when one could determine what the earliest form of things had been, one had come closest to establishing what the *best* form of things had been. If it turned out to be impossible to prove what the *earliest* form had been, then the best one could do was to demonstrate that a form was early: earlier than most. And so, as a matter of practical politics, the earlier seemed to be *better* than the later.

Benson's belief that history creates its own rules for discriminating between the legitimate and the illegitimate, which if consciously thought out was more sophisticated than any view held by Lightfoot or Westcott, is a kind of theory of development. It is pragmatic and phenomenological rather than an attempt to define quasi-philosophical principles governing the development of ideas such as Newman had ventured. Benson does not ever seem to have felt the two needs which Newman plainly felt, to assert that there could be only one organism properly called the Church, and to define, in large and general terms, precisely how its doctrine can evolve legitimately. In both these aspects, Benson's approach was very much more down to earth. The Church with which he was concerned was the actual Church of England; the developments which he regarded as legitimate were those which had actually taken place in accordance with the rules; the appropriate rules were those which had grown up in the course of the history of the Church of England. It was these which enabled one to discriminate between right and wrong when there were actual disputes within the Church. Unfortunately, perhaps, what seemed compellingly objective and unbiased to a learned archbishop did not appear in quite that light to those engaged in the disputes.

5

SEPARATE SPIRITUAL TRUTH:
The Essays in *Lux Mundi*

ONE important aspect of the relationship between history and faith is the question of the historicity of the documents which describe the object of faith, Jesus the Christ. Jowett's refusal to face the implications of that question inevitably gave the impression that he thought them insignificant. Another aspect of the relationship is that faith itself has a history and will develop within it. In very different senses, Newman and Benson were each concerned with the problems that arise from that fact. Both these aspects were implicitly touched upon by the collection of essays published in 1889 as *Lux Mundi*; with the significant subtitle, 'A Series of Studies in the Religion of the Incarnation'.[1]

The conventional account of the volume's origins and history represents it as the Catholic movement in the Church of England coming to terms with scientific knowledge and critical scholarship. The original Tractarians had been extremely conservative in theology and had been unwilling to budge from a belief that the Bible was literally true in every detail. *Lux Mundi*, it is said, was responsible for bringing the heirs of the Tractarians into the modern age and Charles Gore himself, who contributed an essay on biblical inspiration, is sometimes given the personal credit for creating the new attitude of mind. But this account needs correction in several respects because it actually ignores the sophistication of some of the essays in the book and therefore obscures its real significance. When it is placed in its proper context, it is clear that *Lux Mundi* is better understood as effect rather than cause of a widespread change in attitude.

Lux Mundi was, after all, essentially a volume whose context was Oxford in the 1880s and it has to be assessed and interpreted in

---

[1] References in this chapter are to the 4th edition of *Lux Mundi*, published in 1890.

terms of what was happening to Oxford theology in general in that period. One of the most important facts to be taken into account is that theology had only very recently become a subject in which undergraduates could be examined. This is often lost sight of because of the important role played by religious and theological issues in the history of the university in the early part of the nineteenth century. Religious tests, religious observances, and religious instruction are so significant in that history that it is easy to forget that academic theology was not part of the curriculum for any undergraduate. It is true that they were all expected to study the Thirty-nine Articles and what was referred to as 'the elements of religion'. This consisted of acquiring some basic knowledge of the official doctrine of the Church of England and the emphasis was upon contemporary notions of what constituted orthodox belief. The only available degrees in theology were the BD and DD, which were taken after one became an MA, and the examinations for these degrees had become vestigial and composed of largely formal exercises.

Moves for the creation of a theology school began as early as 1848 when Benjamin Jowett and A. P. Stanley had published a pamphlet arguing that the reform of the university, then very much in the air, should include the creation of such a school, which they hoped would revitalize theology by encouraging an Arnoldian approach to the Bible.[2] Pusey was opposed to any such proposal not only because it would have included the critical study of the Bible but also because he objected to the teaching of the history of dogma. Such a subject seemed to him to imply that the faith had not been unchanged through the ages.[3]

One of the important ways, moreover, in which Pusey's significance in the history of mid-nineteenth-century Oxford has to be reassessed is as university politician and controversialist. Previous generations of historians, perhaps, allowed veneration for the saintly leader of the movement, which came to be called 'Puseyite', to prevent their seeing Pusey as an obstinate and partisan member of committees. Recent scholarship has begun to take note,

---

[2] *Suggestions for an Improvement of the Examination Statute*, and see L. Campbell, *On the Nationalization of the Old English Universities* (London, 1901), 74.

[3] I. Ellis, 'Pusey and University Reform', in P. Butler (ed.), *Pusey Rediscovered* (London, 1983), 300.

again, of an aspect of his character of which his contemporaries were very well aware.[4] Pusey would not, indeed, have been in the least ashamed of the fact that he fought strenuously and unremittingly for the orthodox cause; nor would he have seen any virtue in being even-handed in his attitude to truth and falsehood. But in the 1860s, because the liberals were losing ground and he was confident that the supremacy of conservatives would ensure that teaching and examining would be in the hands of the orthodox, he began to support the introduction of a theology school.[5]

It was, therefore, almost inevitable that, when the school was founded in 1870, it should reflect the conservatism of Pusey and his allies. The statutes required a knowledge of the *subject matter* of virtually the whole of the New Testament together with four books of the Old. In dogmatics candidates had to have studied the catechetical lectures of Cyril of Jerusalem, Book III of Irenaeus, *Adversus Haereses*, the Thirty-nine Articles, and the first two books of the seventeenth-century Bishop Bull's *Defensio Fidei Nicaenae*. In apologetics the set texts were Butler's *Analogy*, Tertullian's *Apologia*, and Book I of Hooker's *Laws of Ecclesiastical Polity*. The liturgics syllabus included a study of the Book of Common Prayer as well as the ancient liturgies.[6] This syllabus subtly propagated the Tractarian belief that nineteenth-century Anglicanism preserved a continuity with the 'Catholicity' of the early Church. By stressing the importance of orthodoxy over against heresy and by prescribing texts which were drawn from the Patristic period or from classical Anglicanism it sought to teach that the early fathers and the Anglican divines were the great champions of the truth.

It is possible to understand Pusey's anxiety to control the new school. Most of the candidates in the honour school were Anglican ordination candidates and the theology degree was just beginning to be regarded as a vocational qualification. (Previously mere

---

[4] A. Livesley, 'Regius Professor of Hebrew', in Butler (ed.), *Pusey Rediscovered*, 108 and cf. P. Hinchliff, *Benjamin Jowett and the Christian Religion* (Oxford, 1987), 92 for Jowett's view of Pusey as a controversialist.

[5] W. R. Ward, *Victorian Oxford* (London, 1965), 250 ff.

[6] There were also papers in the history of the early Church and in textual criticism, though the examiners indicated that for candidates not desiring 'high honours' they could be content with much less than the full syllabus. See *Oxford University Student's Handbook* (1873), 156 ff.

attendance at either Oxford or Cambridge and a period of theological reading, prescribed by the bishop's examining chaplain, had been thought a sufficient qualification for ordination.) At the same time the proportion of ordinands who had read other subjects was beginning to decline, even though bishops were more and more inclined to insist on a period at theological college for all intending clergymen. Whoever controlled theology at Oxford, therefore, might hope to control the attitude of mind of a significant proportion of those about to be ordained.

In the early days the final examination placed the same stress on factual knowledge as did the statutes. A favourite question asked what *urim* and *thummim* were and how they were used. Candidates were asked to write about the geography of Palestine, the design and contents of Solomon's temple, and even 'The private life and arrangements of St. Paul during his journeys'.[7] Apart from an occasional question which admitted doubt as to whether Paul had written the Epistle to the Hebrews, 'higher' critical issues were ignored. Such issues first made an appearance in the apologetics paper and candidates were openly directed to *refute* the theories of the critics. In the examination set in Michaelmas 1874 no fewer than three questions required a knowledge of the arguments advanced by a Dr W. H. Mill against a 'mythical' interpretation of the gospels. In the Trinity term of the following year there was, for the first time, a question about the relationship between the synoptic gospels, and in 1879 a question in the Old Testament paper asked for the arguments for and against the Mosaic authorship of Exodus. Otherwise it was simply assumed that the Bible was to be understood in the most literal sense and that doctrine had been unaffected by historical development.

Pusey's confidence in the conservatives' ability to control the appointment of examiners seems to have been justified in these years. In 1875 the examiners were Thomas Espin, Edmund Ffoulkes, John Nutt, and George Rawlinson. The first two had been fellows of colleges twenty years before but Espin had become warden of The Queen's College in Birmingham and rector of Wallasey. Ffoulkes was rector of Wiggington and shortly to become vicar of the university church. They were both therefore among the

---

[7] Examination papers of the Honour School of Theology, Trinity term 1873, New Testament II, question 4.

usually conservative non-resident clergy whom reformers thought to exercise far too much power in the university. (Ffoulkes had actually become a Roman Catholic in 1855 and had only recently been readmitted to the Church of England.) Nutt, sub-librarian of the Bodleian, was appointed, primarily, to examine in the biblical languages. Rawlinson, the professor of Ancient History, had delivered the Bampton Lectures of 1859 (the year of Darwin's *Origin of Species* and the year before *Essays and Reviews*) on the 'truth of the Scripture records'. The impression of conservatism conveyed by the schools' questions is, therefore, almost certainly a reflection of the examiners' own beliefs.

From 1882 onwards the examiners appear to be a rather more mixed collection of people. In that year they were the eccentric Old Testament critic, T. K. Cheyne; the non-resident Edward Bernard; and the High Churchman John Wordsworth, about to become the Oriel professor of the Interpretation of Holy Scripture. Wordsworth had produced a critical edition of the Vulgate but was very conservative in his approach to higher criticism. Candidates were, nevertheless, invited to discuss whether the fourth gospel and the Apocalypse were by the same author.[8] They were also expected, in a more traditional manner, to be able to 'disprove the proposition that a miracle is unworthy of God'.[9] In the autumn examination of the same year they were asked to 'deal with' objections to the Pauline authorship of certain epistles. But the question specifically excluded consideration of Hebrews and the Pastoral Epistles as though their non-Pauline provenance were conceded.[10]

Ten years later Charles Bigg (whose 1886 Bampton Lectures on the Christian Platonists of Alexandria by no means treated patristic theology as unchanging) was an examiner. One is not surprised to find candidates asked whether they detected an 'Alexandrine influence' in the Epistle to the Hebrews. By this time questions of such a kind were not at all unusual. In the previous year, when Bigg had also been an examiner together with Liddon's future biographer J. O. Johnston, a variety of critical questions had been asked. Candidates were expected to be able to argue 'the most probable

---

[8] Examination papers of the Honour School of Theology, Trinity term 1882, Apologetica II, question 1.

[9] Ibid. Apologetica III, question 9.

[10] Examination papers of the Honour School of Theology, Michaelmas term 1882, Apologetica II, question 4.

theory of the relation of St. Mark to St. Matthew and St. Luke'.[11]
There was even a question on Acts which seems to assume a
knowledge of the theories of F. C. Baur, published fifty years
earlier;[12] and in 1892 Bigg and Johnston, with Francis Woods the
vicar of Chalfont St Peter (who had himself taken a first in the
Oxford theology school at its most conservative in 1873),
authorized a very daring question on the criteria to be used in
determining the date of a psalm. What is significant is that non-
resident clergymen and identifiable members of the 'Catholic' party
were willing to accept responsibility for asking questions of this
kind. The examiners were, after all, required to take collective
responsibility for the examination papers.

It is difficult to resist the impression that one of the most
important factors in the change that had taken place in Oxford was
the death of Pusey himself in the autumn of 1882. Descriptions of
his funeral, the enormous procession of friends and admirers from
all over England, speak of the devotion he had evoked from others
and, by implication, of the authority he could exercise over them.[13]
But admired and loved though Pusey had been, he was a survival
from an earlier generation and his death removed a powerful
conservative force. His indomitable opposition had held back the
tide of new theological ideas but, once he had gone, it was almost as
if, with a sigh of relief, even those who had regarded him as their
mentor and hero began to relax some of the rigid positions that he
had imposed upon them.

For a while H. P. Liddon, the man upon whom the mantle of
Pusey had fallen, did his best to exert the same conservative
influence as his master; but either he was a less powerful
personality than Pusey or the times had changed so much that it
was no longer possible to hold back the new ideas. Liddon himself
had a reputation for inflexible Tractarian orthodoxy. In the later
1850s he had said, in a sentence worthy of Pusey, that 'moderate
opinions are not a fair and tolerable representation of the
Revelation of God.'[14] Yet when he was preparing his Bampton
Lectures for 1867, Liddon had been tempted to argue that Christ,

---

[11] Examination papers of the Honour School of Theology, Trinity term 1891, St
Mark and St John, question 4.

[12] Ibid. Acts of the Apostles, question 3.

[13] H. P. Liddon, *Life of Edward Bouverie Pusey*, 4 vols. (London, 3rd
impression, 1898), ii. 386 f.

[14] O. Chadwick, *The Founding of Cuddesdon* (Oxford, 1954), 88.

as human, was limited in his knowledge in precisely the same way as were all other human beings. When Pusey saw the draft of what he proposed to say, he was deeply shocked.[15] If Christ could be ignorant, he could not be God. Liddon bowed to the pressure from Pusey and adopted that argument in his attack on Colenso's critical work.[16] All right-thinking Tractarians in the 1860s, when Liddon delivered his Bamptons, would have accepted that argument without much hesitation.

When *Lux Mundi* appeared in 1889, Liddon attempted to use the same argument against Gore's essay.[17] This time the argument was wholly ineffective. Gore revered Liddon as a good man and a devout priest. He was deeply hurt by Liddon's criticism and considered resigning the principalship of Pusey House. There were many who came to believe that Gore's later relatively conservative attitude to critical scholarship was a result of Liddon's attack on *Lux Mundi*.[18] But he does not appear to have considered changing his attitude to Scripture and he was adamant that he could not abandon his position because of an argument based on what he regarded as a false dilemma.[19]

In view of the fact that Gore was such a committed Anglo-Catholic and so loyal to the Tractarian tradition, the obvious question to be asked was why he was willing to risk being condemned by the leadership of the old guard for his critical opinions. The answer must be that he had become conscientiously convinced of the necessity of a critical approach to Scripture, which he seems to have learnt from Westcott at Harrow and from Jowett at Balliol.[20] Gore himself always maintained that he had become convinced, as early as 1876, that a generally critical approach to the Old Testament was not inconsistent with the Creeds.[21]

It seems to be widely held, indeed, that the early 1880s were

---

[15] G. L. Prestige, *Life of Charles Gore* (London, 1935), 103.

[16] H. P. Liddon, *The Divinity of Our Lord*, 8th edn. (London, 1878), 454 ff. and 469 ff., and cf. P. Hinchliff, *John William Colenso, Bishop of Natal* (London, 1964), 178.

[17] e.g. in *The Spectator*, 5 Apr. 1890.

[18] Prestige, *Gore*, 102 ff. and 112 ff., and cf. S. A. King, *Charles Gore, the Founder of the See and First Bishop of Birmingham, 1905–1911*, printed version of a public lecture given in Birmingham in 1945, p. 13.

[19] See e.g. *The Ecclesiastical Chronicle*, 23 Apr. 1890.

[20] D. Newsome, *Two Classes of Men: Platonism and English Romantic Thought* (London, 1972), 120 ff., and Hinchliff, *Jowett*, 171 ff.

[21] G. Crosse, *Charles Gore: A Biographical Sketch* (London, 1932), 14.

precisely the time when a new and critical approach to biblical scholarship was becoming acceptable in the Church of England as a whole. Frederick Temple's Bampton Lectures on science and religion were delivered in 1884 and have been described by Owen Chadwick as making Darwin's evolutionary hypothesis respectable.[22] The following decade has been identified as the period when the 'scientific revolution' in the understanding of history took place.[23] It has also been characterized as the decade when the majority of scholars and a fair proportion of educated laity in each of the British Churches accepted the general idea that a critical approach to the Scriptures was not incompatible with faith.[24] Pusey's own successor as professor of Hebrew at Oxford was S. R. Driver, beyond question an exponent of critical ideas, however moderate. Yet Driver met with very little opposition even from High Churchmen. Indeed, he very soon came to be widely regarded as typifying moderate good sense.

One suspects that Gore and his fellow contributors to *Lux Mundi* were not the only younger Anglo-Catholics to accept the ideas which became so widely current in this period. Johnston's case suggests the opposite. He had been one of Liddon's assistants in the work of preparing the life of Pusey and after Liddon's own death, in 1890, he became the latter's biographer.[25] He might have been thought therefore to represent the conservative tradition for which Pusey and Liddon had stood. He was the principal of Cuddesdon when *Lux Mundi* appeared and was, therefore, a senior clergyman, responsible for educating future priests, not someone to be swayed lightly by new ideas. He was not a member of the *Lux Mundi* group, though his vice-principal (Robert Ottley) was. If one of the two were to influence the other, one would normally expect it to be the senior man, Johnston. Yet it was Johnston who seems to have changed. By 1892 he was ready, as an examiner with Bigg and Woods, to authorize critical questions in the theology honour school.[26] It is difficult to avoid the impression that a wide variety of younger Anglo-Catholics had come, like Gore, to recognize the validity of a moderately critical approach but had been deterred by

[22] O. Chadwick, *The Victorian Church*, 2 vols. (London, 1966), ii. 23.
[23] V. A. Harvey, *The Historian and the Believer* (London, 1967), 68 ff.
[24] D. L. Pals, *The Victorian 'Lives' of Jesus* (San Antonio, 1982), 152.
[25] J. O. Johnston, *Life and Letters of Henry Parry Liddon* (London, 1904).
[26] Above, p. 104.

the influence of Pusey and Liddon, so long as they lived, from expressing their views.

On such a view the great contribution of Gore and his friends was not that they came to adopt critical views and then persuaded other Anglo-Catholics of their truth, but that they first had the courage to express these opinions in spite of pressure from the older leaders of the movement—not that the contributors to *Lux Mundi* were really very young. Gore had been born in 1853 and was, therefore, 36 when the volume was published. Illingworth was later to say that there was a tone of what he called 'fortyness' about the book which made it duller than he had hoped.[27] It is not entirely clear from the context what he meant by 'fortyness' but it is possible that he was referring to the approaching middle age of many of the contributors.

The stated object of the contributors was to attempt to relate traditional 'Catholic' orthodoxy to contemporary critical and scientific thinking. The doctrine of the incarnation was to be their key concept, and it was not just that the essayists took this doctrine, in some formal sense, as the basis for understanding and interpreting various crucial aspects of Christian doctrine and life. It was specifically a kenotic understanding of incarnation, the self-emptying of the divine in order to be truly human, which lay behind their whole approach. Again and again one comes across statements made by members of the group which indicate how excited they were by their encounter with a kenotic Christology.[28] They seem to have believed that this understanding of the relationship of the human to the divine in Christ would permit them to maintain the Tractarian belief that truth was given, authoritatively, in revelation while recognizing the validity of the liberal position that even religious truth could legitimately be subjected to the tests of human reason.

It is in Moberly's essay on 'The Incarnation as the Basis of Dogma' that this issue is most clearly dealt with. Moberly began by referring to the distinction conventionally made between 'speculative' and 'dogmatic' theology. He said that:

Some think . . . that to practical men exactnesses of doctrinal statement, even if true, are immaterial. Others think that any exactness of doctrinal

[27] A. L. Illingworth (ed.), *The Life and Work of John Richardson Illingworth edited by his wife* (London, 1917), 159.
[28] Ibid. 33 and Crosse, *Gore*, 26.

statement is convicted, by its mere exactness, of untruth; for that knowledge about things unseen can only be indefinite in character.[29]

This seems a fair summary of the 'liberal' position based on Kant, Locke, and Arnold.[30] Moberly rejected that point of view, insisting that a revelation, an incarnation, is not an impossibility and that, if it happened, it has made it possible to speak with exactness about dogmatic truths. That is a claim to stand squarely in the traditional Tractarian position. But he went on to argue that that position did not preclude the use of the rational, intellectual faculties, and that religious knowledge was not acquired in an entirely different way from scientific knowledge. Like scientific truths, religious truths ought not to be accepted without proper and convincing evidence. 'If any man is asked to accept them, without any intelligent ground for the acceptance, we may be bold perhaps to assert that it would be his duty to refuse.'

Moberly's conclusion on this issue was:

To 'take religion on trust', then, as it is sometimes derisively called, is not really an act of defiance of, or apart from, reason. It is an exercise of reason up to a certain point,—just so, and so far as, the experience of the person warrants. He sees what to trust, and why. He sees where understanding and experience which transcend his own would point. And he seeks for the rational test of further experience in the only way in which it can be had. He defers to the voice of experience, in faith that his own experience will by and by prove its truthfulness.[31]

This theme reappears often in the volume, though never so clearly stated, and suggests that the essayists aimed to find and to justify a position from which they could both recognize the validity of secular scholarship and maintain the truth of the cardinal beliefs of classical Christianity. It also enabled them to give expression to their sense of the Christian religion as something passionate, all-embracing, demanding total, disciplined obedience. A kenotic Christology, they believed, enabled them to insist on the reality of the human life of Jesus and on a degree of autonomy for human history, knowledge, and will: when God intervened in history, he did so within the limitations of created nature. This approach might hope to preserve belief in both the activity of God and the genuine independence of history, science and human life. What they did not,

[29] *Lux Mundi*, 217 f.   [30] Above, p. 33 f.   [31] *Lux Mundi*, 223.

perhaps, fully perceive was that their insistence that God might sometimes act directly and outside this framework (as in miracles) introduced a degree of inconsistency into their approach.

The contributors to *Lux Mundi* had met together over a considerable period to plan what they would say, so that the volume might be a coherent survey of the main themes of Christian doctrine. The group seems to have grown out of the so-called 'Holy Party' which Henry Scott Holland had first assembled on the Isle of Wight in 1875. There is some doubt about the identity of the two groups,[32] but they were clearly composed of much the same people.

In spite of the period of preparation, the coherent editorial policy, and a unifying purpose, the essays were not of uniform quality or importance: nor were the contributors. Scott Holland himself wrote about 'Faith', rather surprisingly leaving the subject of Christianity and politics to a tutor of Keble called Campion. Aubrey Moore contributed an essay on the doctrine of God. J. R. Illingworth, in whose rectory at Longworth much of the planning of the volume was done, wrote about the problem of pain and also a more important piece on 'The Incarnation in relation to Development'. R. C. Moberly, who was later to be very well known for his work on the atonement, provided a key article on the incarnation as the basis for Christian doctrine. Lock, the sub-warden of Keble, wrote about the Church, and R. L. Ottley, who had succeeded Gore as vice-principal of the theological college at Cuddesdon, about ethics. Two more senior men, Francis Paget, the professor of Pastoral Theology, and E. S. Talbot, who had been warden of Keble before becoming vicar of Leeds, contributed essays on the sacraments and on 'The Preparation in History for Christ' respectively. It was Gore, however, as the editor of the book and the author of the essay 'The Holy Spirit and Inspiration', who attracted most attention and most hostility.

There are points in all the essays which, in some sense, bear on the relationship between theology and history. Scott Holland's essay on faith, for instance, contained his version of the theory of progressive revelation under the guise of 'our growing intimacy with God'. But the three which relate most directly to this issue are

---

[32] G. Rowell, 'Historical Retrospect: *Lux Mundi* 1889', in R. Morgan (ed.), *The Religion of the Incarnation: Anglican Essays in Commemoration of 'Lux Mundi'* (Bristol, 1989), 206.

Illingworth on development, Lock on the Church, and Gore on inspiration.

Illingworth's essay displays a characteristic inability, or unwillingness, to back up undoubtedly stimulating ideas with precise arguments or directly relevant evidence. Maurice Wiles has contrasted the way 'the mellifluous tones of Illingworth's prose flow on, giving expression to his confidently holistic view of God's consistent self-revelation to humankind in creation and Incarnation' with his failure to examine his own ideas and statements critically.[33] Rather more serious is Illingworth's failure to fill out his 'confidently holistic view' with the tough detail which alone would make it really significant. Not long after the publication of *Lux Mundi* Illingworth published a volume of sermons one of which was entitled 'The Incarnation of the Word'. The sermon began with the words, 'The Incarnation of our Lord has a bearing upon the problems of science and philosophy, the history of matter and the history of mind, as well as upon the personal hopes of the individual soul',[34] but it contains no concrete examples of how this assertion is true and drifts off into being a meditation upon the first fourteen verses of St John's gospel.

Illingworth's essay in *Lux Mundi* is very similar. It opens with a long, optimistic section which welcomes the way in which the theory of evolution 'is an advance in our theological thinking; a definite increase of insight; a fresh and fuller appreciation of those "many ways" in which "God fulfils himself" '.[35] This optimism was not unique to Illingworth. All the essayists were as determined to come to terms with the evolutionary hypothesis as with biblical criticism, and by this time even the older Tractarians seem to have regarded the acceptance of evolutionary ideas as relatively harmless. Darwin's theory does not appear to have greatly shocked either Pusey or Liddon.[36]

What seems to have happened is that the contributors had learned from T. H. Green an evolutionary way of thinking so that it has been said of *Lux Mundi* that 'Darwin and Hegel, who have in

---

[33] M. F. Wiles, 'The Incarnation and Development', in Morgan (ed.), *Religion of the Incarnation*, 74 f.

[34] J. R. Illingworth, *University and Cathedral Sermons* (London, 1893), 181. I am grateful to my colleague, Dr H. D. Dupree, for drawing my attention to this sermon.

[35] *Lux Mundi*, 4th edn. (London, 1890), 182.

[36] J. R. Moore, *The Post Darwinian Controversies* (Cambridge, 1979), 90.

common an emphasis on development, if nothing else, are always on the authors' minds'.[37] And some of the contributors actually understood Darwin's hypothesis. Aubrey Moore, in particular, seems to have grasped what Darwin really taught and to have preferred Darwinism proper to the more Spencerian versions of evolutionary theory which became popular in the latter part of the century.[38]

In Illingworth's essay there is a positive enthusiasm for the way in which the whole idea of evolution has affected late nineteenth-century thought processes. It was, he thought, the 'category' of the age which simply could not be ignored. When one asks questions about anything in the modern world one is compelled to ask how it came to be as it is. And the same is true of Christian beliefs. If one is to discuss them, one must discuss their history—'religious opinions, like all things else that have come down on the current of development, must justify their existence by an appeal to the past'.[39] Yet, when he wrote about development, Illingworth did not appear to be thinking (as one might have expected an Anglo-Catholic to think) of Newman's theory. He used 'development' as a synonym for 'evolution' and his whole treatment of the development of Christian thought is more akin to that of Caird.[40] A large part of the essay was devoted to 'other religions'. Here Illingworth's conclusions were very different from those of Caird. It was, nevertheless, quite clear that, like Caird, he was convinced that the mere existence of these religions had implications for the Christian understanding of the nature of God.

In so far as Illingworth did discuss the internal history of Christian thought, he was really concerned with trying to show that the doctrine of the incarnation, as he understood it (that is to say as 'bearing upon the problems of science and philosophy, the history of matter and the history of mind'), was not some nineteenth-century invention. He quoted from Patristic texts to show that the Fathers also thought of the incarnation as a constituent element in redemption which was a 'reconsecration of the whole universe to God'.[41] He then attempted to show why later periods of history lost sight of this understanding of doctrine as a whole. On the question

[37] S. H. Major, 'Lux Mundi; A Reassessment', The Church Quarterly Review, 166 (1965), 76.
[38] J. Durant (ed.), Darwinism and Divinity (Oxford, 1985), 22.
[39] Lux Mundi, 182 f.   [40] Below, pp. 139 ff.   [41] Lux Mundi, 181.

of the sense in which the atonement can actually be said to have reconsecrated the whole universe to God, or how, and why, that concept of redemption first developed in Christian thought, Illingworth did not have much to say.

Caird's concern, as we shall see, was really to cut Christian truth free from its historical roots because he believed that it was its historical character which laid Christianity open to attack from the critics. He was therefore anxious to render supposed statements of historical fact as metaphysical statements of eternal truths. There is no such concern in Illingworth's essay. Indeed, he was so certain that there could be no conflict between science and religion, so certain that the theory of evolution made it easier to hold the true doctrine of the incarnation, that he could not even have begun to understand the purpose which Caird conceived his work to be serving. For Illingworth history simply demonstrated the truth of 'Catholic' theology:

And though its own first vocation is to seek and save souls one by one, it consecrates in passing every field of thought and action, wherein the quickened energies of souls may find their scope. It welcomes the discoveries of science as ultimately due to Divine revelation, and part of the providential education of the world. It recalls to art the days when, in catacomb and cloister, she learned her noblest mission to be the service of the Word made Flesh. It appeals to democracy as the religion of the fishermen who gathered round the carpenter's Son. It points the social reformer to the pattern of a perfect man, laying down His life alike for enemy and friend. While it crowns all earthly aims with a hope full of immortality, as prophetic of eternal occupations elsewhere.[42]

Illingworth's essay was not entirely without its touches of brilliance. He had clearly understood many of the objections to Christianity arising from the critical and scientific understanding of things. He perceived, for instance, what many of his contemporaries failed to see, that Paley's argument for the existence of God, based upon evidence of 'design' in the universe, ceases to be convincing if the universe has evolved. He acknowledged that 'if of a thousand forms, which came by chance into existence, the one which happened to correspond best with its environment survived, while the remainder disappeared, the adaptation of the survivor to its circumstances would have all the appearance of design without any

[42] *Lux Mundi,* 213.

of its reality'.[43] More striking still, he had seen the even deeper difficulty about Paley's analogy between the universe and a clockwork mechanism—it has to be shown that the universe is an interrelated, integrated system in which the parts work for the better performance of the whole. To these objections Illingworth replied that it was inappropriate to regard the universe as in any way analogous to a mechanism which exists in order to perform a function external to itself:

... we have now come to regard the world not as a machine, but as an organism, a system in which, while the parts contribute to the growth of the whole, the whole also reacts upon the development of the parts; and whose primary purpose is its own perfection, something that is contained within and not outside itself, an internal end: while in their turn the myriad parts of this universal organism are also lesser organisms, ends in and for themselves, pursuing each its lonely ideal of individual completeness.[44]

For all that it suffers from Illingworth's persistent over-confidence, this is a clever and percipient argument.

If Illingworth's essay is much too optimistic about the relation-ship between Christian theology and human history as a whole, Lock's seems equally over-sanguine about the relationship between 'Catholic' theology and Anglican history. His initial purpose appears to be to establish that the nature of the Church is parallel to the nature of the incarnate Christ—a divine life manifested through what is concrete and earthly. He insists that the idea of there being an ideal, invisible Church which is the true Church, is foreign to the genuine Christian tradition. He argues that 'the ideal is never thought of [by St Paul] as something different from the real; the ideal is not simply in heaven nor the real simply on earth; the real is the ideal, though not yet completely developed; the ideal is the actual basis of the real as much as the goal to which the real is tending'.[45] And again, 'The idea of an invisible Church to express the body of true believers, who alone are the Church, to whatever community they belong, so that the visible Church becomes an unimportant thing, is an idea entirely at variance with Scripture and all pre-reformation teaching.'[46]

One begins to believe that the theme of genuine humanity, indissolubly linked, in spite of its weakness, with the truly divine,

[43] Ibid. 189.   [44] Ibid. 190.   [45] Ibid. 375.
[46] Ibid. 375 f.

will develop into vigorous argument for a particular understanding of the Church. This never quite happens. The essay is, for the most part, a simplistic and jejune presentation of conventional, moderate Anglo-Catholic opinion, for its heart is a sustained assertion of the continuity of the Church of England with the Church of the apostolic age. It begins in a section devoted to the Church as a spiritual organization, from which the passage quoted above about the real and the ideal Church is taken, and it goes on into a section which deals with the Church as a school for truth. In it Lock's summary of Irenaeus plays a crucial part:

Truth is essentially a thing *received*; it was received by the Apostles from Christ. He *was* the truth Himself; He revealed it to His Apostles; they embodied it in their writings and handed it on to the Bishops and Presbyters who succeeded them; hence the test of truth is to be sought in Holy Scriptures and in the teaching of those Churches which were founded directly by the Apostles.[47]

Here Lock was, by implication at least, adopting the line which Jowett thought distinctive of the *Lux Mundi* position. By enhancing the teaching authority of the Church one is able to compensate for the loss of a verbally inerrant Bible.[48] Moreover, Lock's emphasis upon the truth as something *received* put him firmly in the Tractarian tradition which Pusey had upheld. Even though he claimed simply to be summarizing the teaching of Irenaeus, his own sympathies seem clear.

At least Lock had got Irenaeus right at a point where 'Catholic' sympathies might have led him in another direction. He did not represent him as an exponent of a 'hands-on-heads' apostolic succession. It is the apostolic witness which guarantees the continuity of the Church. The Church exists primarily to maintain that witness to the central truths ('the Fatherhood of God, the Person and work of Jesus Christ, the Redemption of all mankind, the origin and purpose of human life'[49]). There are other truths which are open questions—a rather curious notion—and the test of truth, of course, is defined by Vincent of Lerins. Lock stated the Vincentian canon, however, in an unusual form, so that it appeared chiefly to prohibit additions to Catholic truth though permitting some element of 'development'.[50] This simplistic view of the continuing Church is repeated again and again in the essay. Christ

---

[47] *Lux Mundi*, 385.
[49] *Lux Mundi*, 387.
[48] Hinchliff, *Jowett*, 178 f.
[50] Ibid. 388 f.

founded the Church by choosing his apostles; they appointed bishops; the Church of Rome has added the distorting 'test of communion with itself';[51] the reformers have 'rejected the whole principle of historic continuity'.[52] By implication, only the Anglican Church remains faithful.

It may be unfair to caricature Lock's essay in this way. He did recognize some of the difficulties faced by anyone who writes theologically about the Church. He made a passing reference or two to the fact that the events of history are capable of being interpreted in ways other than those he used himself, but it is extremely difficult to avoid the feeling that he has evaded all the really crucial questions and, in doing so, has failed to meet his own challenge to present the Church as the extension of the incarnation, both human and divine.

Gore's essay is a much more carefully constructed argument than either Illingworth's or Lock's although, presumably for tactical reasons, he adopted a very circumspect approach for it. It began from a discussion of the doctrine of the Holy Spirit, which may have been an attempt to soften the blow of his critical approach to Scripture, but it also enabled him to talk about Christian experience as a present reality, and thus to claim that the faith was not just about something that lay in the past. The doctrine of the Holy Spirit, he asserted, is concerned with the point at which God most nearly touches man. That gave him the opportunity to turn to a consideration of the whole of God's relationship with creation and, in particular, of man's capacity for conscious fellowship with God. This theme, so typical of *Lux Mundi*, led on to a consideration of the incarnation and its extension in Pentecost and the birth of the Church.

Gore proceeded to assert that the activity of the Spirit in the Church is social, in that it recognizes that man cannot realize himself in isolation, and yet nourishes individuality. This assertion was plainly intended to provide a framework for the discussion of authority which followed. Gore attempted to define authority in terms of what he called the 'principle' of *credo ut intelligam*. The creeds represent 'the catholic judgment, the highest knowledge of God and the spiritual life granted to man by the Divine Revelation': yet there was, he maintained, room for individual judgement within the framework of this authority.

[51] Ibid. 380 f.   [52] Ibid. 381.

This was, perhaps, the least convincing part of the essay. Gore wrestled with the problem of how far individual judgement ought to bow to authority and how far it ought to insist on free enquiry. He was unable to come to any real conclusion on the matter except to say that both had their part to play. His failure to provide a more successful account of the relationship of Church to individual judgement was a major weakness in his essay and in his theology. He believed that what made his Anglican Catholicism a *liberal* Catholicism was the fact that Scripture and one's own conscientious judgement set limits upon sacerdotalism and an exaggeration of ecclesiastical authority.[53] Therefore a failure to define precisely where the limits of each lay was a tacit admission that his theological position was not worked out altogether thoroughly.

Successful or not, it was only after all this groundwork had been done that Gore turned to the question of the inspiration of the Bible. The Scriptures, he argued, contained the record of historical facts and were, therefore, the source of evidence and inseparably linked with the creeds as statements of belief, but the facts were not simply presented as facts in the gospels. Faith was a necessary ingredient, too: the revelation contained in the creeds was continually renewed in the heart of the Christian. Belief in the inspiration of Scripture needed to be held in the context of belief in the action of the Spirit upon the Church and the individual. It was, therefore, difficult 'to believe in the Bible without believing in the Church'. The authority of the New Testament was unique because it consisted largely of the words of the apostles, the accredited witnesses of Christ; but the apostles themselves were, in another sense, only the beginning of the Church's tradition from which they cannot be separated.

In coming to deal, at last, with the actual business of a critical approach to Scripture, Gore reminded his readers that much of revelation took place in the *history* of the people of Israel. However, its significance was chiefly to be found not in the facts themselves but in the way in which the writers interpreted them as the hand of God in history. The records might contain factual errors because the inspiration of those writers 'did not consist in a miraculous communication to them of the facts as they originally happened'. Nevertheless, he argued, the account of events from the

---

[53] P. Avis, *Gore: Construction and Conflict* (Worthing, 1988), 22.

time of Abraham onwards was, in a general way, 'really historical'. It was possible, therefore, for him to accept the work done by moderate critics on much of the Old Testament—the Pentateuch, the Psalms, the Books of the Chronicles—and he specifically did so at some length. What was important was to read each part of Scripture 'in the same spirit in which it was written', that is to say regarding the spiritual truths contained in it as authoritative without necessarily being bound by the supposedly factual detail of the narratives.

In the case of the New Testament he was much less thorough in applying this distinction. He believed that the Church was entitled to insist on the historical character of the gospels and that the miraculous element could not be lightly dismissed. He would have agreed with the point made by Illingworth's essay, that to rule out the miraculous is to have made up one's mind in advance about what one will recognize as admissible evidence.[54] Gore's very different attitude towards the two testaments—and in each case it was the way in which he treated the supposedly historical and factual statements which was at issue—raised precisely the question which Liddon thought to use against the essay. On a surface reading at least, Christ appears to accept the Old Testament as literally true. He is represented as speaking of David as the author of the Psalms and Moses as the author of the Pentateuch. The New Testament writers appear to share Christ's assumptions in these matters. Was it not inconsistent to insist on the historical accuracy of the New Testament but not on that of the Old, if those who wrote the former appeared to accept the inerrancy of the latter? Gore's kenotic answer was to assert that Christ's teaching did not go beyond the knowledge natural to his time and place in history except in revealing the spiritual truths about God and his relationship to creation and to man. He claimed, in other words, that he was being thoroughly logical and consistent at a rather deeper than surface level. The crucial distinction between factual and spiritual truth was maintained throughout his argument.

This distinction was Gore's most significant contribution to the debate. It was also, perhaps, the really significant achievement of *Lux Mundi*. It is clear that the conventional view, that the volume brought the Catholic movement into line with critical thought and modern science, needs considerable modification. It is equally clear

[54] *Lux Mundi*, 207.

that contributors like Illingworth thought of themselves as setting out the positive advantages of science for theology rather than attempting to win over a movement hitherto ignorant of science. In spite of the fact that the old guard objected strongly, and vociferously, to a critical approach to the Bible, the contributors to *Lux Mundi* were not the only younger Anglo-Catholics to have abandoned a literalist position. What *Lux Mundi* had done was to assert *publicly* that there were 'Catholics' who were also critical and, as a consequence of this action, others were also encouraged to come out into the open. The contributors had, at least to their own satisfaction, successfully related their critical opinions to the Christian tradition in such a way as to escape from the dead-end into which, for instance, Jowett's liberalism had taken him. Above all, they had made the vital distinction between factual and spiritual truth. It shifted the whole ground of the debate on the authority of Scripture so that the emphasis was no longer on an inspired text but on inspired authors. This enabled them to take account of the point made by people like Jowett about the original meaning of the text, what the author had intended, while asserting in very clear terms that they still regarded the Bible as authoritative.

Even this was not entirely new. A correspondent, writing to the *Church Times* in the aftermath of the publication of *Lux Mundi*, pointed out that there 'have been *five* different theories as to Inspiration, and four, if not five, have been held tenable within the Church of England.'

These are:

1. The *Organic* theory, which holds every word of Scripture to have been supernaturally imparted.

2. The *Dynamic* theory, which holds that the books of Scripture were committed to writing under the guidance of the Holy Spirit, that their *truths* are inspired but not their words, which were the choice of the individual writers.

3. The *Essential* theory, which holds that the Bible *contains* the Word of God, and is the Divine record of Revelation, but that its inspiration is to be predicated of *doctrine*, *faith*, and *morality*, and not necessarily of secular and scientific matters, allusions, and passing events.

4. The *Illumination* theory, which recognizes *degrees* of inspiration.

5. The *Ordinary* theory, which holds that the Holy Spirit's influence in the writing of the Holy Scripture was not generically different from the influence on the hearts of good men.[55]

[55] W. W. English in the *Church Times*, 7 Feb. 1890.

The writer thought that the view expressed by Gore in *Lux Mundi* fell into the third category, along with those held by 'Erasmus, Le Clerc, Grotius, by leading divines in the Roman Catholic Church, and orthodox German scholars, Döllinger, our own Bishops Warburton, Lowth, and Sumner, by Paley, Clarke, Baxter and others'.

This no doubt well-intentioned attempt to exonerate Gore, by association, takes away too much of the credit from him, too. His attitude may well have fallen into one of the conventional categories, but most of the others cited as belonging there with him expounded their views before there was any question of applying critical scholarship to the Scriptures. Gore, at least, stated his position plainly. He had made it abundantly clear that he did not believe that the writers of the New Testament had some divinely guaranteed access to the 'facts as they originally happened'. And that gave a nicely logical and consistent appearance to his case by bringing his theory of inspiration into line with his kenotic Christology. Christ's knowledge was as limited as that of his contemporaries, except where spiritual truth was concerned. The writers of the New Testament were given to know no more *facts* than anyone else: they were inspired as to spiritual truth.

But the weakness of *Lux Mundi* and of Gore, in particular, was that this logical consistency was not carried into every aspect of the work. The favourite word used by historians about Gore is 'paradox'. They disagree about precisely where the paradox lies but they agree that that term describes him perfectly. Adrian Hastings believes that the paradox is that he was both a natural radical *and* a natural authoritarian.[56] That would at least explain how Gore came later, as a bishop, to seem to stand for repression rather than liberalism. Paul Avis thinks, with Prestige, that he was both (traditional or 'Catholic') Christian *and* rationalist without any coherent methodology for combining the two.[57] The precise nature of the paradox may be elusive; it seems clear that paradox was a characteristic posture. What is worrying is that at so many points in Gore's theology there seems to be little to distinguish paradox from simple contradiction. In this respect Avis's assessment appears to be correct. Gore had come to be convinced of the truth of a great many things, some of them traditional Catholic doctrine and some of

[56] A. Hastings, *A History of English Christianity, 1920–1985* (London, 1986), 83.   [57] Avis, *Gore*, 113.

them new scientific and critical discoveries. Because he was convinced that they were all true, he must affirm them all even if— at least at the time when *Lux Mundi* was published—he could not reconcile them.

In a sense Gore was the victim of being heir to two conflicting traditions—the liberal and the 'Catholic'—and some of his critics perceived that this was the case. *Lux Mundi* was regarded by the older generation of Tractarians as a kind of treason because it admitted the validity of a critical understanding of the biblical writings. The fault of the liberals, in Tractarian eyes, had always been that they undermined belief in divine authority whether expressed in the Bible or the Church. By asserting that religious truth was a matter of enquiry, like any other knowledge, they had rendered it difficult—if not impossible—to determine truth in religion at all. Gore and his friends appeared to be falling into precisely the same error. Their methodology represented a surrender to liberal assumptions. The orthodoxy of their conclusions, therefore, seemed no more than fortuitous to the older Tractarians; and, indeed, in a strict sense, it was sheer good fortune that the application of rational enquiry did not bring the contributors to *Lux Mundi* to heretical conclusions. It was, perhaps, only their own determination not to surrender any orthodox belief which prevented that. Once one admits the principles of free critical enquiry, it *is* illogical to lay down in advance any requirement that its conclusions shall not conflict with orthodoxy.

The older Tractarians were not the only people who saw what was happening. Probably it took very little perspicuity to do so, for the claim to inherit and reconcile the two traditions was made quite openly. The Tractarians saw it and deplored. The Liberal Protestant Jowett saw it, just as clearly, and gave a rather muted cheer. He told Tennyson that, though it still exhibited the typical High Church 'haze and maze', *Lux Mundi* was much more friendly to liberalism than the theologians of that party had been before.[58] Jowett's judgement, which Ieuan Ellis has described as the most interesting comment made about *Lux Mundi*,[59] has never been taken seriously enough. It is treated as if it merely illuminated Jowett's character and opinions, and not as evidence about the attitude of the

[58] E. Abbott and L. Campbell, *Life and Letters of Benjamin Jowett*, 2 vols. (London, 1897), ii. 377.
[59] I. Ellis, *Seven Against Christ* (Leiden, 1980), 263.

essayists, of whom both Gore himself and Scott Holland had been Jowett's pupils. It is usual to claim that T. H. Green (one of Jowett's colleagues and allies at Balliol) had very considerable influence on *Lux Mundi*, but that Jowett himself had none.[60] Even if that assertion could be substantiated, it would still be evidence of the dual inheritance. Green's liberalism was very much more radical than Jowett's.

Gore and his friends would not, of course, have thought of themselves either as attempting to inculcate a more friendly attitude to liberalism or as arriving at an orthodox conclusion merely by accident. To them it would simply have proved the truth of their position that they should seem to be able to combine rationality with Catholic dogma. Gore plainly thought he had harnessed critical scholarship in defence of Catholic orthodoxy. He was always happy to use arguments which were untraditional or were derived from modern philosophers whose presuppositions were different from those of the Fathers. But his conclusions always had to be compatible with the traditional beliefs of the Church, as embodied in the creeds. The creeds, for Gore, occupied a special place as representing the way in which the ancient Church had interpreted the Bible doctrinally. The creeds were therefore the essential Christian truth. Gore was not, however, always careful enough about asking whether, at a level deeper than verbal agreement, the argument and the eternal truth really belonged together. Even towards the end of his life, in the trilogy called *The Reconstruction of Belief*, he was never happier than when he could assert that such and such ought to be believed because the Fathers had said similar things in the fourth century, the findings of modern science looked as though they would confirm it, and it is what we all know anyway.[61] The pity is that he never seemed able to define rigorously the proper spheres of rational enquiry and revealed truth.

[60] e.g. G. Rowell, in Morgan (ed.), *Religion of the Incarnation*, 208. I have assembled the evidence for a different view in *Benjamin Jowett and the Christian Religion*, 171 ff.

[61] e.g. C. Gore, *Belief in God* (London, 1921), 10.

CUT LOOSE FROM HISTORY
British Idealism and the
Science of Religion

THERE were those who would have found Gore's attempted distinction between spiritual and historical truth far too modest a way of dealing with the problem. For philosophical idealists it often seemed that religion was best served by being freed from its historical context altogether. If it were possible to develop a version of Christianity which was founded upon eternal verities rather than upon supposedly historical events, Lessing's argument that necessary truths cannot be proved by the contingent facts of history could lose some of its sting. In that case, moreover, Christianity would cease to be vulnerable to the work of the biblical critics. The early British Idealists clearly believed that this was the right line to explore.

The British Idealist movement really began with Thomas Hill Green, Whyte's professor of Moral Philosophy in the University of Oxford from 1878 until his death four years later at the comparatively early age of 46. But it was more securely established as a movement by his friend and former pupil, Edward Caird. Caird was actually a year older than Green, having been born in 1835, but whereas Green was a product of Rugby and Balliol, Caird had had a rather uncertain early education. This was partly because his father had died whilst he was very young and partly because he was, himself, subject to a great deal of ill-health. He was, at any rate, a student at the University of Glasgow on and off between 1850 and 1856, and at St Andrews in 1856 and 1857. He was therefore already 22 when he took his first degree, at a time when undergraduates on the whole were significantly younger than they are now. Up to this point the two people who had influenced him most were his own brother John, and John Tulloch of St Andrews.

John Caird was fifteen years older than Edward, who lived in his household for several years and to whom he became a sort of surrogate father. John Caird seems to have been a solitary person and it may be that Edward filled a gap in his life, providing one of the very few close relationships he was to have.[1] John had been ordained in the ministry of the Church of Scotland in 1845 and had been deeply hurt by the events of the Great Disruption. As a parish minister he was always something of an odd man out, reckoned a great and popular preacher but, also, always suspected of possible heterodoxy, so that he had a curiously ambivalent reputation.[2] His theology was certainly eclectic. At some point in his life he took up with Hegelian philosophy,[3] which he employed in defence of a more or less orthodox Calvinist stance, which also owed a good deal to Anselm and Augustine. The elder Caird was a great admirer of John Mcleod Campbell, who had been removed from the parish of Row in Dumbartonshire by the General Assembly in 1831 because of his universalist teaching.[4] He appears to have borrowed conservative critical ideas from leading Free Church scholars like Bruce,[5] with whom he seems to have been rather closer than he was with the biblical scholars of the established Church. At all events he soon earned the reputation of being a man who, for good or ill, 'liberalized and humanized Scottish theology and secured faith against scepticism by revealing its intrinsic reasonableness'.[6]

Tulloch was principal and professor of Theology at St Andrews from 1854, shortly before Edward Caird became a student there. He, also, was something of a paradox, a man who was very respected and influential but, at the same time, suspected of holding not entirely orthodox opinions. In fact, like John Caird, his own motivation seems to have been a desire to develop a liberal, rationally defensible orthodoxy in the Church of Scotland and to establish the broadly comprehensive character which he believed its formularies already possessed.

Edward Caird's biographers suggest that the two things which he

---

[1] There is a memoir of John Caird by Edward in the first volume of John's Gifford Lectures, posthumously edited by his brother; J. Caird, *The Fundamental Ideas of Christianity*, 2 vols. (Glasgow, 1899), i. pp. xi–cxli.

[2] Ibid., p. xv.

[3] Ibid., p. lxxvii for Edward's description of John Caird's somewhat ambivalent attitude to Hegel.

[4] I am indebted for help in understanding John Caird to J. B. Arthur whose BD dissertation at Glasgow University was on the theology of the elder Caird.

[5] Below, pp. 83.

[6] H. Jones and J. H. Muirhead, *The Life and Philosophy of Edward Caird* (Glasgow, 1921), 23 ff.

chiefly learnt from Tulloch were an interest in other religions and the thought that the supernatural was simply the spiritual manifesting itself in a particularly intense form.[7] John Caird and John Tulloch would both, then, have had a generally liberal influence on Edward, convincing him primarily of two things; first that it was perfectly possible to construct a version of Christianity which could be defended by rational argument and, secondly, that—in order to support an essentially orthodox view—it was sometimes necessary to advance an argument which was, or appeared to be, unusual, untraditional, or even actually heterodox. Edward very quickly moved to a position which, while it claimed to give very general support to the Christian position, was in fact completely at odds with traditional orthodoxy.

He became an undergraduate at Balliol in 1860 (when he was already 25). Here T. H. Green was his tutor and soon became his close friend. It is easy to understand why Green should have seemed to Edward Caird to be expounding ideas which he had already half perceived but had never fully understood before.[8] Green himself had been introduced to Kant and Hegel by Jowett, but had developed an idealism of his own which came, in the end, to earn Jowett's disapproval. This was partly because Jowett thought it had become a 'system' to which Green tried to make converts and partly because he had come to believe that Kant and Hegel were rather transient excitements.[9] But Green, who is usually described as a neo-Hegelian, was in fact an original thinker who took Kant as his starting point and then thought his way along lines which ran parallel to, rather than being directly derived from, Hegel.[10] His idealism began to be developed, moreover, at about the very time that Caird was one of his pupils. As early as 1862 he was asserting:

When the mind has come to see in the endless flux of outward things, not a succession of isolated phenomena, but the reflex of its own development into a variety of laws on a basis of identity—when the laws of nature are raised to the character of laws which regulate admiration and love—when

---

[7] H. Jones and J. H. Muirhead, *The Life and Philosophy of Edward Caird*, 18.
[8] P. Hinchliff, *Benjamin Jowett and the Christian Religion* (Oxford, 1987), 211.
[9] Ibid. 166 f.
[10] Green's own contemporaries seem to have recognized this: see A. Seth and R. B. Haldane (eds.), *Essays in Philosophical Criticism* (London, 1883), 5; and cf. R. L. Nettleship (ed.), *Works of Thomas Hill Green*, 3 vols. (London, 1886–1890), i. pp. lxxxv f.

experiences of life are held together in a medium of pure emotion, and the animal element so fused with the spiritual as to form one organization through which the same impulse runs with unimpeded energy—then man has made nature his own, by becoming a conscious partaker of the reason which animates him and it.[11]

Green was to argue that it was of the essence of being a follower of Hegel to 'hold that the objective world, in its actual totality, is thought, and that the processes of our intelligence are but reflections of that real thought under the conditions of a limited animal nature'.[12] But the deficiency in Hegel's system, which he believed his followers must attempt to make good, was in the very conception of thought itself. 'If thought and reality are to be identified, if the statement that God is thought is to be more than a presumptuous paradox, thought must be other than the discursive activity exhibited in our inferences and analyses, other than a particular mode of consciousness which excludes from itself feeling and will.'[13] He believed that the world was, indeed, a unity, governed by a single law, animated by an undivided life, constituting a whole; and the strength of Hegelianism seemed to him to be that it enabled one to make sense of that whole and fit oneself and one's actions into it. It was a philosophy 'having for its professed object to find formulae adequate to the action of reason as exhibited in nature and human society, in art and religion'.[14]

Both Green's determination that life should be understood as a coherent whole and his admiration for Hegel's philosophy, because it provided 'formulae adequate to the action of reason', meant that he linked his religious and political ideas within his idealist system. He was passionately concerned, not only with the broad sweep of moral and political thought but with the practical, even boring, detail of politics at the most mundane and local level. It was all a way of translating the ideal into the actual. Indeed, one of the key concepts in all his thought was that religion is the link between political philosophy and social practice.[15] It was, however, a somewhat unusual form of the Christian religion which he believed provided the best possible form of the link between philosophy and practical politics. In spite of the fact that he came from a clerical

[11] Nettleship (ed.), *Thomas Hill Green*, iii. 22.   [12] Ibid. iii. 143.
[13] Ibid. iii. 142.   [14] Ibid. iii. 125.
[15] A. Vincent and R. Plant, *Philosophy, Politics and Citizenship: The Life and Thought of the British Idealists* (Oxford, 1984), 12.

family he sat rather lightly to formal religion, saying, towards the
end of his life, that the clergy seemed to content themselves with
polishing 'a pebble or two' in 'a corner of the beach on the great
sea-shore'.[16] Green aimed to achieve something more significant.
He set himself to present Christianity in a form in which what had
been supposed to be history was converted into metaphysics, so
that the religious ideas of the gospel might thus be protected from
the attacks of historical criticism.

Green seems to have become interested in F. C. Baur's Hegelian
approach to the history of doctrine. The distinctive feature of
Baur's technique was to substitute a historical for a systematic
theology. But, unlike more conventional Liberal Protestant attempts
to burrow back behind developed dogma to the supposed simple
and original Jesus of history, Baur treated the historical developments as themselves significant. Hegelian concepts were echoed by
two principal characteristic features in his thought, though the
resultant hypotheses were not without supporting historical evidence. He believed that the earliest Christian Church was the
synthetic product of violent opposition between Paul's followers
and the Judaizing faction. He also believed that there was an overall
unity, harmony, and continuity observable in history. In Christian
history, in particular, Baur maintained that a serious and objective
observer could perceive the working out of a controlling idea; and,
if one believed with Hegel that history is the absolute Spirit's
realizing and actualizing of itself, then it was possible to see that
development as in some sense intended and intentional. His ideas
on the relationship between faith and historical knowledge have
been summarized thus:

On the one hand, historical-critical theology is dependent on authentically
subjective faith, for it is only through the freedom thus achieved that the
historical theologian is able to transpose himself critically into the
objectivity of the historical data. On the other hand, faith is dependent on,
or must be instructed by, historical knowledge, since the content of faith is
mediated historically and knowable historically-critically, and because
authentic faith requires the continual prodding and testing of historical
criticism, for its certainty is of a different order than the empirical
certainties of this world.[17]

[16] S. Paget, *Henry Scott Holland: Memoir and Letters* (London, 1921), 31.
[17] P. C. Hodgson, *The Formation of Historical Theology: A Study of Ferdinand
Christian Baur* (New York, 1966), 174.

This aspect of Baur's thought Green did not immediately take up. But he set himself to write an essay on dogma, describing the speculative basis of his own brand of Christianity. This was so firmly based upon, and so clearly worked out from, his own philosophical position that there is no way to separate the two. It was not that he accepted a faith and then had to reconcile it with a philosophy; or even that he had to develop a rationale for a religious position he had come to adopt for other reasons. It was, rather, that the two developed together. Since all existence was to be conceived of as the expression of God as universal mind, and since God was, therefore, the real self, he did not find it difficult to conceive of an incarnation in Christ in which God could be made known to man. His difficulty—if his theology is understood in terms of traditional orthodoxy rather than in Green's own terms— was to say clearly how God-in-Christ could be thought of as different from God's presence in any other human being.

Green lectured on the New Testament regularly in Balliol. Though he does not seem to have followed Baur's distinctively historical approach, he claimed to find his ideas about the New Testament stimulating. Yet Green insisted that the fact that Paul had not known Jesus was a positive fact that made it possible to construct a Christian faith impervious to historical criticism.[18] He therefore attempted to represent his own conception of God as the ideal self as a reworking of Paul's 'the witness of God', arguing that it was necessary 'to reproduce with as much exactness as modern phraseology admits of, and without any conventional use of theological language, the essence of St. Paul's belief in Christ'.[19] Christ is one with God, so that what Christ did—God did. Therefore a death to life, a life out of death, must be in some way of the essence of the divine nature; must be an act, 'which, though exhibited once for all in the crucifixion and resurrection of Christ, is yet eternal, because the act of God himself'. Christ as God is also present and operative in man, and so man has to re-enact in himself this eternal act of God, going out of himself and thus being conformed to the being of God, to whom he is at every point related.

This essential, fundamental identity between God and the self caused him to be uneasy about miracles. Founding religion upon

---

[18] Vincent and Plant, *Philosophy, Politics and Citizenship*, 13.
[19] Nettleship (ed.), *Thomas Hill Green*, iii. 235.

supposedly supernatural events seemed to imply a belief that the
energy which creates the order of nature 'reveals itself by annulling
the order in which it is implied and apart from which it has no
reality'.[20] And so, by miracles, God would uncreate himself. Such a
misconception, as he conceived it, of the true relationship between
God and nature seemed to be responsible for the dogma relating to
the person of Christ, the Chalcedonian formula of the one person in
two natures, human and divine. Christ, he believed, had been
'gradually externalized and mystified' by the Church.[21] The truth
would be better expressed if one claimed that in Jesus the spirit of
life out of death was present in an exceptional way. So he disliked
attempts to reconstruct the original teaching and character of Jesus
from 'uncertain documents', preferring to base what he said on a
reinterpretation of Pauline or Johannine theology.

Perhaps the best summary of Green's religious thought is in his
own words:

It has sometimes been remarked that if all the New Testament had been
lost to us except some half-dozen texts, the essence of christianity would
have been preserved in these, so that out of them everything in it that is of
permanent moral value might have been developed; and if there can be an
essence within the essence of christianity, it is the thought embodied in the
text, 'The word is nigh thee;' the thought of God not as 'far off' but 'nigh',
not as a master but as a father, not as a terrible outward power, forcing us
we know not whither, but as one of whom we may say that we are reason
of his reason and spirit of his spirit; who lives in our moral life, and in
whom we live in living for the brethren, even as in so living we live freely,
because in obedience to a spirit which is our self; in communion with
whom we triumph over death, and have the assurance of eternal life.[22]

The average reader may be forgiven for feeling that, in spite of
Green's claim to be using Pauline ideas and language, this bears
very little relationship to anything intended by New Testament
writers. But it is easy to see why it might appeal so deeply to, and
awaken so many echoes in, the Edward Caird who had been
trained by his brother and by John Tulloch to welcome ways of
restating Christianity so as to make it defensible by philosophical
argument. Green's thought would be especially attractive to him
because of the way in which it found expression in political and
social concerns. Caird had already become a devotee of the early

[20] Nettleship, *Thomas Hill Green*, iii. 128.   [21] Ibid. iii. 242.
[22] Ibid. iii. 221.

writings of Carlyle, whose morality condemned poverty and oppression and expressed 'disgust at the mean achievements of what we call civilization ... generous wrath at the arbitrary limitation of its advantages, [and] deep craving for a better order of social life'.[23]

Having been for a brief while a fellow of an Oxford college, Caird returned to Glasgow as professor of Moral Philosophy in 1866. His brother was already the professor of Theology there and was to become principal of the university in 1873. Edward Caird's biographers suggest that he acted as his brother's ally, and perhaps agent, in introducing a number of radical policies into the university—widening the range of subjects taught, lifting the restriction which forbade persons not members of the Church of Scotland to be taught divinity, opening education to women, and appointing younger lecturers so as to break the teaching monopoly of the occupants of the endowed professorial chairs.[24] In fact, the records indicate that, though all these things may be true, they were true in a much more muted way than that account suggests. John Caird's chief work was the completion of the establishment of the university on its new site after its move from the centre of the old city in 1870—complete with stuffed animals from the museum, if one is to believe a delightful watercolour by the wife of the professor of Mathematics at the time.[25] There was a great deal of restructuring to be undertaken but, if there was any deep-laid plot by the two brothers to radicalize the university, it took second place to the more immediate demands of day-to-day academic politics.

Additional subjects were certainly introduced, such as naval architecture in 1883, but it is not clear that attendance at divinity classes had ever been restricted to members of the Church of Scotland. There seems, in fact, always to have been a greater flexibility than in English universities. Undergraduates behaved much more like the wandering students of medieval times. What mattered most at Glasgow was that they should pay their fee for attending the lectures. (The professors had to collect these fees in person until as late as 1879 when it was agreed that the assistant

[23] E. Caird, 'The Genius of Carlyle', *Essays on Literature and Philosophy* (Glasgow, 1892), 230 ff.

[24] Jones and Muirhead, *Edward Caird*, 106, 114, and 149.

[25] R. Fairley (ed.), *Jemima; The Paintings and Memoirs of a Victorian Lady* (Edinburgh, 1988), 158.

clerk might collect lecture fees on their behalf.)[26] Moreover, the so-called 'professors' who controlled the training of ministers in the smaller 'free' denominations, seem to have encouraged their students to attend university classes as well as their own. Nor had Glasgow ever possessed a tradition of excluding other Churches. As early as 1843 and 1844 the university had conferred honorary doctorates in divinity on ministers of the Relief Synod,[27] and this was, of course, long before either Caird became a professor of the university.

The same sort of picture emerges in the matter of university reform in general. The senate of Glasgow University spent far more time agonizing over the cost of making the enormously detailed returns required by the Scottish Universities Commission, and trying to persuade the commission itself to pay for it, than in any discussion of actual proposals for reform.[28]

In the matter of women's education Caird's record is a little more impressive. On 8 November 1877 a memorial from the Committee of the Glasgow Association for the Higher Education of Women was read to the university senate showing that various professors, including Caird, had agreed to deliver courses of lectures to ladies and 'prayed' to be allowed to use their class-rooms for the purpose. There was some opposition to the permission being extended in the following year and the senate flatly refused to contemplate examining the women in what they had learnt. Caird proposed both motions.[29] And so the story proceeds. Education for women inched forward (but far more quickly than in England). Caird was always among those in favour of its extension but was seldom conspicuously in the lead, except that he served as chairman of a committee appointed to look into the requests made by the women's association. It has to be said that one of the very few Edward Caird items in the university archives is a letter of April 1887 to Miss Galloway—the leading local activist in the matter of

---

[26] Minutes of the Senate: 1 May 1879.

[27] W. Mackelvie, *Annals and Statistics of the United Presbyterian Church* (Edinburgh, 1873), 198 f. The two ministers concerned subsequently became ministers of the United Presbyterian Church, which is why they are listed in this work.

[28] Minutes of the Senate: 8 and 22 Mar. 1877. There is no further reference to the work of the commission in the minutes of senate until 14 Oct. 1879, by which time the report of the Royal Commissioners upon the Universities of Scotland (1878) had already been published.   [29] Minutes of 21 Mar. 1878.

women's education—but the letter itself is very uninformative. It merely refers to a report which is no longer attached to the letter.[30] By that time the senate had agreed to examine women. They were eventually permitted to form Queen Margaret College and the college itself finally became part of the university in 1892, the year before Edward Caird left Glasgow to return to Oxford to become master of Balliol.

The only other matter of general educational reform which the senate seems to have debated, and Edward Caird was one of the most vigorous campaigners for the proposal, was the question whether to set up in 'provincial towns' courses of lectures for the benefit of 'those who are debarred from the special advantages of University Education' (specifically 'clerks in mercantile offices and others engaged in non-professional business who could not afford to leave their work even for a single year') and women.[31]

If Caird was, perhaps, less committed to the day-to-day minutiae of small-scale politics than his friend and mentor T. H. Green, that is not to say that he had no interest in political questions. This was a troubled time in British politics for men with a liberal conscience. In 1895 the Jameson Raid into the Transvaal aroused suspicion that there had been a plot to engineer the collapse of the Boer republic. It was thought that Joseph Chamberlain, who had become Secretary of State for the Colonies in the same year, might have been implicated in it as well as Cecil Rhodes, Prime Minister of the Cape Colony. A parliamentary committee in 1897 censured Rhodes but exonerated Chamberlain. Two years later the Boer War broke out and until 1902 Britain was in the uncomfortable position of being the large bully attacking a small (but white) independent state in Africa. The discomfort was not felt universally. The so-called Khaki election of 1900 produced a sweeping Conservative victory. In these circumstances Caird was capable of courageous and unconventional political action. He caused great offence in Oxford by opposing the conferring of an honorary degree on Cecil Rhodes, which was thought very improper behaviour in the head of a college.[32]

Caird's conviction that political action was important because it gave concrete expression to eternal truth, sits rather oddly with his

---

[30] Glasgow University Archives; Accession DC/233/2/3/6.
[31] Minutes of the Senate: 18 Mar., 1 Apr., and 28 Oct. 1880.
[32] Jones and Muirhead, *Edward Caird*, 153.

belief that in Christianity the eternal truth could be cut off from the historical actions that were its roots. But he was, after all, primarily a *moral* philosopher and it was the *morality* of politics which chiefly interested him. The very reason why he was such an enthusiastic disciple of Hegel was precisely because he believed that Hegel related philosophy to the real and corporate life of human beings. Hegel 'materialized and socialized' Kant's thought and, in so doing, secured the moral and religious basis of human existence. Caird's political theory was essentially a moral one; as his moral theory was essentially religious. At its heart was the belief that the law of liberty is 'to retain permanently the consciousness of the better self in subjection to which alone we can be truly free'.[33]

What Caird meant by 'materializing and socializing' Kant is best illustrated by a quotation from one of his later addresses:

To believe that we can, here and now, make our lives ideal, that the round of duties that seem commonplace and secular,—these family ties, this college companionship, these professional occupations of law, or education, or commerce, these civic and political relations,—furnish the very environment that is needed for the realization of the highest of which we are capable, that is the most difficult of all things. We form an ideal picture of some better state of the world, in which the commonplace and secular aspects of life have no longer any room and duties are at once more heroic and more easy, forgetting that there is no act but derives its character, its greatness or its pettiness, from the spirit which manifests itself in the doing of it. The only world worthy of being regarded as ideal is that which carries within it the present world with its meaning understood, and its worth deepened. It is our own world given back again, item by item, with all the elements that constitute it multiplied a hundred-fold in value, raised to a higher spiritual power: and it is realized, not without effort nor by leaps and bounds, for it comes 'with persecutions', but by the more faithful and full performance of the duties, commonplace as they may seem, of the station in which we stand.[34]

When he engaged in local or university politics Caird saw himself as deliberately expressing his conviction that the morality of one's daily life ought to be an endeavour to unite the finite with the infinite. This engagement 'materialized' morality, giving it secular and temporal expression; and 'socialized' it, turning it away from

[33] Quoted by Vincent and Plant, *Philosophy, Politics and Citizenship*, 27.
[34] E. Caird, *Lay Sermons and Addresses delivered in the Hall of Balliol College, Oxford* (Glasgow, 1907), 70 f.

the selfishness of the individual. For this reason he was associated with the new ethical societies, which were almost an embodiment of a humanist religion based on Kantian ethics and aimed at combating the individualism and divisiveness of industrial society.[35] But his humanism was essentially a religious humanism and his liberalism was an application of idealist religious ideas to public affairs. Society was a corporate entity in which the whole must care for each of its members.

All this he tried to express in his teaching in Glasgow. Manuscript notes taken at some of his lectures survive in the university archives.[36] These notes suggest that the lectures were dictated verbatim for they are written in the first person as if by Caird himself—'In my last lecture I argued . . .'. If that was the case, they were probably dictated rather slowly, for each lecture occupies only about 7 pages of the quarto notebooks; or it may be that Caird actually delivered his lecture less formally and then ended it with a dictated summary.

How much of what was said was actually understood by the student who took the notes is far from clear: Caird evidently employed a good deal of philosophical jargon. And this is a point worth remembering when one is considering the influence of any thinker. It applies to the sermons of Newman and Jowett as much as to Caird's lectures. An audience does not always receive precisely what a speaker or writer intends to communicate. Certainly these lecture notes are not nearly as impressive as surviving notes said to have been taken at lectures delivered by Green in Oxford in the same period.[37] This does not necessarily imply that in the 1870s the standard of Balliol undergraduates was very much higher than that of the students at Glasgow University; the editor of Green's *Works* may well have polished the material before publication. But it is quite clear that Caird's students were very young indeed and there is plenty of other evidence that the professors of the University of Glasgow were accustomed to treating their pupils as children.[38]

---

[35] Vincent and Plant, *Philosophy, Politics and Citizenship*, 54.

[36] Glasgow University Archives; Accession Nos. 31355/6. Two volumes (vols. II and IV) of Notes taken by John L. Steven of 329 Sauchiehall Street, Glasgow, from the lectures on Moral Philosophy delivered by Professor Edward Caird MA.

[37] Nettleship (ed.), *Thomas Hill Green*, iii. p. vi.

[38] On 22 Dec. 1880 the senate passed a regulation providing for a fine of five shillings for snowballing. It then immediately imposed the fine retroactively on 'William Eadie who was caught in the act of throwing snowballs by one of the

Although Caird's lectures are described as being on moral philosophy they were actually about the history of philosophy and of religion. An extract from the penultimate lecture in the student's notes gives a flavour of what Caird was saying, how far he tried—or failed—to gear his idealism down to the level of the class he was speaking to, and what the student made—or failed to make—of it:

I was speaking of the development of Pantheistic religion and of the two Categories of thought employed. In the first Pan the negative side prevails. In so far as these religions go out from Infinite to finite their defect lies in this that they are illogical and arbitrary. They are broken up into a confused Polytheism. What was wanting was that the Infinite and finite sh'd be brought together. Hence in religion like Greeks on same basis there is the best representation by the Reflective Categories that is thoughts in pairs. Hence we have the idea of *necessity* in the Greek religion. Connected with this is a peculiar kind of moral heroism. Its a heroism that reconciles itself with necessity. What must be must be. Ancient heroism does not accept law of world as a good law but merely as something that is good. This attitude has a kind of grandeur about it. At the same time it is a kind of sublimity that is imperfect. At the same time it can't be said that this is the highest attitude it is an attitude of despair.[39]

In spite of the fact that this particular student seems not entirely to have grasped the point Caird was making, some, at least, of his students at Glasgow did understand and appreciate his teaching. One of them later said that what he remembered as the chief things Caird had taught him were:

Such teaching as: that revelation cannot act outside reason or it becomes incomprehensible; that the Spiritual and the Rational can never be opposed to one another; that revelation is Spirit, and must be *to* Spirit, in whatever external form; that the action of Spirit in history cannot be erratic; that there can be no isolation of any subject for exclusive treatment apart from the ordinary conditions of reason and life; that we cannot divide up the human consciousness into separate compartments, such as will, thought, feeling; that arbitrary or traditional methods of thought must give way to methods in which organic relations and groupings are supreme.[40]

In 1877 Caird published his *Critical Account of the Philosophy of Kant*, which was later expanded into the two-volume work, *The*

professors'. At this period, too, the university sports field was always referred to as 'the playground' in the senate minutes.

[39] Glasgow University Archives: Accession No. 31356, vol. IV, lecture civ.
[40] Quoted in Jones and Muirhead, *Edward Caird*, 74 f.

Critical Philosophy of Immanuel Kant of 1889. He was also the author of a relatively small book on Hegel which was regarded as important because it helped to spread an understanding of Hegelian idealism in Britain.

There seems to have been some opposition to Caird in his early days at Glasgow and some criticism of his theological and philosophical opinions. It came principally from supporters of the Scottish 'common-sense' school of intuitionist philosophy,[41] rather than from die-hard upholders of biblical literalism, or traditional theology. Sir William Hamilton, who had died a decade before Caird's appointment, had been the last great leader of this school but there were many of his followers still in the Scottish universities. Initially developed as an answer to Hume, intuitionist philosophy under Hamilton maintained that metaphysical certainties were impossible because all knowledge is relative and conditioned, and that perception of external reality was an immediate awareness through the senses.[42]

The link between intuitionism and orthodox theology is not immediately obvious but it was possible to develop Hamilton's ideas so as to insist that revelation was the only possible source of knowledge of God and that natural science was capable of only a very limited and narrow kind of knowledge. The gulf between intuitionists and idealists, who stressed the supreme value of a metaphysical architectonic and took science seriously because it, too, was part of the manifestation of the divine, was therefore a wide and immediate one. As professor of Moral Philosophy, Edward Caird set himself to reassert the possibility of metaphysical certainty because he believed that, without that certainty, there could be no secure foundation for morality at all.[43]

Both Cairds had, in fact, begun to take an interest, in the 1870s, in what they described as the philosophy of religion but which was, as were Caird's ordinary lectures in the university, really concerned with the history of religions. The brothers were anxious to try to establish what they called a 'science of religion', finding a scientific, objective, and therefore widely acceptable basis for the study of

[41] Ibid. 68.
[42] A. M. Quinton, 'Absolute Idealism', *Proceedings of the British Academy*, 57 (1971), 315.
[43] Cf. Thomas Arnold's conviction that there could be no certainty or unanimity, in religious ideas, above, pp. 33 f.

religious ideas. This would—they hoped—provide a means of deciding which were the permanent, or highest, or 'true' features of religion. Such an approach assumed, of course, that all actual religions were expressions of the same basic universal religiousness, a way of looking at things that was the very reverse of any idea of real historical development. The only sense in which one could really talk of development at all, within this framework, was by trying to identify the form of religion in which the universal and eternal religiousness was most perfectly or fully expressed. In the Cairds' case it was assumed that Christianity came nearest to being the ultimate manifestation of religion. John seems to have thought that this could be said even of conventional, more or less orthodox Christianity: Edward was—at this stage, at any rate—more inclined to think that it applied only to a refined version of it.

In 1878 John Caird gave the Croall Lectures at Edinburgh, following a course of lectures in his own university in the previous year.[44] These lectures contained a lengthy section on the significance of other religions.[45] All religion, he maintained, existed in order to enable the human spirit to surrender itself to the Divine Spirit. The true religion (i.e. Christianity) was that which did this most perfectly. What gave the whole history of religion a unity and cohesiveness in John Caird's thought was the quasi-Hegelian idea that each religious tradition was part of a single organic evolution of a single spiritual principle.[46]

The Cairds' campaign continued through the 1880s and became intertwined with the establishment of the Gifford Lectures in four Scottish universities in 1887.[47] Their own concerns were perhaps reflected in the decision by the University of Glasgow to appoint Max Müller as the first lecturer on the Gifford foundation there.[48] It was expected that Müller would lecture on the non-Christian

---

[44] J. Caird, *Introduction to the Philosophy of Religion* (Glasgow, 1880), and cf. University of Glasgow, Minutes of the Senate: 16 Jan. 1877.

[45] J. Caird, *Philosophy of Religion*, 321 ff. I am indebted to Paul Supple, a graduate student who is working on nineteenth-century attitudes to other religions, for drawing my attention to these lectures and also to John Caird's contribution on 'The Religions of India: The Vedic Period—Brahmanism' in *The Faiths of the World* (Edinburgh, undated), 1–36.

[46] J. Caird, *Philosophy of Religion*, 323. It is difficult to know precisely where John Caird acquired the at least superficial Hegelianism of some of his ideas, unless he borrowed them from Edward.

[47] See the Minutes of Senate for 10 Mar. 1887 and 12 Jan. 1888.

[48] Minutes of Senate: 9 Feb. 1888.

world religions. This was something of a distortion of the intention of Lord Gifford himself, who desired the lectures to be on 'natural theology', which primarily meant proofs of the existence of God and related questions.[49] But it was argued, very strongly, that natural religion must include the study of those actual religions which are not the consequence of the Judaeo-Christian revelation.

Max Müller accepted the lectureship with alacrity, but his tenure did not proceed smoothly. He was, apparently, slow to give the lectures but quick to request payment of his stipend.[50] When it was time to consider the appointment of the next lecturer, a majority of the members of the senate signed a letter proposing that John Caird himself should fill the post. It was foolish, they thought, to go outside the university when there was someone so peculiarly well qualified in Glasgow.[51] Caird declined on the ground that, as principal, he was too busy: Max Müller was reappointed. There was still some difficulty in getting Müller to deliver his lectures as regularly and frequently as the senate desired and, by 1892, rather more serious trouble over the content of the lectures themselves. A petition from the faculty of Theology desired the senate to make it clear to the general public that 'the sole responsibility for the mode in which the subject may be treated rests with the Lecturer'. The principal prevented the petition being discussed by moving the previous motion, which was carried by 5 votes to 4 with 7 abstentions.[52] Neither this device nor a successful move (seconded by Professor Dickson, Müller's principal critic) to have John Caird appointed as Gifford Lecturer for the next two academic years, settled the issue. There was a storm of protest about both the content of Müller's lectures and the use of a procedural device to stifle discussion.[53]

In the same year as all this controversy Edward Caird published his own first set of Gifford Lectures, *The Evolution of Religion*.

---

[49] See S. L. Jaki, *Lord Gifford and His Lectures: A Centenary Retrospect* (Edinburgh and Macon, Ga., 1986), 5 ff. It should be noted, however, that this is not really a history of the lectureships but rather a summary of the contents of the various lectures.

[50] Minutes of Senate: 28 Feb. 1889. See also Glasgow University Archives, Accession 1613 Mfn/Misc, letter from Müller to the University's solicitors, asking what the income of the Gifford Fund was, as though he was suspicious that he was not being paid the full amount.

[51] Minutes of Senate: 30 Jan. 1890.

[52] Minutes of Senate: 15 Jan. 1892: Edward Caird was not at the meeting.

[53] Minutes of Senate: 11 Feb. 1892.

Though delivered at Edinburgh and not Glasgow, the lectures were plainly conceived by Caird himself as part of his campaign for the rediscovery of moral truth by demonstrating that religion could be treated as an object of *scientific* enquiry and as the subject of an evolutionary process. If there is no reference to the surviving intuitionists in his lectures that is not surprising. Caird disliked controversy and believed that to omit to mention one's opponents was to deal them a fierce and punishing blow.[54]

Caird's motive in writing *The Evolution of Religion* is set out in the preface to the published version of the lectures:

I have specially had in view that large and increasing class who have become alienated from the ordinary dogmatic system of belief, but who, at the same time, are conscious that they have owed a great part of their spiritual life to the teachings of the Bible and the Christian Church. To separate what is permanent from what is transitory in the traditions of the past is a difficult task which every generation has to encounter for itself. In the present day there are many who are divided between two feelings: perplexed on the one hand by a suspicion that in clinging to the orthodox forms of the creed of Christendom, they may be untrue to themselves, and may even seem to assent to doctrines which they have ceased to believe; and checked on the other side by a fear that in discarding those forms they may be casting aside ideas which are essential to their moral and spiritual life.[55]

'What they want, above all,' he added, 'is some principle or criterion, which will make it possible for them to distinguish what is tenable from what is untenable in the opposite claims which are made upon their belief—claims which, on both sides, they cannot help to some extent acknowledging.' Caird believed that 'for the first time' there was now an available yardstick for measuring religious truth and for distinguishing between the permanent and the transitory in religion. That yardstick was 'the idea of development'.[56] In using the term 'development' he does not appear to have had Newman's theory in mind at all: he was using it simply as an alternative to 'evolution' in the scientific, biological sense. He believed that by analysing the concept of evolution in relation to

[54] Jones and Muirhead, *Edward Caird*, 68 f.

[55] E. Caird, *The Evolution of Religion*, 2 vols. (Glasgow, 1893), i. p. viii.

[56] Ibid., p. x; what Caird meant by using the idea of development as a yardstick is set out below in the discussion of his application of the concept of evolution to religion.

religion he would be able to establish a means of distinguishing between essential and inessential aspects.

The lectures were concerned, then, with the possibility of a 'science' of religion and with 'the idea of development'. It is interesting to compare Caird's approach with that of Baring-Gould, the third edition of whose work had been published a year earlier than *The Evolution of Religion*.[57] Baring-Gould tried to give his treatise a 'scientific' character by opening the work with a discussion of physics and physiology by means of which he hoped to be able to locate the 'seat of the religious sentiment'. What Caird meant by 'science' in this context—the discovery of 'law, order, and reason in what seems at first accidental, capricious and meaningless'—was very different. The progress of science, he maintained, resulted from specialization: what he called 'the division of the sciences'. As 'science' became divided into its separate fields of enquiry it became possible to tackle more and more complex problems and to understand, more fully, the orderliness of the subject. He believed, however, that orderliness, rational explanation in terms of causality, and the consistency of things in terms of 'law', though they existed throughout the universe, were not always on the same level: moral science or science of religion would be different from the physical sciences. But he went on to argue that what had made it possible to treat religion scientifically, were two concepts which had only recently been generally accepted, the *unity* of man and human *development*. Caird proposed, in fact, to develop a kind of dialectic from the paradox that, while progress in any science depended on specialization, the science of religion depended for its very possibility upon the unity of man and his unity with the rest of existence.

Though there were difficulties in combining Caird's view of the scientific consistency of religious phenomena, in terms of law,[58] with any concept of evolution, it appears that he intended the title of his lectures seriously. Though he did not precisely analyse and apply the concept of evolution in its biological sense to the study of religion, he often employed its language. 'The different religions are not merely co-ordinate species varying one in this direction, the other in that, from a single general type. They are in many cases at

---

[57] S. Baring-Gould, *The Origin and Development of Religious Belief*, 3rd edn. (London, 1892). The work had been written some thirty years earlier than that date.

[58] Above, p. 134 and 136.

least, to be regarded rather as successive stages in one process of development, in which the later include and presuppose the earlier.'[59] He did not believe that religion evolved in a form precisely analogous to biological evolution but he held that, nevertheless, all religion could be regarded as part of a 'development', even when there was no historical connection between the different manifestations of it. Indeed, he thought that there was little point in enquiring into the similarities between differing religions which *had* a direct historical connection, like Christianity and Judaism, or Buddhism and Brahmanic Hinduism. That, he maintained, would be like asking what there was in common between 'the bud, the leaf, the flower and the fruit of a tree'. Therefore one could not treat such religions as 'co-ordinate species'. Even those religions which possessed very little historical connection, or none at all, could not be treated as 'reciprocally exclusive logical species which are united only by a common generic quality'.[60] They are really 'phases of religious belief, which represent different stages in the development of the *idea of religion*'.[61] In other words, Caird did not think that the science of religion consisted of tracing the *historical* development of one form of religion out of another, but in examining the developing way in which the human mind *conceived* of religion. He believed that it was possible to demonstrate that there was a common course followed by such development and that each phase evolved out of what went before it.

This meant that nothing was to be gained by comparing a variety of religions, for that would imply that they all stood at some roughly comparable point in relation to the supposed 'origin' of religion. He proposed to show, moreover, that the 'development' was not in a straight line. He believed that pantheism, for instance, was the 'culminating' phase of polytheism but that monotheism 'always arises in direct opposition to both'.[62] There was a dialectic here, in other words, which made it clear that the evolution of religion was quite different from biological evolution because it was the evolution of ideas not of physical entities. In the evolution of ideas, what was evolved became the environment for the evolution of new forms in a more obvious way than in biological evolution. Moreover there was another, and equally important, aspect of

[59] E. Caird, *The Evolution of Religion*, i. 40.   [60] Ibid. 41.
[61] Loc. cit.: the emphasis is not in the original.   [62] Loc. cit.

Caird's thought implicit in the words '*always* arises'. It is the same point that was noted by his former student and quoted above—'that the action of Spirit in history cannot be erratic'.[63] Essentially what enabled him to treat religion 'scientifically' was his belief that the spiritual manifested itself with a consistency analogous to the consistency which is assumed as the basis for all scientific enquiry.

The reason why Caird thought that the term 'evolution' was appropriate to the science of religion also emerged in his second lecture. This lecture, really the nub of his whole argument, contains the words, 'any definition [of religion] which we might derive from the analysis and comparison of the higher forms of religion would be too lofty and comprehensive to apply to the superstition of savages; yet in these superstitions we recognize the obscure beginnings of religious experience, and they could not be left out of account in any definition of religion'.[64] If different religions are stages or phases in a single development, then it might be thought that it was precisely in these '*beginnings*' that the common element is likely to be found—'*ex hypothesi* the simplest religion must still contain the essence of religion, and it will contain little or nothing else to disguise that essence from us'. Stated in such a form, of course, the weakness of the search for a common element in all religions was obvious—'it would constrain us to define religion in terms of the lowest possible form of it'; and if one were forced to recognize that some forms of religion were a reaction against earlier forms—as Caird believed—'then we should be obliged to reject from our definition even the elements that appear in its earliest form'.[65]

So he came to think that no simple definition of religion was possible. In a lengthy passage he compared understanding religion—rather as he had already done with his analogy of bud, leaf, flower, and fruit—with understanding a human being. It is possible to understand an adult's nature by looking back at the child, but that will not explain everything about him. It is equally possible to forecast what a child may become, but only because we have knowledge of what adults are. We fully understand what a human being is at the point at which the child becomes an adult. It was only in this sense—treating religion, in effect, as if it were an

---

[63] Above, p. 134.
[64] E. Caird, *The Evolution of Religion*, i. 42.
[65] Ibid. i. 42 f.

individual instance within a species—that he felt able to apply the analogy drawn from evolution.

Development is not simply the recurrence of the same effects in similar circumstances, not simply the maintenance of an identity under a variation determined by external conditions. Hence it is impossible, from the phenomena of one stage of the life of a developing being, to derive laws which will adequately explain the whole course of its existence. The secret of the peculiar nature of such a being lies just in the way of regular transition in which, by constant interaction with external influences, it widens the compass of its life, unfolding continually new powers and capacities—powers and capacities latent in it from the first, but not capable of being foreseen with any definiteness by one who had seen only the beginning. It follows that, in the first instance at least, we must read development *backward* and not *forward*, we must find the key to the meaning of the first stage in the last; though it is quite true that, afterwards, we are enabled to throw new light upon the nature of the last, to analyse and appreciate it in a new way, by carrying it back to the first.[66]

It was in this sense that Caird thought he had found an appropriate yardstick for distinguishing between the permanent and the transitory features of religion.

Caird began his third lecture by reasserting this point in a different form—'that history is just religion defining itself'[67]—and from that point on the book is really an explication, in detail, of the scheme that he had already adumbrated in the attempt to define religion. Some very interesting points emerge and new and important ideas and distinctions are introduced. For instance, Caird defined his concept of the unity of finite and infinite over against the theories of Max Müller and Herbert Spencer, arguing that the first made the infinite wholly other and that the second, in attempting to define an infinite out of existence, had really got rid of the cosmos too. He made a careful distinction between what he called objective (theistic) religion and subjective religion (i.e. religions which have no concept of an objective God). There are interesting sections on the connection between religion and morality; on the role played by the imagination in 'objective' religion; on the relationship between goodness and happiness in the Old Testament.

But in essence Caird had already given a brief outline of his

---

[66] E. Caird, *The Evolution of Religion*, i. 45.   [67] Ibid. i. 61.

argument: God is infinite but not—as in Kant—transcendent, since he is the unity that includes and fulfils all things.[68] Spirit manifests itself through everything that exists, consistently and not erratically. It does so, supremely, through the human mind. Since all existence has a consistent unity, humanity also possesses a unity, both in itself and with the rest of the universe. Because religion is an aspect of the human mind and because the rational is the spiritual, religion will also manifest a consistency and a unity which makes it possible to treat it 'scientifically', as a developing, living organism. Surveying religion in this way; tracing its development and understanding why it has taken the forms it has; perceiving which are the 'higher' and which the 'lower' forms of religion, will enable one to distinguish what are the permanent features of genuine religion and exclude those aspects of it which are merely conditioned by the needs and the limitations of earlier times.

The two volumes of the book survey what Caird obviously believed to be the most important stages in the development of religion. Much of what he wrote was hardly scientific, in the sense of being objective and demonstrable. A great deal of it was simply an expression of his own personal view of the nature of the religions he was considering. For instance, he attributed to Paul and to the author of the fourth gospel the 'separation of Christ from humanity and a kind of identification of him with God, which is practically a return of the Jewish opposition of God and man'.[69] Caird himself believed that one of the essential aspects of the gospel of Jesus was the unity of the human and the divine, not in the classical sense of the one person in two natures, but in the sense that man cannot be true to himself unless he is able to see himself in God. Caird was not alone, of course, in holding such views but they are not self-evident. Caird ought to have produced arguments in support of his opinion, not merely asserted it; so, although he was able to set out a scheme which seemed to provide a firm basis for his own religious beliefs and his rejection of some aspects of orthodoxy, the scheme was a good deal less watertight than he assumed it to be.

The Evolution of Religion was published in 1893, the year in which Caird succeeded Jowett as master of Balliol. Three years later, as president of the Oxford Society of Historical Theology, he

---

[68] See Quinton, 'Absolute Idealism', 309, describing these lectures.
[69] E. Caird, *The Evolution of Religion*, ii. 214.

delivered an address on the question of Christ and history.[70] The society was so called to make it clear that one could be a member without being committed to particular dogmas, but Caird seems to have treated the occasion as an opportunity to construct a version of F. C. Baur's kind of historical theology. The lecture is in some ways a puzzling piece of work. It is curiously concerned with the importance of history, for someone who believed that the way to protect Christianity from the attacks of the critics was to cut it free from its historical roots. It also develops the broad, general thesis of *The Evolution of Religion* in such a way as to involve Caird in contradicting some of the points of detail he had made in the Gifford Lectures. In particular, in the brief period between delivering the lectures and giving his presidential address, he had changed his attitude to the role of Paul and the fourth gospel in the history of Christian thought.

For this very reason, perhaps, he began the address with the words, 'Everyone would admit that the true interest of theological controversy lies not ... in proving that some writer has contradicted himself, or admitted ideas which if developed would be fatal to his fundamental principles, but in bringing out the full implications of different lines or tendencies of thought, and the possibility or impossibility of reconciling them.'[71]

In fact the paper has little to do with the actual facts of history and much more with Caird's concept of the nature of history. He argued that there was a general tendency 'to look for the explanation of a thing to its origin, and even to treat the first form in which a principle or idea manifests itself as the true form of it'.[72] This, he thought, as one might expect from the author of *The Evolution of Religion*, was a serious mistake. Those who seek to return to the beginning in the hope of finding the essential idea, forget that they cannot escape from their own consciousness of problems of which the person whose work seems to them so splendid was unaware. Then they read into the original a more complex or a fuller meaning than the original author intended.

Precisely the same danger threatened those who urged, ' "Back to the simple original Gospels;" and back through them,—as interpreted, many would add, by the modern resources of criticism—to

[70] 'Christianity and the Historical Christ', *Abstract of the Proceedings of the Oxford Society of Historical Theology*, 22 Oct. 1896.   [71] Ibid. 5.
[72] Loc. cit.

the image of the original Founder of Christianity, expressed in his authentic words and deeds.' Citing Principal Fairbairn's work[73] as an example of the tendency, Caird continued:

It seeks by a study of the original records, in the light of all the historical and critical aids now open to us, and guided by the modern idea of Evolution, to bring us face to face with Jesus of Nazareth, to listen to his direct words of wisdom; and it seeks also to enable us to trace all the steps of his spiritual advance, all the steps by which he grew into the Messiah of Israel and of humanity, giving the deepest interpretation to the prophetic dream of his nation, and lifting it into that higher region in which the freely accepted Cross became the necessary means to the deliverance of man. The highest, though of course impossible, goal of such criticism would be to annihilate space and time, and to enable us to live over again the life of the disciples who enjoyed the personal communion of their Lord, who immediately received his new interpretation of life in apothegm and parable, and felt the growing power and pathos of his utterance, as he became more and more conscious of the inevitable end and prepared to meet it. It is a very natural feeling that makes us suppose that, if this were possible, we should attain to the pure source of inspiration, and learn what is the real, the genuine Christianity, in which there is healing for all our mental and moral difficulties.[74]

Caird then attempted to show that such a hope was an illusion by quoting some remarks of Jowett's on the impossibility of re-constructing an accurate picture of Christ[75]—but, having had a dig at Fairbairn, he could not resist the opportunity to treat his predecessor in a similar manner, pointing out that his comments were 'not altogether consistent with one another'. Caird's own, more solid, argument depended on what he called 'two contra-dictory impossibilities'. First: 'We cannot live in the first century and revive the thousand details of a life that has passed away. We cannot verify the exact words and deeds which have reached us through the medium of a different language, and coloured by the memories of many persons who were not trained to be solicitous about verbal accuracy.' And then, returning to the first real point in his paper, 'if we could translate ourselves into the past, we should

---

[73] Below, pp. 190 f. Ironically, Fairbairn proposed the customary vote of thanks at the end of the presidential address, according to the entry in the Society's minute book for 22 Oct. 1896.
[74] E. Caird, 'Christianity and the Historical Christ', 9.
[75] See above, p. 65.

not get from it what we wish, except as interpreted by all those experiences, all those controversies and conflicts of the subsequent time, from which we seek to escape,—controversies and conflicts of thought and life which could not be present to the mind of Jesus or to his disciples, but which have been evolved in the effort to work out the ideas which they expressed.' Even the uniqueness of Christ, he thought, could not lift him out of his context in the history of human development. If we could re-create the Christ of the first century, he would not be able to tell us what to do in the modern world.

It becomes plain, in fact, that Caird had adopted a view very like that of Baur who had argued that:

The historian of dogma can take his position only from the standpoint of the most recent dogmatic consciousness. His task is to follow Christian dogma from its first origins through all the periods and moments of its development up to the most recent points of its development ... The historian can move back into the past only from the present. His whole task is to move backward through the same course by which the subject matter ... has come down to him, in order to complete the movement, which the subject matter has completed only objectively, also in his consciousness of it.[76]

Caird had become, in fact, very suspicious of the Liberal Protestants—though he does not use that term—who attempted to divest the 'simple gospel' of everything that had happened since. They 'regard the whole history of dogma, from the first to the eighteenth century, as a kind of interlude during which men lost themselves in scholastic subtleties, and forgot the simple morality of Christ as it is presented in the Synoptic Gospels'.[77] Pursuing the argument of the Gifford Lectures that the essence of a religion is to be found in its whole history, Caird felt himself obliged to point out that, if one took away from one's concept of Christ everything that belonged to the way he had been interpreted and understood in the past, one would be divesting him of everything that made it possible for him to be the centre of one's religious faith. Christ must, in other words, be interpreted 'by that which sprang from him, by the whole impression which he made upon his own and the immediately succeeding generation'. And, if we admit that, then we cannot

[76] *Dogmengeschichte*, I/1, 12–13, quoted in Hodgson, *Formation of Historical Theology*, 171.
[77] E. Caird, 'Christianity and the Historical Christ', 13.

maintain that there is a point at which the understanding and interpretation of later generations becomes invalid. Christ is to be treated like an idea or a spirit which continually finds new ways of expressing itself. If we do not recognize this, we 'are trying to separate the fact from its interpretation, and forgetting that if we were quite successful, there would be no fact left to interpret'.[78]

The remainder of the paper develops this point, attempting to show how the various gospels are, in fact, different interpretations of Jesus and how the history of doctrine is, in a sense, a continuation of the process of interpretation and has been necessary for the preservation of truth. 'There are some writers,' Caird said, 'who are so zealous against the idea of a Christianity without Christ, that they are in danger of teaching a Christ without Christianity.'[79] It was not, he pointed out, 'Christ after the flesh' that was needed but the Christ embodied in the long struggle of the Church, in the sense of those animated by the spirit of Christ, to overcome the world and adhere to the living principle which is working itself out in their lives.

It was an interesting conclusion for Caird to reach and, in spite of the very obvious Hegelianism of that last point, a more orthodox one than might have been expected. His idealism which had first led him to cut his Christianity free from the historical Jesus, so as to make it invulnerable to the attacks from higher criticism, was now leading him to argue that it was the history of dogma rather than the history of Jesus which enshrined the essential truth. Moreover he had repeatedly insisted in the paper that he recognized the value and importance—as well as the limitations—of the critical enterprise; and that too represented something of a change in his position.

Caird was now isolated from almost every other imaginable position. Jowett would not have approved of the place given to the Church in his scheme of things. Whatever Jowett meant by talking about an 'idealized life of Jesus',[80] he certainly would not have wished to represent Jesus as a spirit embodied in the Church's history. Yet Caird's attitude to history would not have been approved by Fairbairn either, for whom the Christian's chief hope of knowing Christ was precisely through the historical means about which Caird had been so scathing. On the other hand, more

[78] Ibid. 15.   [79] Ibid. 19.   [80] Hinchliff, *Jowett*, 138.

'Catholic' thinkers like Newman and Gore would have found him too undiscriminating. The great advantage they possessed, which was denied to the Liberal Protestants, was their declared determination to be faithful to the Christian tradition. This implied, in turn, an ability to define the *true* Christian tradition. Newman, Benson, and Gore, each in his own manner, had regarded it as essential to distinguish between the true and the false in the way in which Christ had been interpreted and understood in the course of Christian history. Caird seemed to have no such concern. Even those ways of understanding Christ with which he felt least sympathy (the medieval, for instance) had their part to play in the historical embodying of the Christian spirit.[81] He believed, after all, that 'development is always regress as well as progress'.[82] In this, as in so much else, his final position was very like that of Baur.

Of all the thinkers whose ideas are surveyed in this book, Caird is the one whose personal religion, piety, or faith—whatever one is to call it—is most difficult to assess. In part this is because he was the most reserved and private of them all, and few of them wore their hearts upon their sleeves. There can be no doubt that he cared passionately for moral values. There can be no doubt that he possessed a strong sense that God moved in, and controlled, history, but it is very difficult indeed to understand what his Christ-not-after-the-flesh actually meant to him. He was certainly not merely indulging in donnish speculation as a means of keeping himself occupied in the Oxford afternoons: he was far too austere in conscience for such an attitude to theology. As a young man he had founded, with a group of friends, the Old Mortality Club. It was given its name because they had each suffered from fairly serious illness and might not have long to live (though, in fact, most of them seem to have survived to a reasonably ripe age). At one of its meetings Edward Caird argued that God must be capable of suffering because his manifestation of himself in history necessarily implies that he is involved in, and with, all aspects of human existence.[83] But this glimpse of what might be a deeply personal application of his Hegelian notion of God to his actual life and experience, is rare. More often it seems, as in his address on the idealization of ordinary daily life, a way of demonstrating the worth of an extremely demanding morality.

[81] E. Caird, 'Christianity and the Historical Christ', 18 f.   [82] Ibid. 17.
[83] Jones and Muirhead, *Edward Caird*, 31.

The great strength of idealism was that it seemed to offer sound arguments in support of theism. Christian theologians, influenced by Caird and Green, believed that their philosophy provided a climate of thought in which Christianity could flourish. The climate survived for a surprisingly long time.[84] What was, perhaps, not so obvious was that idealism could not provide *more* than a friendly climate. Because thinkers like Caird appeared to be vigorously defending the Christian tradition, and to be doing so with a systematic and coherent metaphysical apologetic, it was not always realized just how radically different their reinterpretation of Christianity was. A purely metaphysical Christ was no real substitute for a historical one, for the Christ of Christian tradition needed to be related to the Jesus of history.

[84] Quinton, 'Absolute Idealism', 303, suggests that idealism was the dominant philosophy in Britain until as late as the 1940s.

FAITH AND HISTORY
Lord Acton and Catholic Modernism
in Britain

THE history of Christian doctrine, if not the historicity of Jesus, turned out to be more important than Caird had expected, but, because of the influence of Hegel and Baur, he thought himself absolved from having to decide which phases of the history of doctrine really mattered. The problem looked very different, and much more intractable, to those who had been brought up to believe that true doctrine and the history of the true Church were intimately related. When Newman had published his article 'On Consulting the Laity in Matters of Doctrine' in *The Rambler* in 1859, he had said that at the time of the Arian controversy in the fourth century 'the divine tradition committed to the infallible Church was proclaimed and maintained far more by the faithful [laity] than by the Episcopate'.[1] For this he was delated to the Congregation of Propaganda. The question whether the laity had once acted as better guardians of the faith than the bishops was regarded as not so much a matter of historical fact as of doctrine. The authenticity of the received tradition had acquired something of the sacrosanctity which dogma possessed. That meant that dogma might seem to be proved untrue if history did not support it. There would also be considerable temptation to tamper with the truth of history, in order to make it seem to support dogma. It was this connection between history and dogma which brought Catholic Modernism into existence in the last decade of the nineteenth century, though the dilemma itself was nothing new.

Writing about a 'movement' carries with it its own very beguiling temptation. One can argue almost indefinitely about whether the name commonly given to the movement is an appropriate one; about whether the people usually reckoned as members of the

---

[1] I. Ker, *John Henry Newman: A Biography* (Oxford, 1988), 482.

movement really were such; about the dates during which the movement can properly be said to have existed; how it originated, and where it got its ideas from. This can defer any discussion of the significance of events and people, and yet, by a sort of sleight of hand, is able to suggest that one has done so at a particularly profound level.

Nevertheless, the origin of the movement *in Britain* is of some importance. There has been a good deal of discussion of the question whether Newman was a precursor of Modernism or influenced the Modernists or was a Modernist in advance of Modernism. Just as, in Newman's own lifetime, there were some who thought of him as a dangerous heretic, while others believed him capable of restating traditional orthodoxy for the new world of the nineteenth century, so, since his death, some commentators have attempted to show that he was responsible for the dangerous ideas that circulated at the end of the century, and others have been just as anxious to show that he was perfectly orthodox and, therefore, in no sense responsible for Modernist errors. In very general terms, the fact that the 'British' Modernists were so often tempted to use history as the yardstick for measuring the truth of theology, even if in the end they tended to take refuge in separating the two, makes it fairly certain that their attitudes and ideas did not derive from Newman. For Newman was, himself, convinced that someone who did no more than argue his faith out of history was not, in any real sense, a 'Catholic'.

At a more scholarly level, perhaps, there is less disagreement. A collection of essays which examines various ways in which Newman might be said to have influenced the Modernists seems to come to the conclusion that that influence was something which the Modernists *found* in Newman, rather than something which Newman *intended* to exert on other minds. The very first essay in the volume starts by making the crucial point that Newman ought always to be taken at his word, provided, always, that that word is taken in context.[2] Newman clearly set his face against liberalism in theology; a liberalism which must be understood, again, in Newman's own terms. Nor can there really be any doubt that what

---

[2] P. Misner, 'The "Liberal" Legacy of Newman', in M. J. Weaver (ed.), *Newman and the Modernists* (Lanham and London, 1985), 3. For a different view of the relation between Newman and Modernism see J. Ratté, *Three Modernists* (New York, 1967).

Newman was attacking was the idea that the human intellect was competent to sit in judgement upon the truth about God when that truth was a matter of miraculous divine revelation.[3] All too often the Modernists did, at least implicitly, claim that they could decide where, and how, the traditional formulation of the faith was incompatible with, and must give way to, the modern understanding of truth. They often preferred the human and the historical to the metaphysical and transcendent.

For, if one is to take Newman at his word, then it is equally proper to take others at their own word, also. The Modernists, on the whole, were not very anxious to claim Newman as their spiritual progenitor. Alfred Loisy, one of the best-known names among the Modernists, admired the *Essay on Development*, but Newman's influence on Loisy is not overwhelmingly obvious. Perhaps Newman gave him the beginnings of a theological vocabulary which could serve as an alternative to that of scholasticism; and Loisy may even have intended to develop Newman's thought and adapt it for a world which had changed drastically since the 1840s.[4] If that was the case, the task was never accomplished.

George Tyrrell, the other person whose name is always associated with Modernism, was, for a time, clearly influenced by Newman and was keen to acknowledge that influence, but he later turned away from Newman, declaring that his concept of development was unsatisfactory because it was not an evolutionary one. The walnut, Tyrrell pointed out, was not the same thing as the walnut tree which grew from it. The original revelation was not a fixed deposit of doctrine but a spiritual impulse eventually burgeoning into a more fully developed truth. Therefore, theological formulations are, and must be, continually subject to change and improvement through the human experience which is faithful to the original impulse.[5]

---

[3] Above, p. 35.
[4] R. Burke, 'Was Loisy Newman's Modern Disciple?', in Weaver (ed.), *Newman and the Modernists*, 147 ff., and cf. B. M. G. Reardon, *Roman Catholic Modernism* (London, 1970), 226.
[5] Reardon, *Roman Catholic Modernism*, 45, and see also N. Sagovsky, ' "Frustration, Disillusion and Enduring Filial Respect": George Tyrrell's Debt to John Henry Newman', in Weaver, (ed.), *Newman and the Modernists*, 97 ff. Sagovsky thinks Tyrrell embraced the method of the *Essay on Development* but rejected its suppositions.

The truth is that Newman belonged to a different world from even the older Modernists like Loisy and Tyrrell. 'A generation apart, they stood on opposite sides of the shift from classical to modern times.'[6] Loisy and Tyrrell believed that they had no option but to take contemporary scholarship and attitudes seriously. Newman, having expressed his dislike of rationalistic modern forms of enquiry (such as biblical criticism), felt able, simply, to ignore them. It was the kind of thing which belonged to 'the minute intellect of inferior men', 'men who excel in a mere short-sighted perspicacity'.[7] It was always, in Newman's opinion, easy for the rationalists to win an argument with some simple display of apparent logic. The truth had to be expounded and argued for in complex, compounded, circumambulating discourse that seemed— at least on the surface—so much less convincing.

It has been argued that, of all the members of the Modernist generation, the one most clearly influenced by Newman is the author of his biography, Wilfrid Ward. That influence was so powerful that Ward, in writing Newman's life, felt compelled to side with his subject rather than with his own father, who had been a leading Ultramontane.[8] Certainly, Ward has sometimes been counted almost as a 'fringe' Modernist, in spite of the fact that both his writings and his actions make it perfectly clear that he believed that obedience to the *magisterium* was the only stance proper to a member of the Church. He presented Newman, in the biography, as a man exhausted by his efforts to occupy a would-be mediating (but actually isolated) position between liberal Catholics and Ultramontanes. Many of the Modernists were Ward's friends but, in the last resort, he was forced to reject them because he believed in the necessity of authority. At the same time, he rejected the tyrannical abuse of authority and could understand the rebellion of those who opposed it, and he 'felt deeply the intellectual bankruptcy of the hyper-orthodox judges who condemned them'.[9]

The most radical of the British Modernists, Edmund Bishop, was in no doubt as to the person to whom he owed his own attitudes—

---

[6] Burke, 'Was Loisy Newman's Modern Disciple', 152.

[7] See above, p. 34 f.

[8] S. Gilley, 'Wilfrid Ward and his Life of Newman', *Journal of Ecclesiastical History*, 29 (Apr. 1978), 177 ff., and cf. N. M. Lahutsky, 'Ward's Newman: The Struggle to be Faithful and Fair', in Weaver (ed.), *Newman and the Modernists*, 47 ff.   [9] Gilley, 'Wilfrid Ward', 180.

and it was not Newman. At the time of the papal encyclical
Pascendi he wrote to his friend and namesake, the Anglican
W. C. Bishop (who, by a curious coincidence, shared his interest in
liturgy and had some marginal influence on the history of liturgical
revision in the early twentieth century),[10] to say that he had been a
Modernist long before Modernism. He also told Baron von Hügel
that it was a consequence of his being influenced by the *Home and
Foreign Review*—that is by the ideas expressed in the 1860s by
Lord Acton. And there is something much more plausible in
Bishop's professed debt to Acton, whose understanding of history
was much the same as that of the Modernists, than in any supposed
Modernist debt to Newman, whose attitude to history was so very
different.

John Emerich Edward Dalberg-Acton was related to half the
nobility of Europe and had links with every kind of ruling circle
from the English Whigs to the papal and the Neapolitan courts. He
was born in Naples in 1834. His English as well as his Continental
ancestors had been Roman Catholics and he was educated at
Oscott and in Munich. In Munich the great historian Ignaz
Döllinger assumed personal responsibility for his education. In
1857 the two men went on a visit to Rome together, when Acton
had (at second hand) his first experience of working with archival
material and so of modern scientific historical research. Back in
England, Acton entered public affairs. In 1859 he became, through
his stepfather's influence, Whig MP for the Irish constituency of
Carlow but does not seem to have given a great deal of his time and
energy to fulfilling his parliamentary obligations. Though he was to
become an ardent admirer of Gladstone, who persuaded the Queen
to make him a peer, practical politics was never to be his first
concern.

In the year before that in which he began his brief career as an
MP, Acton had taken over the editorship of the journal called *The
Rambler* which already had something of a reputation as a liberal
ecclesiastical gadfly. He thus commenced his real career as a thinker
and writer whose principal interest was the Roman Catholic
Church and its place and influence in the world. He found himself
in conflict with the ecclesiastical authorities, more or less from that

---

[10] A. R. Vidler, *A Variety of Catholic Modernists* (Cambridge, 1970), 135, and
see also P. Hinchliff, *The South African Liturgy* (Cape Town, 1959), NB 17 ff. for
W. C. Bishop's influence on the revision of the Prayer Book in southern Africa.

moment until the end of his life, because of his determination to fight for liberty, morality, and truth—as he perceived them—against religious authoritarianism. *The Rambler's* history continued to be stormy. In one attempt to placate the authorities Newman became editor for a brief period. Three years later the journal's name was changed to *Home and Foreign Review*. Neither manœuvre was effective. 'Ultramontane' was the dirtiest word in Acton's vocabulary at a time when the Ultramontanist party was dominant in the Church. He was bound, therefore, to be suspected of disloyalty. The *Home and Foreign Review* was threatened with a formal veto from Rome in 1864. Acton abandoned the journal rather than risk this kind of censure.

His opposition to the prevailing ideology in the Church did not cease. He strongly opposed the *Syllabus of Errors* of 1864. As his biographer notes, the description of the opinion attacked in the final anathema of the *Syllabus* reads like an exact summary of Acton's most passionate beliefs.[11] By this time he was no longer on friendly terms with Newman to whom he assigned 'the permanent label of enemy'.[12] Perhaps this was, as the same biographer asserts, because he wished to rest the defence of Catholicism on the facts and evidence of impartial history, whereas Newman preferred the evidence of personal belief. Or perhaps Acton was becoming more and more inflexible in his conviction that it was the job of the historian to judge the morality of everyone's actions, and had made up his mind that Newman was one of the most culpable of Ultramontanes.[13]

Acton went to Rome in 1869 to organize resistance to those who were working to ensure that the first Vatican Council would define papal infallibility. He co-operated closely with his old mentor Döllinger to ensure that information about the inner proceedings of the Council should receive the widest possible publicity. His objective was to demonstrate to the world that the whole thing was a corrupt, dishonest, and hypocritical attempt to force through a

[11] G. Himmelfarb, *Lord Acton: A Study in Conscience and Politics* (Chicago and London, 1952), 61. The final anathema condemned those who said that the Pope 'can, and ought to, reconcile himself to and agree with, progress, liberalism, and modern civilization'. [12] Himmelfarb, *Lord Acton*, 31.
[13] H. A. MacDougall, *The Acton–Newman Relations: The Dilemma of Christian Liberalism* (New York, 1962), 140 f. MacDougall places the final break between Acton and Newman after 1874, but see R. Gray, *Cardinal Manning, A Biography* (London, 1985), 183 f.

false doctrine.[14] When Acton's campaign failed he found himself in a peculiarly difficult position but he never actually broke with the Roman Church.

In the end Acton was not compelled to choose between submission and excommunication, though Manning may have wished to force him to that decision.[15] He managed to live quietly, as a faithful member of the Church, protected by his lay status and his social position. In his later years most of his energy went into being a professional historian. He became the Regius professor of Modern History at Cambridge in 1895 and was responsible for the planning of the *Cambridge Modern History*, though he died in 1902, before the greater part of it was even written.

Discovering precisely what motivated Acton in all this is not easy. He has been represented as the great champion of liberty; or as the self-righteous moralist determined to pass judgement; or simply as someone who was paralysed because he could not reconcile the conflicting claims of faith and truth. What does seem clear is that his opposition to infallibility was historical and moral rather than theological.[16] Perhaps the place to look for the most illuminating clue is in his inaugural lecture delivered at Cambridge after his appointment as Regius professor. It was a model of what an inaugural should be, surveying the state of the discipline, declaring the new professor's interests, and describing how he believed the subject should be taught.[17]

The chief interest of the lecture, however, for someone who wishes to understand Acton is that it was written by a man who had reached the final phase of his life and who, in talking about history, religion, and politics—the subjects of the lecture—could hardly be (or hope that others would be) oblivious of the dramatic events in which he had been a protagonist and obtained some notoriety twenty-five years earlier. There is no evidence that Acton was a particularly insensitive or thick-skinned person but he would have had to be remarkably thick-skinned to pontificate publicly about the proper way for a historian to behave if he believed that his own

[14] Cf. Gray, *Cardinal Manning*, 231 and 233.
[15] Himmelfarb, *Lord Acton*, 120, and cf. Gray, *Cardinal Manning*, 236, and, for earlier relations between Manning and Acton, 179 ff.
[16] J. V. Conzemius, 'Lord Acton and the First Vatican Council', *Journal of Ecclesiastical History*, 20 (Oct. 1969), 285 f.
[17] J. E. E. Dalberg-Acton, 'The Study of History', in *Lectures on Modern History* ed. J. N. Figgis and R. V. Laurence (London, 1912), 1 ff.

earlier, and very public, actions had been themselves improper. His lecture gives not the slightest hint that he thought he had ever behaved without integrity or contrary to the principles he was enunciating.

Acton was plainly aware that the chief criticism levelled at his own behaviour, as a man and as a historian, was that he was an inflexible moralist who made it his business to sit in judgement on others. But the first part of his lecture is, in the main, a defence of liberty. To write a history of liberty was his great ambition and the lecture sets out the framework for what that history might have been. He lumped Newman with James Anthony Froude and Carlyle as men who believed that 'anxious precaution against bad government is an obstruction to good, and degrades morality and mind by . . . dethroning enlightened virtue for the benefit of the average man'.[18] Acton, himself, of course, would be more likely to fear the authoritarianism even of good men. Allowing rulers the freedom to repress the ruled is hardly the way to advance the cause of liberty.

Perhaps the most 'professional' part of the lecture is Acton's attempt to describe what he thought was new and different about the historical discipline in the late nineteenth century. The most radical innovation was the opening of the archives of Europe to scholars but, he added, 'the main thing to learn is not the art of accumulating material but the sublimer art of investigating it, of discerning truth from falsehood and certainty from doubt. It is by solidity of criticism rather than by plenitude of erudition that the study of history strengthens, and straightens, and extends the mind. For the critic is one who, when he lights on an interesting statement, begins by suspecting it.' 'The maxim that a man must be presumed to be innocent until his guilt is proved is not for him.'[19]

It was only at the end of the lecture that Acton turned to the question of the place of morality in history, and it is at this point that it becomes perfectly obvious that he was aware of the controversy that surrounded his conviction that the historian's function *is* to sit in judgement. He was concerned that historians should be at pains 'never to debase the moral currency or to lower

---

[18] Ibid. 11.
[19] Ibid. 14 ff. In the last sentence quoted the final 'him' is ambiguous. It is not clear if it refers to the historian who is doing the investigating, or the source which is being investigated. The significance is the same in either case.

the standard of rectitude but to try others by the final maxim that governs your own lives and to suffer no man and no cause to escape the undying penalty which history has the power to inflict on right or wrong'.[20] The alternatives are either to withhold judgement altogether or to judge an individual or a cause by the moral standards of their own age. Acton did briefly consider what he believed to be the reasons why these alternatives were more popular than the course he advocated, but what he really seemed to be saying was that one cannot have one moral standard as a person and another as a historian; that history does not have moral standards of its own and cannot, for that reason, teach morality; that history itself needs the judgement of morality if there are to be any constant values and virtues in the world.[21]

It is possible to make sense of a good many of the otherwise puzzling episodes in Acton's life if one takes what he said in the inaugural lecture seriously and assumes that he was attempting to describe the principles that had governed his behaviour as a man as well as a historian. He could not, with any logic, have been prepared to recognize a distinction between the two. Morality was morality. One could not have one moral code for life and another for history.

It was probably from Döllinger—and not from Newman—that Acton had first learnt to understand the development of doctrine, for he always believed that Christianity was essentially a history, rather than a dogmatic system. Like Newman, he believed that dogma is not fixed for all time but is always undergoing development and change; dogma clearly has its own history. But Acton thought that historical evidence and fact were the real test for the truth of dogma, not whether it fitted logically and coherently into a metaphysical scheme, such as Newman had tried to develop. Newman was interested in the metaphysical coherence of a dogmatic system and in defining the theory of how such a system might develop. Acton was interested in the actual facts of history as they related to the development of doctrine and to the morality of that history. Nor did he have Newman's grudging attitude towards change. Newman's notes for distinguishing true

[20] J. E. E. Dalberg-Acton, 'The Study of History' in *Lectures on Modern History*, 24.

[21] Cf. Herbert Butterfield on the 'bloodless' relativism of historians who evade the duty to interpret events, *Christianity and History* (London, 1957), 33.

from false developments imply that the less change there is in doctrine the more likely it is to be true. Acton's attitude is much more that the truth of a belief *is* in its history. He opposed the promulgation of the dogma of the immaculate conception because it had never been given, in earlier periods of history, the status of a divinely revealed truth.[22]

For Acton the idea that the essence of a thing lies in its history, rather than in systems of thought, or doctrine, or ideology did not apply to Christianity alone. He thought that the history of liberty exemplified it also and that one would understand the necessity of maintaining freedom if one studied its history, rather than one or other of the many possible definitions of liberty.[23] His admiration for Burke was, in part, derived from the way in which that statesman's approach to the British constitution was a pragmatic one. The truth or justice of the constitution lay in its history not in some theoretical definition of the inalienable rights of man.[24] Acton believed that history was the demonstration of religion because the world improves, even if it does not become perfect.[25]

Acton's distaste for supposedly inalienable human rights was probably the reason why he was never an enthusiastic Whig Member of Parliament. It may also explain why he, like most Englishmen at the time, sided with the South in the American Civil War. In this, as in some of the early things he wrote about religious persecution, Acton seemed to misapply his own liberal principles: of the principles themselves he was always quite sure. His hatred of ecclesiastical authoritarianism derived from his belief that even the most exalted authority must be subject to law. He was as unwilling to accept the concept of the sovereign will of the people as he was to accept the dogma of papal infallibility.[26]

In the end, this unwillingness created a situation from which there appeared to be no escape. Acton continued still to cling to history. Though the dogma of papal infallibility had been promulgated as a consequence of an Ultramontane victory, it did not follow that the truth it contained was the truth which the Ultramontanes attributed to it. He lived always in the hope that the

[22] Himmelfarb, *Lord Acton*, 26.
[23] Acton, 'The Study of History', 12 f.
[24] Himmelfarb, *Lord Acton*, 70.
[25] Acton, 'The Study of History', 12.
[26] Himmelfarb, *Lord Acton*, 73.

dogma would come to be seen in some very different light and one which he could accept. Therefore he was determined not to deny the truth of the dogma formally, since that would involve being cut off from the Church, and he was equally determined not to affirm it since he did not believe it to be true.

Acton's fierce statements about morality, as the ultimate judge of history, were by no means vague or abstract generalizations; nor were they merely an enjoyably self-righteous judging of others. They were an expression of the values by which he lived as a man and as a historian. In the 1870s, in the aftermath of the Vatican Council, Acton broke with Döllinger, whom hitherto he had almost hero-worshipped. The quarrel obviously hurt Acton very deeply but this did not stop him from labelling Döllinger thenceforward as—like Newman—Ultramontane and, therefore, immoral. Acton came, in fact, to the conclusion that Döllinger suffered from the moral relativism of the romantics.[27] To say that one would not condemn, for instance, the Inquisition, because it belonged to another age when men had different values, was to sell the pass and to admit that there was no clear line between good and evil. For the Church to pretend that moral judgements were not decisions between absolutes of right and wrong would be to divorce herself altogether from Christian history, which *was* Christian reality.

In his attitude to history and its relation to doctrine, in his understanding of the nature of development, in his passionate resentment of authoritarianism, coupled with an apparently para-doxical refusal to consider the existence of a Church apart from Rome, Acton was very like the Modernists and rather different from Newman.

The Modernist movement began in the last, ecclesiastically rather quiet, years of Acton's life. It is usually dated from 1890, when Leo XIII became pope. Like his predecessor, Pius IX, the new pope had the appearance and reputation of being somewhat liberal in his outlook, but Leo's liberalism was almost as illusory as that of his predecessor. He was, perhaps, less openly opposed to the new ideas of the nineteenth century: he seemed to be a sophisticated, urbane intellectual. But he was, in fact, quite as much of an Ultramontanist as his predecessor and he was determined to make

---

[27] Ibid. 148. It may be that Acton was also angered by other actions of Döllinger—the Munich declaration of 1871, for instance; but even if that were the case, different moral standards would still have been the issue between them.

neo-scholasticism the only theology acceptable in the Church. His aims and object remained exactly the same as those of Pius IX; his methods were less obviously repressive. Nevertheless, his pontificate gave the Modernist movement an opportunity which rapidly disappeared under his successor, Pius X. Modern writers delight to hint that the latter pope's repressive tendencies were a consequence of his peasant birth. The implication seems to be that he had a peasant's inability to cope with theological flexibility and a peasant's sense of security, which depends on things being patently black or white. Be that as it may, it was Pius X who put an end to Modernism as a movement, by the decree *Lamentabili* of July 1907 and the encyclical *Pascendi* of September of the same year.

That it is possible to say with such confidence that the movement came to an end soon after the publication of the papal condemnation is significant. Whoever drafted the documents, for no one seems to suppose that the pope was capable of writing them himself (another consequence of his peasant origins), gave Modernism the appearance of being a consciously and systematically designed doctrinal programme. This was, no doubt, quite deliberate. If Modernism were presented as a system, then it could be made to appear more sinister, more like a cunning plot, than if the condemned propositions were variously attributed to a number of different individuals, none of whom subscribed to all of them. Indeed many of the Modernists themselves hastened to assert, with a fair degree of unanimity, that they had never subscribed to *any* of the doctrinal propositions condemned by the pope.

On the other side, two things could be said. One was that, on the principle that one should hate the sin but love the sinner, it was better to condemn propositions than named individuals, because this allowed them the opportunity to recant and submit. It could also be said, with some justice, that there was nothing new about the excuse that the heretics did not hold the opinions condemned as heresy. It had been advanced again and again, from Nestorius's *Bazaar of Heracleides* in the fifth century, to the Jansenist response to the 'five propositions' in the seventeenth, and so, as a defence, seemed a little shop-soiled. But the case of the authorities was somewhat spoilt by the fact that the Modernists were accused of committing every conceivable error. They were charged, among other things, with holding, as Kant had held, that one can only *know* that for which there is empirical evidence. In fact, a more appropriate complaint would have been that the Modernists taught that one should not claim a historical basis for one's beliefs unless there was historical evidence to support it.

Nevertheless, there was a real sense in which the Modernist movement did actually come to an end at this point. It is significant that Baron von Hügel, in the last period of his life, became more and more critical of Modernism. In part, this was because his own ideas had changed somewhat and he had developed a fear of the immanentist tendencies which he now perceived within Modernism. He continued to believe that the Christian faith should be modern, in the sense of being expressed in ways which did not make it appear obviously untrue for his contemporaries; but he regarded the idea of a Modernist *movement* as appropriate only to the pontificate of Pius X, and any attempt to persist with it in later years as perverse.[28] Since von Hügel seems to have been the person who really welded individual modernizers into a Modernist movement, his later attitude is of some importance; and Loisy, who is one of the two paradigm figures of the movement, was even more unwilling to encourage its continuance. After his own excommunication in 1908, he regarded Modernism as a finally defeated cause.[29] The fact that he was content to be thought of as a humanist during the last phase of his life only partly explains his apparent cynicism. Much more weighty was his sense that a movement such as theirs, was no longer at all appropriate.

The truth is that none of the Modernists had the slightest belief in a Christianity that was outside the Holy Catholic Church and the jurisdiction of the Roman see. They all believed that a refusal to subject dogmatic tradition to critical historical enquiry encouraged rather than diminished scepticism. They all wished that that Church might engage with the modern world and express its ideas in terms that made sense to modern thinkers. But for none of them was there any sort of viable alternative to that Church. In 1905 H. C. Corrance, a convert from Anglicanism who eventually threw in his lot with the Modernists, made the shrewd comment that the High Church party in the Church of England 'had been built up on the theory of the necessity of tracing dogma in its present form to as early a period as possible, which of course does not conduce to

---

[28] Vidler, *Variety of Catholic Modernists*, 123 ff.
[29] Reardon, *Roman Catholic Modernism*, 16.

creating the detached state of mind necessary to an historian'.[30] He attributed this need to search for support from antiquity to the fact that Anglicans had nothing which could be described as 'the general faith of the Church'. Because the Roman Catholic Church, the true Church, possessed such a 'general faith', a clear, certain, corporately held body of teaching, it had no need to prove that it could trace a dogma unchanged to the earliest times. There was less temptation to falsify history. Roman Catholics alone, therefore, could be both Christian and critical.

History was to demonstrate that this argument was very largely a matter of wishful thinking. The attitude toward the Church expressed in it, however, was clearly reflected in the Modernists' determination to stay with an unmodernized Roman Catholicism, rather than look for a congenial home elsewhere. It may also explain what seems at first sight to be absurd—the way in which both the Modernists themselves and their interpreters have tended to exaggerate the differences between Catholic Modernism and Liberal Protestantism. Since their goals seem to have been very similar, why should everyone be so anxious to stress that there was absolutely nothing in common between the two movements?

It begins with the Catholic Modernists themselves. George Tyrrell, after all, wrote in *Christianity at the Cross-Roads*, generally reckoned to be his most theological work: 'Whatever Jesus was, He was in no sense a Liberal Protestant.'[31] The main theme of Loisy's *L'Évangile et l'Église* is an attack on von Harnack's typically Liberal Protestant understanding of the history of Christian doctrine.[32] Von Harnack believed that the original simple gospel about the individual's relationship with God the loving Father had become distorted and complicated by the intrusion of metaphysics and mysticism. Jesus of Nazareth, whose original role—von Harnack was convinced—had been as the preacher of this gospel, had become, himself, the divine subject of the dogmatic system

[30] Quoted in Vidler, *Variety of Catholic Modernists*, 149. The truth of the judgement seems to be borne out by the attitudes of Benson and his friends: above, pp. 95 ff.

[31] G. Tyrrell, *Christianity at the Cross-Roads* (London, 1909), p. xxi. Tyrrell added, 'All that makes Catholicism most repugnant to the present modes of thought derives from Him': an idea that needs some unpacking.

[32] For a discussion of the differences between Loisy and von Harnack see S. Sykes, *The Identity of Christianity: Theologians and the Essence of Christianity from Schleiermacher to Barth* (London, 1984), 123 ff.

which had replaced it. It may well be that Loisy chose to present his ideas in the form of an attack on von Harnack's Liberal Protestantism because that was the way to make them least offensive to the Vatican;[33] but there is a sort of passion to his argument that does not sound like a merely clever tactical device. The heart of it is that there could be no gospel, at all, if it were not for tradition; that what we know of Christ we know by, in, and through the tradition of the Church.

On the other hand, so many of the things the Modernists said might equally well have been said by some of the Liberal Protestants. In his *Mémoires* Loisy maintained that what mattered in religion was the sense of duty and of what is good; an understanding of Jesus as the exemplar of self-sacrifice and moral perfection. This is the kind of thing that many a Liberal Protestant taught. Loisy added that, though abstract dogma is of little significance, religious practices are important because the Christian ideal lives and works in the ceremonies of the cultus.[34] This would not have seemed to the Liberal Protestants to be so worthy of an enlightened teacher of the modern world.

The immanentism which von Hügel came to see, and to fear, as the chief characteristic of Modernism, was precisely the theological approach adopted by many of the Liberal Protestants, and there were other characteristics in common. Loisy wrote to von Hügel in 1900, 'I distrust systems, because they are all false'.[35] What he meant was that true ideas could be falsified by being forced into a supposedly logical system which distorted their significance. This is almost exactly what Jowett had said about systems several decades earlier—'a final system can never be constructed; at best a system is but a synthesis of what we know in the present state of our experience. He who adopts a system closes the eye to the mind; he becomes blind to the facts which controvert his theory.'[36] Nor is this simply the chance agreement of a phrase or two taken out of

---

[33] Von Hügel described Loisy's book as 'richer and both more radical and more traditional' than von Harnack's and added that most Roman Catholics 'will be glad enough of his general conclusion but will fear his premisses'. B. Holland (ed.), *Baron Friedrich von Hügel: Selected Letters, 1896–1924* (London, 1927), 112.

[34] A. F. Loisy, *Mémoires pour servir à l'histoire religieuse de notre temps*, 3 vols. (Paris, 1930–1), i. 364 f.

[35] Vidler, *Variety of Catholic Modernists*, 55.

[36] One of Jowett's followers summarizing his teaching, quoted in Hinchliff, *Jowett*, 77.

context. The two men actually *meant* much the same thing, and Edmund Bishop, who claimed to have been a Modernist long before there was a Modernist movement, even thought that von Harnack was more likely to be right than Loisy was.[37] If it is possible to find instances in which Modernists and Liberal Protestants were not very far apart in their opinions (and one could cite many other examples), how is it that the received opinion is that they had almost nothing in common?

It is probable that the explanation is partly that the similarities and connections have simply been overlooked. Vidler, for instance, who is one of the authorities most clearly responsible for propagating the view that the two movements had nothing in common, failed to notice contrary evidence on at least one occasion. In *A Variety of Catholic Modernists* he printed a list of sympathizers whom Mgr. Mignot, Archbishop of Albi and one of the people on the fringes of the Modernist movement, had met during his visit to England in 1904. There are twenty names in the part of the list that referred to friends in Oxford. Von Hügel, who drew up the list, had underlined once the names of those who had been exceptionally helpful and underlined twice the names of those sufficiently important to be sent, if possible, a copy of one of the archbishop's works. Those underlined are a select few, of course, but they include Edward Caird (once) and two of his Balliol colleagues, Strachan Davidson and J. A. Smith (both twice). Caird certainly cannot be regarded as anything other than liberal and Protestant in his sympathies. Davidson, who was to be his successor as master of Balliol, had been a close colleague and associate of Jowett.

The only other Oxford people to have their names underlined twice were: one of the younger von Hügels and his wife; George Young, a notable English sympathizer; Archdeacon Lilley, the Anglo-Catholic whom Vidler actually includes among his 'Variety of Catholic Modernists'; and Dom Cuthbert Butler, at that stage an intimate friend of Edmund Bishop and much exercised in his conscience about his future as a Roman Catholic scholar.

Vidler simply ignored the three Balliol names on the list. His remarks emphasized the significance of those sympathizers like A. E. J. Rawlinson, the future bishop of Derby; and this was

---

[37] Vidler, *Variety of Catholic Modernists*, 149.

entirely natural, since he had set himself the task of writing about people, whether Roman or Anglican, who could be plausibly described as both 'Catholic' and 'modernizers'. But none of them had his name underlined on the list. If close friends, disciples, and admirers of Benjamin Jowett were also members of the small group of most valued supporters of the Modernist movement, then there was less of a gulf between the two schools of thought than Vidler would sometimes have us believe. (It may be, of course, that Vidler simply did not regard English Broad Churchmen as the same thing as 'Liberal Protestants', a term which he chiefly applied to Germans.)

The most probable explanation of all the facts would seem to be that the Catholic Modernists were glad to have the support and sympathy of influential Broad Churchmen (or Liberal Protestants). As part of what they had to achieve they needed to be able to convince their audience that some beliefs and opinions were indeed untenable in the modern world. If liberals were able to produce evidence to back up that claim, so much the better. Where they differed, in fact, was not in the *conclusions* to which they came but in *the use to which they intended to put them.* While Liberal Protestants usually sought to devise an individual modification of traditional Christianity to suit their own particular needs and difficulties, such an approach would be of no help to Catholic Modernists. They had to modernize the Church, to persuade the Church itself to accept their conclusions, or they had failed altogether.

Moreover, both movements were essentially trying to determine how far the historicity of the earliest Christian tradition could be reconciled with the findings of historical criticism. Reardon has argued convincingly that 'from correlating old beliefs with new knowledge a wide variety of views is likely to result, depending partly on what is held to be fundamental in religion'.[38] If that is true, then Roman Catholics, inheriting a much more tightly defined deposit of dogma and a strong sense of corporate order and discipline, were much more likely to agree among themselves about what was fundamental in religion and, therefore, less likely to arrive at *widely* differing conclusions.

Yet there were significant differences among the Modernists themselves. Modernism has been defined as 'the attempt to

[38] Reardon, *Roman Catholic Modernism*, 9.

synthesize the basic truths of religion and the methods and assumptions of modern thought, using the latter as necessary and proper criteria',[39] or as 'to hope and to work for the modernizing of catholicism' and to 'believe in its possibility'.[40] If one takes Loisy and Tyrrell, once more, as the prime examples of Modernism, one is not immediately struck by the similarity of their theological positions, and it is Loisy who seems more to fit the definitions of Modernism that have just been quoted. Biblical study he found to be a disillusioning process since orthodox theology seemed to require one to persevere in a credulity which would be totally unacceptable in any other sphere of life. There is some doubt whether Loisy continued to be, in any real sense, a believer. Vidler, who makes a good case for saying that he did, quotes one of Loisy's friends as explaining that by 1904 he 'had no longer faith, if one means by faith adherence of the mind to revealed dogmas. But he still has faith, if one means by that a profound, suprarational, in a word mystical, adherence of the whole being to the invisible realities of which he still believes the Catholic Church is the principal and the indispensable guardian.'[41]

In the sense that he was also impatient with the idea that faith was, principally, an adherence to dogma, Tyrrell may fairly be classed with Loisy.[42] Like Loisy, too, he was distressed by the inability of conventional Roman Catholic teaching to stand up to historical criticism, but he seems to have lacked Loisy's ability as an original critical scholar, though he came later in life to imbibe some of Loisy's ideas. What made him a rebel against conventional doctrine was not so much a conviction that it was incapable of meeting the challenge from modern thought but a disillusionment with scholastic theology which he had once greatly admired. Tyrrell, in fact moved from one theological position to another with a fair degree of rapidity until he found himself in the Modernist camp. He was born in Ireland in 1861, brought up an Anglican Evangelical, and educated at Trinity College, Dublin. But he was much influenced by some of the leading Anglo-Catholics in the 1870s and became a Roman Catholic in 1879. Even before his

---

[39] Ibid. 9.   [40] Vidler, *Variety of Catholic Modernists*, 61.
[41] Ibid. 45.
[42] There is a recent biography of Tyrrell, N. Sagovsky, *On God's Side, A Life of George Tyrrell* (Oxford, 1990). The author has chosen quite deliberately to focus on the events of Tyrrell's life rather than on his theology.

formal submission he seems to have been quite clear in his own mind that he wanted to be, not only a Roman Catholic, but also a Jesuit and so he entered the noviciate of the Society in the following year. He was ordained priest in 1891 and sent to Stonyhurst to teach moral theology. He was moved to Farm Street in 1896 where he fell under the influence of von Hügel who encouraged him to follow up the ideas of Loisy and other Modernists.

It was at this point that Tyrrell became hostile to scholasticism. At first he claimed that the new scholasticism of the nineteenth century was not, in fact, Thomist and he maintained that he was a true disciple of the real Aquinas in his opposition to the kind of theology that was then in favour. For a brief period he professed himself to be a great admirer of Newman but this did not persist for very long, nor was there any profound or lasting influence. Tyrrell seems to have become more and more anti-intellectual, insisting that what mattered was not how belief was formulated but how it was lived and experienced. After an unconventional and rather angry article on the Church's teaching about hell (he called the article 'A Perverted Devotion') Tyrrell was sent to think things over at the Jesuit mission house in Yorkshire and his final rupture with the Society came in 1906. He was suspected of being, perhaps, more radical than he really was; of teaching that Christianity was not the final and absolute truth but might only have something to contribute to the ultimate and universal religion. It may be that this suspicion really derived from his immanentism and his fierce denial that truth could be encapsulated neatly in theological formularies.

The story of Tyrrell's death is a pathetic one. He had to be buried in an Anglican graveyard because the Roman Catholic authorities refused him burial, but this was at least as much the fault of his friends as of his enemies. Sagovsky says that on the evening before Tyrrell's death 'at the bidding of the Bishop of Southwark, John Pollen came from Farm Street' and gave him absolution. Maude Petre, whose enormous personal devotion to Tyrrell had not made their relationship always an easy one, sent a letter to *The Times* saying that he had been given absolution without recanting his views. 'It was this letter' in Sagovsky's view which 'made a Catholic funeral impossible'.[43] The service was conducted by another ex-

---

[43] Ibid. 260 f. The story is told, slightly differently, from Henri Bremond's point of view in H. Hogarth, *Henri Bremond; The Life and Work of a Devout Humanist* (London, 1950), 14 f. There is also an account of the events surrounding the funeral,

Jesuit, Henri Bremond—a French priest with liberal, anti-authoritarian sympathies—who wore no vestments other than a soutane, used only the most vestigial of rites, but gave a very moving address.

Tyrrell's 'anti-intellectualism', at first sight, seems very different from the acute, critical scholarship of Loisy, but it was, after all, Loisy who said that Jesus is 'more God' than the Council of Nicaea said and is more really present in the eucharist than the Council of Trent said. He also insisted that 'in speaking of Jesus, I could not represent him as if he had been God preaching publicly in Galilee and Jerusalem and dying on the cross'.[44] It is perfectly clear, however, that Loisy's intention was not to deny the divinity of Christ but to present it in a more vivid form which would evoke in response a specific kind of moral living. This is precisely what many liberals in Britain, Anglican and Protestant, were equally determined to achieve, and much of what Tyrrell wrote towards the end of his life has manifestly the same intention. The book which he called *Through Scylla and Charybdis: Or the Old Theology and the New* captures, in the symbolism of its title, the essence of the Modernist programme. Their course needed to be steered between the rock of tradition and the whirlpool of modern progress in science and historical criticism. In *The Church and the Future* Tyrrell ventured into his own little exercise in critical history. While others might abandon traditional beliefs because of their serious doubts about the literal truth of the Bible or the failures of an idealized Church or papacy, his sticking point was the tradition that the apostles, having received the *depositum fidei* from the Lord, handed it on to St Linus, Peter's successor in the see of Rome.

A savagely sarcastic passage in *A Much-Abused Letter* suggests what it was that really irritated him about theology (and also possibly explains the almost personal vindictiveness that seems to colour the action taken against him by the ecclesiastical authorities).

I have often wondered whether, if all the circumstances were known, the priest and Levite, whose conduct is contrasted with that of the Good Samaritan, might not have had much to urge in extenuation of their

and the text of Bremond's address, in M. D. Petre (ed.), *Autobiography and Life of George Tyrrell* (London, 1913), 422 ff. The first volume of this work consists of Tyrrell's own account of his first twenty-three years; the second volume is Maude Petre's continuation of the story.

[44] Quoted in Vidler, *Variety of Catholic Modernists*, 53.

apparent heartlessness. There are duties of non-interference, of minding one's own business; there are the evils of indiscriminate charity; there are the perils of impulsiveness to be considered. A large experience of 'distress cases' often teaches the priest and the Levite a slow caution which seems callousness to the tender-hearted amateur philanthropist. It may be that their charity was not less than the Samaritan's, but that it was more educated; that a prudent casuistry had taught them to balance the claims of conflicting duties; and that before their mental debate was finished they had passed by and left the sufferer behind.[45]

The real central issue was still theology rather than history. In *The Church and the Future* Tyrrell argued that we can know God only as he reveals himself, not as he *is*. God's revelation of himself always has to be, it seems, a concurrent obscuring of himself, too, because of humanity's inability ever to know him as he truly is. God was not more disguised, Tyrrell thought, when he was described anthropomorphically as walking and talking with Adam in the garden in the cool of the day than he is when he is described by theologians as personal. He realized very well that this would give offence to

. . . those who fancy that their conception of him as a personal Spirit has an adequate ontological, and not merely an equivalent practical truth. And the like is to be said of all particular beliefs of the creed wherein the Christian dogma of the Trinity is expanded, and which serve to fix, characterize and develop more fully the Spirit of Divine charity by which they have been inspired and shaped. In the measure that we live in the light of these doctrines of the Trinity, the Incarnation, the Atonement, the Virgin Birth, the Resurrection and Ascension, Heaven and Hell, Angels and Devils, the Church and the Sacraments, the Communion of Saints—we shall be brought into closer spiritual harmony with the 'Absolute' which reveals itself to us in these forms through and in the mind of the Christian Church, stimulated and guided in its selection of beliefs by the Spirit of Christ. In no fuller way can God reveal himself than in man's thought about God, in man's reflection on the nature and meaning of the Spirit that strives with his own. No voice from the clouds 'mid the thunders of Sinai could win credence till submitted to that inward tribunal of the secret conscience.[46]

The ending of this passage seems to be as strongly individualistic as anything that a Liberal Protestant might have written.

Tyrrell's anti-intellectualism and his individualism would have

---

[45] G. Tyrrell, *A Much-Abused Letter* (London, 1907), 25.
[46] *The Church and the Future* (London, 1910), 91.

made him suspect, in the end, to the other—and probably much more significant—Modernist located in Britain. He was the Austrian baron, Friedrich von Hügel, who had been born in Florence in 1852 to a Scottish mother, herself a convert from Presbyterianism to Roman Catholicism. His education was almost as cosmopolitan as his ancestry,[47] but eventually he settled in England and, after his marriage in 1874, in Hampstead in particular. His health was always poor but he was, nevertheless, a great traveller and his religious zeal and devotion were beyond question. He was something of a mystic and he wrote about spirituality. He visited the blessed sacrament every day, made his confession weekly, and made regular use of such aids to devotion as the rosary.

Because of his obviously genuine piety, perhaps, his role as the real creator of the Modernist *movement* was ignored for a long time. There was a reluctance, while Modernism was still thought of as the most dreadful of nineteenth- and twentieth-century errors, to admit that the man chiefly responsible for its existence was also someone whose ideas on mysticism and spirituality were widely used by the undoubtedly orthodox. However, some of the theological emphases deriving from the second Vatican Council have made it less necessary to defend von Hügel and he is now recognized as the person who drew together the leading Modernists, kept them in touch with one another, tried to co-ordinate their activities, and planned strategies for them.[48] The truth is that, although von Hügel was many other things besides (internationally known aristocrat, devout mystic, unofficial spiritual director), he was also—at least in earlier years—a typical Modernist. He had that aversion from scholastic theology which Loisy and Tyrrell also had. He shared with them, too, a passionate dislike of ecclesiastical authoritarianism, but he was also a biblical scholar in a way that certainly Tyrrell, and perhaps even Loisy, never were. Like other biblical critics von Hügel attracted attention to his views by writing for the *Encyclopaedia Britannica*. His article in the eleventh

---

[47] L. F. Barmann, *Baron Friedrich von Hügel and the Modernist Crisis in England* (Cambridge, 1972), 1 ff.

[48] See e.g. L. R. Kurtz, *The Politics of Heresy* (Berkeley, Los Angeles, and London, 1986), 110 ff., and Vidler, *Variety of Catholic Modernists*, 116 ff. Vidler also discusses, pp. 113 ff., the reasons why von Hügel's role as instigator of others' Modernism was formerly minimized.

edition, on the authorship of the fourth gospel, is said to have convinced William Sanday, the great Anglican New Testament scholar at the turn of the century, that the traditional opinion was quite untenable. It also openly advertised the fact that von Hügel's views were comparatively radical.

At this stage he was certainly a radical spirit. His critical historical scholarship compelled him to radical conclusions. He found that he had much in common with the Protestant theologian and philosopher of history, Ernst Troeltsch, with whom he struck up a personal friendship.[49] If von Harnack may be thought of simplistically as a 'simplifier' in his search for an original, essential Christianity, Troeltsch may be regarded as a 'complexifier'. He maintained that Christianity must be looked at historically, which implied that it must not expect to be exempted from the normal rules of historical enquiry. 'Historical explanation . . . necessarily takes the form of understanding an event in terms of its antecedents and consequences, and no event can be isolated from its historically conditioned time and space.'[50] Inevitably this forced upon the enquirer a scepticism difficult to reconcile with faith. It was possible, nevertheless, provided one viewed Christianity in terms of history in general, of history at the point at which it became almost philosophy, to assess it as a whole and not simply as the 'teaching of Jesus'. The impartiality of the historian, Troeltsch rightly argued, does not lie in a destructive, sceptical spirit but in being conscientious in the interpretation of material from one's own standpoint. His view was, rather, that 'if one wants to do essence reconstruction at all, one is bound to accept the fact that the concept will be formed by the judgement of the historian'.[51]

Von Hügel came to believe that Troeltsch had taught him 'how profoundly important is Church appurtenance, yet how much appurtenance never, even at best, can be had without some sacrifices—even of (otherwise) fine or desirable liberties'.[52] It is not easy to say why *that* should have been the obvious lesson for von Hügel to learn from Troeltsch; but, in spite of the fact that the

[49] Vidler, *Variety of Catholic Modernists*, 117.

[50] V. A. Harvey, *The Historian and the Believer* (London, 1967), 15.

[51] S. Sykes, *The Identity of Christianity*, 115.

[52] Barmann, *Friedrich von Hügel*, 244, and cf. Holland (ed.), *Friedrich von Hügel: Letters*, 113, for von Hügel's anxiety lest he should have been responsible for creating intellectual difficulties for Tyrrell by introducing him too abruptly to the ideas of, *inter alia*, Ernst Troeltsch.

relationship between theology and history was one of the baron's principal interests, his approach was never quite the same as that of his close friends and associates Tyrrell and Loisy. Their critical attitudes were primarily concerned with establishing what could be said at a human and historical level about Christ and the Church. Von Hügel thought that what was really important was what could be said about *God*. *The Reality of God and Religion and Agnosticism* was the significant title given to that part of his projected Gifford Lectures which was eventually published (for he was too ill actually to deliver them).[53] Though, at first, he had been rather inclined to distrust the metaphysical, he came, in the end, to believe that religion required a metaphysical and transcendent dimension, and to be very fearful of the effect that the immanentism he perceived in some of his allies might have upon their thought.

In his later years immanentism became the great enemy in his eyes and he was hesitant about some of the ideas he had previously supported. In earlier years he had berated those of his associates who submitted to ecclesiastical authority or soft pedalled their Modernism; yet, after Tyrrell's death in particular, he often seemed to treat twentieth-century attempts to maintain the movement as perverse.[54] By the end of his own life von Hügel had come to distinguish two senses in which the term 'Modernism' could be used—as describing a general and unceasing struggle to express the 'old Faith' in terms of new thought, and as the name of the more specific movement of the reign of Pius X.[55] Modernism, in the latter sense, was over and done with though in the more general sense the struggle had to continue. He was never formally censured by the ecclesiastical authorities, perhaps because he was both a layman and an aristocrat.[56] By the end, he had almost entirely lived down his radical past and had become a venerated authority on spiritual things.

In fact, it seems that the real radical among those Modernists who can in any sense be described as 'British' was the one who attracted least attention, Edmund Bishop. He escaped notice partly, perhaps, because he, too, was a layman. The son of a Devonshire hotel keeper, he was born in 1845 and received no more than secondary education. He was, then, in a very real sense the

[53] Edited by E. G. Gardner and published in 1931.
[54] Vidler, *Variety of Catholic Modernists*, 123 ff.
[55] Barmann, *Friedrich von Hügel*, 243.
[56] But see ibid. 231.

antithesis of the aristocratic, cosmopolitan von Hügel. He became a Roman Catholic at the age of 21 and though he tested his vocation at Downside and was in some sense attached to the abbey for most of his life, he was never a religious, held no position in the Church, and his scholarship—which was immense—was in the history of liturgy, which was not a field which appeared to have much direct practical bearing on the life of the Church in the nineteenth century. Even Anglicans had no great interest in the development of the early liturgies until the very last years of Bishop's life. When he died, in 1917, the moves towards the 1927/8 revision of the Prayer Book in the Church of England had hardly begun. Roman Catholics would not have believed it possible that the post-Tridentine rites would ever be changed. Bishop's great learning was not really recognized until long after his death, when he began to be quoted as an authority from whom there was little appeal.

The apparent remoteness of Bishop's discipline may have served to protect him from attention. An article about whether the cope was, in origin, the same vestment as the chasuble was hardly likely to attract the wrath of the authorities. One which implied that the feast of the Conception of the Blessed Virgin made its way into England in the tenth or eleventh century as an instance of 'the importation of foreign and outlandish ways', was probably rather more uncomfortable, though hardly dangerous. One which claimed that the *Kyries* were not introduced into the Roman rite until the late fifth century would, no doubt, have upset the more sensitive traditionalists. Bishop's paper on 'The Genius of the Roman Rite', originally delivered in 1899, was probably the most contumacious of his works. It argued that an austere simplicity was the chief characteristic of the early Roman liturgy and that many of the features which the Protestant world regarded as typically Roman Catholic were, in fact, elaborate extravagances derived from the Gallican tradition.[57] But none of these would have been thought of as constituting a major threat to the authority of the Church.

The history of liturgy was, nevertheless, history. And Bishop's approach to history was that of a positivist interested in phenomena, facts, and concrete empirical evidence. He was not much interested in metaphysics and, indeed, he suspected that too great

---

[57] E. Bishop, *Liturgica Historica: Papers on the Liturgy and Religious Life of the Western Church* (Oxford, 1918), 260 ff., 258, 135, and 1 ff.

an interest in the metaphysical might corrupt one's ability to judge the evidence objectively. It was this concern for the objective weighing of evidence which led him in the end to prefer Harnack to Loisy in the debate about the original form of the gospel.[58] He was not, in other words, afraid of the consequences of applying a theory of development to the history of the Christian Church, whether in its worship or its doctrine.

Bishop once said:

The historical and the theological methods of mental training are, in fact, here and now, different, and so different, as to be, at this time of day, almost—I fancy I may say quite—antagonistic . . . The business of the modern historian, the condition on which depends the utility of his labours, is precisely the ascertainment and presentment—as nearly as the material conditions will allow—of the mere truth, on the evidence . . .[59]

In this passage the hesitations and hedgings hide the drastic nature of the point Bishop was making. He may, like many a Victorian, have exaggerated the ability of the historian to produce objective, uninterpreted facts which could 'speak for themselves', but the target and the purpose of his attack were both very clear. Theology, he thought, tended to remake history as it would have liked it to be. History's function was to apply a critical corrective to the fanciful character of some traditions. So he also wrote approvingly of the argument put forward by the French historiographers Langlois and Seignobos that:

it is utterly impossible for us ever to know more than the extant documents tell us. Whatever airs or graces historians may give themselves, whatever their *allures* of mastery or freedom, it is by this inexorable necessity that they are cabined, cribbed, confined. Any past, or any part of the past, not witnessed to by documents is for us as though it had never existed . . . With the recognition that knowledge—at least the only knowledge which the historical inquirer can recognize—is conditioned by record, the importance of as full a presentment as possible of record is a necessary security against error; and in proportion as knowledge is full, a document insignificant at first sight, that tells nothing to most men, may yield up to the practised and informed mind the key to some hitherto insoluble problem or enigma.[60]

---

[58] Vidler, *Variety of Catholic Modernists*, 149.
[59] From a privately printed paper entitled 'History and Apologetic', quoted in Vidler, *Variety of Catholic Modernists*, 136 f.
[60] Bishop, *Liturgica Historica*, 476 f.

The potentially radical effect of the views expressed, particularly in the first part of this extract, may be easily imagined, especially if these remarks about the importance of documentation were to be applied to the study of the New Testament and the Jesus of history. Bishop did not attempt to do this in the article from which the quotation is taken; but Langlois and Seignobos had maintained that there was a human tendency to proceed confusedly—and credulously—in matters of history and to behave uncritically, and incautiously, with such evidence as there was. Bishop, quoting the Frenchmen, went on to apply their criticisms quite specifically to the Church.

The authors have in these two words 'proceeding confusedly' put their finger exactly on the difficulty which is so often the obstacle to bringing people into accord on subjects where agreement not only is but obviously should be possible. This I think to be in some measure the case among Catholics at the present day, especially where the treatment of the past—in a word, history—is concerned. However clearly we may see the case external to ourselves, even a moderate acquaintance with our current literature for the past generation or so must convince the attentive reader that it is not uncommon amongst us to 'proceed confusedly' in historical matters.[61]

Bishop appears not to have had any very optimistic belief in the likelihood of the Church's being brought into the world of modern critical thinking. In that sense he did not conform to Vidler's definition of a Modernist as one who believes in the possibility of modernizing Catholicism. There was at least an appearance of cynicism about his attitude. He believed that the modern world was unable to hear the gospel because the way in which it was expressed made it seem to be nonsense. Yet the ecclesiastical authorities rejected the Modernists' attempt to help the Church meet that problem. Therefore, he concluded, the authorities should be left to devise their own way of defending the Church. The scholar's vocation, under those circumstances, was to become the scientific savant whose knowledge exists for its own sake alone. It was not his responsibility to fulfil any useful purpose in the practical affairs of the Church.

The problem of the relation of history to dogma remained unsolved, but it is possible to detect a shift of emphasis among the

[61] Bishop, *Liturgica Historica*, 478.

Modernists as it became clear that the ecclesiastical authorities were unwilling to listen to them. Their initial concern had been that theology should be subject to the criticisms of history. Once that plea had been rejected, Bishop was not alone in tending to put theology and history into different compartments. Loisy did not totally separate faith and history but he distinguished very sharply between the functions appropriate to each of them. If he did not actually say that what was historically untrue could be true for faith, he certainly came to doubt whether very much could ever be known about the Jesus of history. If he remained opposed to the Christ-myth school of thought, he was sceptical about the degree of support which history could provide for the Church's traditional teaching about Christ. Tyrrell, less of a historian in his own right, made much the same distinction, but von Hügel held it, too, in a form which was more practical than theoretical. His devotion to the Church and its rites and ceremonies remained unaffected by his critical learning. His anxiety to stress the transcendence of God led to his treating history as less important, and the way in which he understood the Church as a corporate reality and the locus of necessary tradition made it impossible for him to use history as a yardstick by which to measure the truth of theology. Since history was essentially what could be said about human beings in human terms, it must necessarily exclude God. Theology is the language for asserting truth about God; history is inadequate for the purpose of testing it.

Edmund Bishop's view was different from both these positions. He believed that history *could* properly be used to test at least some theological truths, since the history of doctrines was closely related to their truth. Hence his support for Harnack against Loisy. On the other hand his conviction that scholarship had an independent sphere of its own, while the ecclesiastics ought to be left to construct theological defences for their theological formularies, implies a clear dichotomy between the two realms.

Like Acton, the Modernists hoped for a liberal Catholicism which was intolerable to the ecclesiastical authorities at that particular time. The Ultramontanes insisted that everything else was subject to the teaching authority of the Church. There was no superior law which that authority could be compelled to obey. Acton had believed that it ought to be subject to the sceptical laws of critical history. When the teaching authority proclaimed its infallibility there seemed to be no alternative left to him but to live in, and with, the Church while evading the final act of obedience which the Church did not quite ask from him. In practice, that *was* to separate faith from history. This was the sense in which Acton was the forerunner of the Modernists. They also were reacting against ecclesiastical authoritarianism, whether in France (where it was a response to anticlericalism) or in England (where it was part of Cardinal Wiseman's determination to bring Roman Catholicism out of the shadows). Their liberalism was as unwelcome and unpopular as Acton's, yet a loyalty to the Church, which made them unable to live outside it, persisted side by side with an intensely critical spirit. It was this which drove history and theology apart for them.

8

KNOWING GOD IN HISTORY
The Scottish Critics and
Principal Fairbairn

WHENEVER questions of historicity were raised, whether by Catholic Modernists or by Liberal Protestants, it was in relation to the text of the Bible that they were felt to be most acute. Ecclesiastical authorities, quite naturally, regarded attacks upon the authenticity of the gospel accounts of the life of Jesus as a most serious threat to the faith. In Scotland, however, controversy about the Bible came rather later than in England and, perhaps for that very reason, the authorities were reluctant to mount large-scale heresy trials. In the Church of England attempts to do that had, on the whole, proved to be unsatisfactory, partly because it was extraordinarily difficult to discover what kind of legal and disciplinary machinery could be invoked to coerce the liberals.[1] Heresy trials also proved to cause more unhappiness and disturbance than the original 'heresy'. In Scotland there was not the difficulty of having to discover whether there was a court competent to act. No one doubted that the General Assembly was the proper ultimate authority. But, however enthusiastic the heresy hunters might be, the ecclesiastical authorities were hesitant and cautious.

The situation in Scotland was complicated by the fact that the eighteenth and nineteenth centuries were a period of unparalleled religious fragmentation. One secession after another took place, almost all of them, in one sense or another, on the question of the role of the state in relation to the Church. Few of the schisms affected the Presbyterian polity or Calvinist doctrines of the Church. Many of them did not even question the principle that the Church should be the *national* Church. The largest of the secessions, the Great Disruption of 1843, which brought the Free

---

[1] Above, pp. 89 f.

Church of Scotland into existence, did not attack the concept of establishment but only the way in which the state was interpreting its role in the partnership with the Church. When, later in the century, there was a proposal for union between the Free Church and the United Presbyterian Church, stalwart defenders of the principles enshrined in the Great Disruption, like Dr James Begg, opposed it vigorously on the ground that the United Presbyterians did not believe in establishment.

It happened that the most notorious attempts to charge critical biblical scholars with heresy were mounted within the Free Church of Scotland. There was, first of all, the case of William Robertson Smith, professor of Oriental Languages and Old Testament Exegesis at Aberdeen Free Church College who, about 1875, wrote certain articles for the ninth edition of the *Encyclopaedia Britannica*, notably one about the Bible and another about angels. It is clear that the College Committee of the General Assembly of the Free Church received many complaints about Robertson Smith's opinions.[2] The College Committee, which consisted of the principals of the three colleges, two other academics from the colleges, six parish clergymen, and eight laymen, was the body responsible for exercising control over the training institutions of the Free Church. It committed the complaints against Robertson Smith to a subcommittee consisting of most of the academics and three other clergymen from the parent committee. The subcommittee gave Robertson Smith an opportunity to comment on the complaints, which he did with a good deal of skill.

He argued, first, that the house rules of the encyclopaedia excluded what he called 'constructive theology', that is to say arguments in support of a specific religious position: he had not, however, considered this a reason for refusing to contribute. He dealt very cleverly with specific charges of teaching contrary to the church's confessional standards, showing that these could, in each case, be interpreted so as to support his view rather than that of the literalists. It has to be said, however, that his interpretation was usually very different from the conventional explanation, without being actually forced or artificial.

The crux of Robertson Smith's defence, however, was his

---

[2] *Special Report of the College Committee on Professor Smith's Article 'Bible'*, Free Church of Scotland (Edinburgh, 1877), 3.

insistence that nothing he had written detracted at all from the authority of Scripture or its divine origins.

So far ... is it from being true that sound criticism is associated with unbelief, that the steps which have raised criticism from the chaotic state in which it appears at the close of the last century in the hands of writers like Eichhorn, are inseparably bound up with the reintroduction into theological circles of the notion of Revelation, which, in the epoch of Rationalism, had almost dropped out of sight ... Belief [in Revelation] says that God first finds and chooses man. Unbelief [in Revelation] says that man first finds and chooses God. The critic has no middle ground between these two positions.[3]

And his claim was that he was unquestionably on the side of belief in revelation.

The subcommittee firmly and wisely declined to act as a court. It was surprisingly sympathetic to Robertson Smith, perhaps because so many of its members were themselves academics. It was plainly afraid that his views might upset his students by suggesting that he did not believe in the authority or inspiration of Scripture—a belief, they were quick to add, which they themselves were satisfied that he did hold.[4] (In view of the fact that the students at the Free Church College in Aberdeen held an enthusiastic meeting at which they presented Robertson Smith with a unanimous address expressing admiration and support, the fear of the subcommittee may have been justified. If the professor was not unsettling his students, he was certainly influencing them very strongly.)[5]

The report of the committee, as it was finally presented to the General Assembly, must have been one of the strangest reports ever written. Of the nineteen members of the full committee, no less than five attached dissenting opinions to the report itself—neither did their dissenting opinions agree together. One member thought that the committee should have condemned the articles or demanded their retraction because Robertson Smith had declared that angels were not separate personal beings, and that prophecies were not primarily written as forecasts of some messiah to come. Another objected to the report's expression of anxiety about the

---

[3] Ibid. 22 f.
[4] Ibid. Appendix I, pp. 11 ff. for the full report of the subcommittee.
[5] A printed account of the meeting of the students in Aberdeen is bound up with the copy of the report of the College Committee in the archives of the Free Church, in the National Library of Scotland, in Edinburgh.

effect of Robertson Smith's views, and a third asserted roundly that, if the committee was going to say more than that there was no cause to prosecute, it should have put the blame where it belonged: on those stirring up trouble and anxiety by making public attacks on the professor.

It was, perhaps, hardly surprising that the General Assembly was slow to take action. The committee itself was so deeply divided. Even the majority report came to no clear decision. It expressed 'grave concern' and came dangerously near finding Robertson Smith guilty by association since it regretted that he should have embraced views which were often held by those who were unbelievers and rationalists. But it had not been able to find evidence to support a charge of heresy.[6] Nevertheless, after discussion in the General Assembly, Robertson Smith was removed from his chair in 1881. The rest of his life was spent in Cambridge, where he became a fellow of Christ's in 1885.

Yet, in a sense, the actual report of the College Committee in the Robertson Smith case established an important precedent and could almost be called a victory for tolerance. At least no single party on the committee had been able to insist that its view, and its view alone, was the only possible orthodox opinion. But one suspects that, at the same time, the decision was—as much as anything—a result of a great weariness with the battle itself or an expression of a feeling that it was not going to be possible to arrive at, and impose, an agreed and final judgement in the matter. What, perhaps, no one realized was that a tolerance born of weariness would, in effect, be a triumph for the liberal belief that there could be no absolutes in questions of metaphysics; that matters lying outside the demonstrative sciences, as Thomas Arnold had argued, were bound to be understood differently by different minds.[7]

The case proved to be the precedent on which all such cases would be judged in the future. It also seems to have given critical scholarship a more respectable reputation. At any rate, in 1889 the General Assembly of the Free Church appointed the Reverend Marcus Dods to the chair of New Testament in its college in Edinburgh, in spite of the fact that he was well known to hold unconventional opinions on the inspiration of Scripture.[8] In the

---

[6] *Special Report: Smith's Article 'Bible'*, 8 f.

[7] Above, p. 33 f.

[8] S. Mechie, *Trinity College, Glasgow, 1856–1956* (Glasgow, 1956), 25.

following year the College Committee received complaints against Dods and also, separately, against A. B. Bruce of its Glasgow College. Its decision, though very different from that in the Robertson Smith case, was arrived at by a very similar path.

Marcus Dods seems to have believed, as Charles Gore did, that inspiration did not somehow guarantee the biblical writers an immediate and infallible knowledge of the historical facts as they had actually happened. 'The apostles', he argued, 'nowhere maintain that their inspiration raised them above the necessity of establishing the fact of the resurrection of Christ on ordinary grounds.'[9] In his view inspiration was, 'in short, a spiritual gift and only indirectly a mental one',[10] that is to say, it illuminates the mind by stimulating and elevating it rather than by communicating factual information to it.

Bruce's views were, if anything, even more conservative than those of Dods.[11] In 1871 he had published *The Training of the Twelve* which attempted to show that the substance of the Christian faith could be arrived at through the exegesis of the gospels, using some of the moderately critical techniques. *The Humiliation of Christ* of 1876 was, however, a thorough examination of the kenotic theory, and more offensive to some. *The Kingdom of God or Christ's Teaching according to the Synoptic Gospels*, which was published in 1889, was the work which was the chief object of attack before the General Assembly. In it Bruce had said such things as, 'Luke had before him the words of Christ in the form reported by Matthew, believed them to have been so spoken and deliberately modified them.'[12]

The College Committee had had some fairly severe, but rather vague and general things to say about the upset likely to be created by the professors' views but concluded 'that their writings do not afford ground for instituting a process against either of them as

[9] Marcus Dods, *Revelation and Inspiration: The Historical Books of Scripture* (A Sermon), 4th edn. (Glasgow, 1877), 19. [10] Ibid. 21.

[11] He was convinced, for instance, that the author of the Gospel according to St Matthew was the Galilean tax collector, see 'The Trustworthiness of the Historical Foundations of Christianity', *Abstract of the Proceedings of the Oxford Society of Historical Theology*, 10 May 1894, 70.

[12] Quoted from the report of the subcommittee of the College Committee in *The Case Stated: Statement by Ministers and other Office-Bearers of the Free Church in regard to the Decisions of the last General Assembly in the cases of Drs Dods and Bruce* (Glasgow, undated), 37.

teaching what is at variance with the Standards of the Church'. The General Assembly approved the report, refusing to take action against either man. Very much to the fury of the conservative,[13] the only 'positive' action the Assembly would take was to reaffirm those doctrines which some had thought that Bruce and Dods were calling in question, and to remind the professors of their duty to teach the faith.

The third important case came after the Free Church of Scotland and the United Presbyterian Church had come together to form the United Free Church. It was the case of George Adam Smith, professor at the Free Church College in Glasgow from 1892. It was initiated by a memorial protesting against the teaching of his book, *Modern Criticism and the Preaching of the Old Testament*. George Adam Smith was, however, a more difficult target to attack than any of the earlier critical scholars. The circumstances had changed, too, in that public opinion at large had become more tolerant of critical opinion. Smith was an interesting man, who had been born in Calcutta, educated in Germany as well as in Scotland, and had travelled extensively in the Middle East. His scholarship and his breadth of experience put him almost beyond the reach of his opponents and he was to become principal of the university of Aberdeen in 1909.

Meanwhile, however, the procedure followed was as in the previous cases. A subcommittee of the College Committee investigated the matter. Adam Smith was given an opportunity to reply to the memorial. He submitted a lengthy statement to the subcommittee, who recommended that no action should be taken against the professor, while expressing misgivings about his methods and the effects they were likely to have. The committee reported accordingly and the General Assembly accepted its advice.

In spite of the fact that the College Committee, once again, made the customary noises about disliking the man's opinions while finding them not to be heretical, its report contained some remarkable good sense. The nub of the report was:

The essential positions of the Pentateuchal criticism have arisen, it must be remembered, from an extraordinarily minute scrutiny of the actual phenomena of the record. It can be argued, certainly, that this scrutiny has been conducted from a point of view, and under the influence of methods,

---

[13] Report of the subcommittee of the College Committee, 11.

which are misleading. But the purely critical and many of the historical results have gained the assent of a very large proportion of competent scholars, including not a few believing men, not predisposed to revolutionary views. These believing men have at the same time maintained faith in the divine revelation embodied in the Old Testament. This is not, in itself, a reason for accepting their views; but it is a state of things which seems to call upon the Church to take no hasty action. The criticism referred to may have erred or gone to excess; but it appears to the Committee that if so, it must be dealt with, not by authority, but by the process of discussion. The Church cannot escape the duty of guarding herself against the results of a criticism which proceeds on naturalistic and unbelieving principles. But this is not the present case, and the Committee are persuaded that it would be wrong to make Dr Smith personally responsible for a system of learned opinion which has for years been entertained by scholars of all the Churches; which is not uncontradicted, indeed, but prevalent, and has to be dealt with in a spirit of faith and patience.[14]

It is against this background of events in Scotland that one has to understand the life and ideas of a man who was to become a very prominent figure in English Free Church circles at the turn of the nineteenth and twentieth centuries, Andrew Martin Fairbairn. He was born in Fife in 1838 and his family background was secessionist. He came, in other words, from precisely the kind of cultural enclave that people have in mind when they talk of Scots religion as narrow and bigoted. He himself, as a young man, joined the Evangelical Union, a denomination led by James Morison, a minister of the United Secession Church, suspended for teaching that the atonement was of universal efficacy. In a sense anti-Calvinist, then, but still fervently Evangelical in an old-fashioned way, Fairbairn was soon studying to become a minister of his new Church.

Fairbairn attended the academy which Morison had founded and became at the same time a student at Edinburgh University. There was nothing very unusual in this. Because the theology faculties of the Scottish universities had always trained the ministers of the national Church, the secessionist bodies (notably the Free Church after the Great Disruption of 1843) set up their own academies with their own 'professors'. The Free Church academies were considerable institutions, deliberately reduplicating whatever the

---

[14] *Special Report by the College Committee Anent the Memorial on Professor George Adam Smith's Work entitled 'Modern Criticism and the Preaching of the Old Testament'*, 6.

established Church had to offer in the universities, as the Free Church was attempting to reduplicate the parish structure of the established Church throughout the country. The 'academies' of some of the smaller denominations, however, were hardly institutions at all. They were a handful of students attached to someone appointed, or elected, as 'professor' in order to train the future ministers of the body concerned.

At this stage of his life Fairbairn does not seem to have had any very impressive reputation as a student. His biographer, though anxious in the fashion of the day to suggest that future events were already casting long shadows before them, was reduced to offering excuses for his hero's modest academic record. 'No doubt the defects in his earlier education made matters very difficult for him and compelled him to devote much of his labour to making up for lost time.'[15] As Fairbairn had been working, as an errand boy from the age of 10 and then as an apprentice stonemason, he really needed no excusing. To be getting himself educated at all was a considerable achievement.

Fairbairn began his pastoral ministry at the Evangelical Union Church in Bathgate in 1860 and moved from there to St Paul's in Aberdeen in 1872. It was in this period that he became, for the first time, significantly interested in theological questions. At Bathgate this hitherto earnest young Evangelical 'lost his faith' and went off from his pastorate, for a while, to study in Germany. In Berlin he was principally influenced by two men. Dorner was a historian of philosophical and theological thought, attempting to use the ideas of Schleiermacher and Hegel in Christian apologetic. Hengstenberg, the man whom Colenso so despised,[16] was among the most conservative of biblical scholars, a powerful but somewhat bigoted figure.

Fairbairn continued to be influenced by Hengstenberg's ideas for the rest of his life.[17] Though he came back to Scotland to resume his ministry, no longer the simple Evangelical of earlier years, it is worth noting by what path he had come to this position. For the most part, the older scholars who had been influenced by critical biblical scholarship or post-Kantian philosophy had begun life as 'simple believers' and modified their religious convictions, in one way or another, in consequence of their encounter with the new

[15] W. B. Selbie, *The Life of Andrew Martin Fairbairn* (London, 1914), 10.
[16] Above, p. 30.   [17] Selbie, *Andrew Martin Fairbairn*, 38.

ideas. Fairbairn's history was very different. He had proceeded from Evangelical fervour to unbelief and then, through critical and philosophical scholarship, even if of a very conservative kind, back to Christianity. For him, therefore, modern scholarship was not a diluter of faith but the positive means for reacquiring religious convictions. His powerful, personal religious commitment, from which he derived the force which was to make him so enormously influential, was a consequence of his encounter with contemporary learning. As a result, he was always rather different from most of the liberals of his generation. Like them he believed that the new critical approach would uncover the real historical person, Jesus of Nazareth, as he actually had been. Unlike them, however, he believed that that Jesus would be manifestly and unequivocally God.

While still ministering in the congregations at Bathgate and then at Aberdeen, Fairbairn began to develop his own theological thought. He was influenced chiefly by Max Müller's work in the field of comparative religion and by critical historical studies. 'He was known to be a student of German theology, a proof in itself that he was dangerous. He was suspected of knowing something of Hindu philosophy, and it was even whispered that he had quoted in his pulpit from the Vedas.'[18] Max Müller gave him some rather condescending encouragement. He managed to get some articles published, and, from Aberdeen, he wrote his first volume of theology, *Studies in the Philosophy of Religion and History*, published in 1876.

The title of this volume is, in modern times, a little misleading. The book is not really about either the philosophy of religion or the philosophy of history, as those disciplines would be understood now. Fairbairn was really writing a broadly sweeping history of religious ideas, as he thought they had developed. His approach was very like that of Edward Caird, both in its breadth and in its idiosyncratic interpretation of events. Yet he was not entirely happy with the science-of-religion approach. 'The book is really a plea for and vindication of the historical method in the study of religion and religious ideas. It is an attempt to escape from the dogmatic and a priori theories common among materialistic scientists on the one hand, and orthodox theologians on the other.'[19] Fairbairn thought,

[18] Ibid. 52.   [19] Ibid. 76.

in other words, that history would provide the means for arriving at an objective, unbiased knowledge of God. Yet it cannot really be said that he was entirely unprejudiced in his understanding of history, either in interpreting events or in relating them to doctrinal issues.

A passage from towards the end of the volume gives a very good idea of the somewhat romantic style he used, as well as of the very generalized history with which he was concerned:

The point our discussion next reaches is one where the Semitic family and the Greek people seem alike broken and powerless. Rome has conquered and rules. Freedom and philosophy have together forsaken Greece; and can hardly be said to live in Rome. Cicero has written elegant if not very profound or original disquisitions on various things philosophical. Lucretius has sung the praises of Epicurus, and done his best to show how atoms could become a world. Stoicism, a creed congenial to the sterner Roman spirit, is making, and is for long to continue to make, noble men in swiftly degenerating times. But Philosophy, as a creative search after truth, has not found a home in the imperial city, and is looking for one elsewhere. The Semitic family seems doomed; its great nations are either dead or dying. Assyria has ceased to be. Phoenicia, aged, withered, feeble, is hardly alive. Carthage is eclipsed; against her the *delenda est* had gone forth. Israel, proud, subject, weeping under an alien king, sits cold in the lengthening shadow of national extinction, and scarcely dares to dream of her ancient hopes. Hebrew is dead; Aramaean lives. Syrians are everywhere, swarm in the capital,

'in Tiberim defluxit Orontes'

and are everywhere useful, used, trusted, despised. The Jew is becoming a citizen of the world, has penetrated to India, to China even, has quarters and colonies in every city of the empire, can count his thousands in Rome and Alexandria. In Nazareth one who shall make the name of Jew at once illustrious and infamous for all time, is beginning to move to love or hate the minds of men. In Tarsus a youth is awakening to the world about him, asking many things, what it is to be, to be a Jew, a Greek. Everywhere within the old the seeds of a new order are falling, and shall yet fructify, causing death while creating life.[20]

---

[20] A. M. Fairbairn, *Studies in the Philosophy of Religion and History* (London, 1876), 385 f. In view of the idiosyncracies of Fairbairn's prose style, one is almost bound to wonder whether Acton's remark to potential contributors to the *Cambridge Modern History*, that the reader should not be able to tell where Stubbs left off and Fairbairn began, was not sardonically intended. See above, p. 12.

In 1877 Fairbairn moved to England and became principal of the Airedale Theological College at Bradford, one of the well-established dissenting academies of English Independency. It has to be said that Fairbairn took to English Nonconformity, like the proverbial duck to water. It seemed to offer him all the freedom to be orthodox in his own way that he had been seeking for a long time. When it was proposed to move Spring Hill College to Oxford and to refound it as Mansfield College,[21] Fairbairn was the obvious person to become the first principal in 1885. He understood Oxford and Anglicanism in a way that few Nonconformists, and even fewer Scots, could claim to do. Oxford Anglicans, or at least those who were less than rigidly High Church, tended to regard Fairbairn as almost one of themselves. It was, no doubt, rather patronizing for William Sanday to say that he regarded Fairbairn as in no way inferior to himself: Fairbairn seems to have retained his independence and integrity in spite of that kind of back-handed flattery. He remained critical of both Oxford and Anglicanism while being willing and able to move with and within them, an astonishing feat for a former apprentice stonemason whose early academic training had been in the makeshift academy of a tiny Evangelical Scottish sect.

He established Mansfield as a centre for all Nonconformity in the university. The Sunday morning sermons in its chapel became the Nonconformist equivalent of the official university sermon. As recently as three years before, when there had been some 200 Nonconformist undergraduates in Oxford, there had been a good deal of anxiety lest—in the absence of a proper provision of pastoral care for them—they might find themselves tempted to join the Church of England.[22] By the time the new buildings for Mansfield College had been completed and consecrated in 1889, with encouragement from Oxford liberals like Jowett and Edwin Hatch, that fear had almost entirely dissipated. Fairbairn further enhanced the status of Mansfield in Oxford by establishing a series of summer schools at which he arranged for scholars like Bruce, Dods, and Sanday to lecture.

---

[21] The Mansfield family had given some of the money to endow the original Spring Hill College.

[22] R. K. Evans, 'The present Religious and Ecclesiastical Situation in Oxford', *Mansfield College Magazine*, Dec. 1910, p. 55—quoting remarks made by T. H. Green in 1883.

It was a remarkable achievement and almost as remarkable was the growth in intellectual stature in Fairbairn himself, which one senses in his later writings. In 1893 he published his theological *magnum opus*, *The Place of Christ in Modern Theology*, which ran to twelve editions in the next few years. There is still recognizable in his style the rather grandiloquent, slightly superficial, over-generalized approach to history of his *Studies in the Philosophy of Religion and History*. This may have been a curious hangover from his days as a traditional Evangelical. One of his friends remembered his lecturing technique, in the years immediately after his return from Germany, in a way that might almost have served to describe his literary style at its worst; 'Fairbairn never used a note: he never spoke for less than an hour. His lectures were full of names and facts and dates and quotations, delivered with unbroken fluency, in a kind of chant, and with much gesticulation.'[23] And the man who supplied that description did not think that Fairbairn's lectures compared at all well with the much simpler, more direct style that he came to employ when preaching.

If one ignores the too grandiloquent generalities and concentrates on the rest, *The Place of Christ in Modern Theology* is a much tougher, altogether more modern, work than his earlier writings. Its theme is that the direction which scholarship has taken has given an entirely new shape to theology, a shape provided by history. The opening section of the work displayed a very firm grasp of precisely how recent developments in critical and historical techniques had affected theology. And Fairbairn clearly believed that the effect had been entirely good. Modern theology, he claimed, had more feeling for Christ because it knew him better in history. Because he was perceived as a historical reality, he had become better known than at any other period in Christian history.

The 'old theology', Fairbairn thought, was primarily doctrinal and only secondarily historical. It came to its knowledge of Christ through the dogmatic traditions, the theology of the schools, and the conventions of denominational teaching. But theology had become primarily historical and secondarily doctrinal: we come to the doctrinal traditions only by way of our historical knowledge of the actual historical Christ. Whereas it used to be the case that history had to be made to fit dogma, now belief has to be

---

[23] Selbie, *Andrew Martin Fairbairn*, 81.

harmonized with history—a more natural, but a more difficult, process because man is always reinterpreting his past in terms of his understanding of himself. (This really rather shrewd and sophisticated point arose because Fairbairn thought—somewhat surprisingly—that the new interest in history had begun with Romanticism, itself a revolt against the Renaissance understanding of humanity in terms of classical antiquity and a reinterpretation of it in terms of the Medieval. The resultant dithyramb is very typical of Fairbairn at his worst.)

The volume proceeds in this fashion. Telling and clearly argued points are interlarded with long and woolly passages of rhetoric. He pointed out, for instance, that the old theology had been prepared to treat doctrinal questions, such as the atoning sacrifice of Christ, exhaustively, endlessly, and with remorseless logic without having any regard to its historical dimension in his actual life. This is an interesting point. Properly pursued it might have enabled him to see why the exponents of historical criticism were often also those most impatient with the traditional theology of the atonement. But it took Fairbairn no less than eight pages to make his point because he simply could not resist the temptation to wrap it all up in an 'imaginative' style, and his insights tended to get lost. But at least the conclusion of this part of his argument was clear enough. He thought it beyond question that 'the second half of our century may be described as the period when the history of the New Testament has, through its literature, been recovered, and in this history by far the greatest result is the recovery of the historical Christ'.[24]

A great many interesting issues are raised by this opening section of the book. There is the fundamental question whether it *is* proper to treat theological issues through historical enquiry. A hundred years later even the most optimistic might be less confident on this point than Fairbairn was.[25] Nevertheless, he possessed a more realistic understanding of the relationship between the two than was exhibited, for instance, in Caird's treatment of the subject, superficially similar though it appears to be.[26] Caird, at any rate by the time he came to deliver his presidential address to the Oxford Society for Historical Theology, had adopted a position in some

---

[24] A. M. Fairbairn, *The Place of Christ in Modern Theology* (London, 1893), 19.
[25] See P. Hinchliff, 'Christology and Tradition' in A. E. Harvey (ed.), *God Incarnate: Story and Belief* (London, 1981), 81 ff.   [26] Above, p. 143 f.

ways similar to that of F. C. Baur. He maintained that to understand Christianity one needed to know the whole of its history and development. Like Baur, he took a very different line from that of Harnack, who sought to disentangle the original, simple gospel from the accretion of later developments. Fairbairn attempted yet another approach and an essentially conservative one. He claimed to be able to construct a *systematic* Christian theology. He believed, in other words, that his historical technique would provide the tools for devising a coherent and logically structured exposition of the main themes of Christian teaching, building synthetically upon the basis of the analysis provided by critical scholarship. The result is by no means an absurd one. The problem is that it is so difficult to disentangle his supposed system from his wanderings in the byways of rhetoric that it is almost impossible to judge how far he succeeded in welding history and theology together.

The work fell into two main parts, each subdivided within itself. Book I dealt with historical and critical matters and its first subsection set itself—perhaps unfortunately—to tackle the theory of development. It was very obviously a revival of his argument with Newman, who had died just three years before the book was published. There is an unhappy smell of vendetta about this passage as Fairbairn repeats many of the old points which Newman had been at considerable pains to rebut by clearing up misunderstandings.[27] This may have been inevitable. Fairbairn clearly felt that he must write about development and that, if he were to do so, he must give Newman the credit for introducing the idea into modern theology. He shared Newman's conviction that it is important to perceive that the Church is an organism whose thought grows and develops. Having done this, he could not forebear to point out what he believed to be the weaknesses of Newman's concepts of Church and of development.

Fairbairn's new, and most telling, criticism of Newman is that his idea of development is not 'biological, historical or real',[28] by which he meant that Newman did not examine the actual way in which development of the organism had taken place in history as a whole. He had really treated it as 'abstract or logical'—the very thing that Newman himself had insisted that one must not do.[29]

---

[27] Above, p. 34 f.   [28] Fairbairn, *The Place of Christ*, 34.
[29] Above, p. 40 f.

Even more, Fairbairn felt, Newman had not looked at the whole organism, the whole process. He had isolated one part of it, however large and important, and in particular had isolated it from the most important part of the whole, Christ himself. Fairbairn insisted that 'in the field of inquiry which concerns us what has been termed the organism is not the Church but the historical Christ—not the created society but the creative Personality'.[30] This is, on the face of it, an important and extremely interesting idea. Clearly, to include Christ himself within the process of organic Christian development would be vital; but Fairbairn set out to do this by an enormously lengthy survey of the history of Christian thinking about Christ through nearly two thousand years. Long though this survey was, it was still not long enough to marshal the evidence to prove the case he wished to make. Moreover, since some of his statements are little more than reformulations of his own prejudices, evidence in support of them would have been difficult to find.

The second part of Book I was yet another survey, this time of modern thought and its effect on Christian thinking, from Lessing to D. F. Strauss and F. C. Baur. It is a more effective survey since it is not concerned to make a case but simply to expound and report. It is, for the most part, well and sensibly done, but all this survey leaves very little space for constructive thought. At the end of it all, Fairbairn came back to the theme of the opening section of the whole work—we are now in a position to know Christ as he really was. He quite clearly believed that this was literally true and perhaps his generation was the last that could actually do so before Schweitzer destroyed that confidence for ever. Fairbairn believed that he was able to know Christ 'as He knew Himself and to understand His mission as it was in His mind and before it had been touched by the spirit of Paul or seized by the coarse hands of controversy'.[31] Therefore, he thought it possible to revive another version of the old idea that the original Christianity was the true one. But he would have nothing to do with the argument that it was the earliest generation of Christians which had the truth. It is only Christ himself. His was, in other words, a fuller version of the old liberal view, expounded briefly by Jowett in *Essays and Reviews*, that knowledge of God comes to a climax in Christ

---

[30] Fairbairn, *The Place of Christ*, 38.   [31] Ibid. 292.

himself and that everything afterwards should look back to that peak.[32] Fairbairn actually thought it was possible to measure precisely how far Paul, the author to the Hebrews, Peter, James, and John departed from what Christ himself had taught. 'Where Paul is greatest is when he is most directly under the influence or in the hands of Jesus, evolving the content of what he had received concerning Him; where he is weakest is where his old scholasticism or his new antagonism dominates alike the form and substance of his thought.'[33] Therefore the method of Christian theology ought to be a return to the source, which is Christ, who is now as never before accessible. A Christian theology, in the sense of a theology concerning Christ and derived from him, 'is more possible today than at any previous moment'.[34]

Book II deals with two different kinds of issues, 'the exegetical, concerned with the source of the Christian concept of God; and constructive, concerned with its explication'.[35] Fairbairn is far ahead of his time in perceiving what a 'New Testament theology' might be. He recognizes that a very great deal of the New Testament is, in fact, theology rather than history, that it consists of 'attempts to construe the person and work of Christ',[36] and that there are a variety of *different* theologies contained within the New Testament rather than a single New Testament theology. He is not so clear in his handling of the question of how these theologies relate to history or what history consists of. Instead of recognizing that history itself always contains a subjective and interpretative element, he tried to maintain that New Testament history is symbolic and allegorical, making it appear very different from any other kind of history. He continued to insist that it was possible to identify Christ's own ideas, and distinguish them clearly from the ideas of the New Testament writers. He believed that he could contrast what he called Christ's own theology from that of the apostles.

His attempt to construct a Christology on this basis is quite impressive. He really did try to be faithful to his own principles though he cannot be said to have constructed, unquestionably or ineluctably, from the analysis of the text, a theological system which everyone would feel compelled to accept. At least he did not,

---

[32] Above, p. 60.   [33] Fairbairn, *The Place of Christ*, 293.
[34] Ibid. 297.   [35] Ibid. 301.   [36] Ibid. 302.

like so many liberals, simply use Hegelian or Schleiermacherian concepts and claim that they were derived from the critical exegesis of the New Testament. At times his arguments seem to be much more dependent upon common-sense ideas, notions derived from nineteenth-century cultural commonplaces or bits of contemporary popular psychology; but often enough he makes a brave attempt at doing precisely what he claimed to be doing.

Fairbairn's Christology, for instance, began from a consideration of the Synoptic accounts of the temptations of Christ. Rather weakly he maintained that these could only make sense if they were describing real, felt, struggles in the soul of Christ. Therefore Christ must be an ordinary, natural human being. But, in an almost conscious mimicry of Anselm, he argued that Christ must be both a natural man and a supernatural person. To do this Fairbairn used the language of 'fit person' and 'fit work'. Christ must, by nature, be the human 'fit person' to do what he must do; but the 'fit work' can only be done by God. His humanity is not miraculous: the miracles belong to the fit work, the supernatural element in the whole, the proclaiming of the kingdom. 'The Word is a miracle, a spirit that quickeneth.'[37]

On this basis Fairbairn argued for a Christ who is both human and divine (though he avoided Chalcedonian language), a kenotic Christ and a passible God. His atonement theology, though it appeared perfectly orthodox, was, in fact, unusual since it was explained in terms of a sacrifice which is made by the Father in giving the Son to die for the sin of the world. There was, thus, no problem in reconciling the love and the justice of God, both of which Fairbairn was anxious to affirm while avoiding what the liberals regarded as the monstrously immoral penal substitutionary theory.[38]

There is an almost Barthian definition of the Trinity (though not serving a Barthian end):

In salvation . . . there is a threefold Divine causality—the Father who gives, the Son who is given, the Holy Spirit who renews and reveals. And these are so united as to be inseparable in essence and in act. The Father is the font, the Son the medium, the Spirit the distributor of grace . . . It is the unity of the whole that constitutes the efficiency of each, yet the difference is as suggestive as the unity. While the Son enables us to understand the being and action of personality within the Godhead, the Spirit enables us to

[37] Ibid. 356.   [38] Ibid. 486.

conceive its being without. There is an immanent presence of God in man, but it represents personal agency not impersonal energy.[39]

In its way, perhaps, Fairbairn's attempt to build up a 'scriptural' systematic theology was almost as brave as Barth's but, in the last resort, one is left with the lurking suspicion that he had really done little more than find apparently critical arguments in favour of the conclusions that he *wished* to reach.

The work ended with a section called 'God as Interpreted by Christ the Determinative Principle in the Church'. It was an unusual climax for a nineteenth-century Nonconformist work of theology. But Fairbairn was passionately interested in the relationship between the institutional structure of the Church and the theological concept it was believed to embody, hence his interest in Newman's theory of development. It was also the basis for his friendship with Edwin Hatch, reader in Ecclesiastical History at Oxford.

On the surface this friendship appeared to be simply an alliance between two liberals who were not particularly interested in denominational labels. But Fairbairn was not, as we have seen, a conventional Liberal Protestant. Hatch, on the other hand, was Jowett's godson and held views that were very similar to those of the arch-Liberal Protestant Adolf von Harnack. Hatch's controversial opinions had attracted attention in 1880 when his Bampton Lectures (translated into German by von Harnack) had attempted to apply to the historical evidence relating to the earliest history of the Christian communities the methods used in any other kind of historical study. Hatch's lectures were intended to demonstrate historical criticism in action, assessing the worth of documents as sources for history, and drawing conclusions from them. He claimed that his generation had seen the growth not only of historical science but of what he called 'the historical temper'. And he went on to say:

Hitherto that science and that temper have been applied almost exclusively, in this country at least, to the facts of civil history: but if we assume, as I propose to assume, that—at least for purposes of study—the facts of ecclesiastical history, being recorded in the same language, and in similar documents, and under the same general conditions of authorship, belong to the same category as the facts of civil history, it is not too much to maintain the existence of a presumption that the application of historical science and

[39] Fairbairn, *The Place of Christ*, 491.

the historical temper to a field of historical phenomena which they have hitherto left comparatively unexplored, may be followed by new results.[40]

His technique was, in a sense, very modern; his conclusions sometimes very radical; but his opinions were often theological rather than strictly historical; and they upset the conservatives, and particularly the Anglo-Catholics, a great deal.

Hatch's Hibbert Lectures a few years later went so far as to assert that the classical post-Nicene dogmatic system was the result of the influence of Greek ideas on the original, simple, peasant religion of primitive Christianity. This was also very much the theme of von Harnack's *Dogmengeschichte*, published in the years between 1886 and 1889. And von Harnack paid tribute to Hatch in the preface to the English edition of this work a decade later.[41] That Hatch's opinions were so close to those of von Harnack makes it, in one sense, even more surprising that he and Fairbairn should become such close allies. For Fairbairn's *objectives*, however much he may have thought that he shared Hatch's modern historical *methods*, were in many ways almost the reverse of Hatch's. Fairbairn believed that his own historical critical work was positive, conservative, and creative, and therefore very different from the negative and reductionist tendencies of much Liberal Protestantism. He was convinced that historical enquiry would enable him to create a wholly orthodox, but critically impregnable, systematic theology.

What Hatch and Fairbairn really had in common was an interest in the growth of Christian institutions and the history of ecclesiological thought. After Hatch's death in 1889 Fairbairn edited, and put in order for publication, the notes for the Hibbert Lectures which appeared in the following year under the title *The Influence of Greek Ideas and Usages on the Church*. Von Harnack did the same for the German edition (and added some extra bits and pieces of his own as well). Though von Harnack's views may well have been closer to those of Hatch, there was certainly no one in Oxford better qualified than Fairbairn to complete an unfinished work on the relationship between Christian theology and ecclesiastical institutions.

---

[40] E. Hatch, *The Organization of the Early Christian Churches*, 8th impression (London, 1918), 2 f.

[41] B. M. G. Reardon, *Religious Thought in the Victorian Age: A Survey from Coleridge to Gore*, rev. edn. (London, 1980), 355 f.

9

OFF WITH THE NEW AND ON WITH THE OLD:
R. J. Campbell and the New Theology

IN the early years of the twentieth century the Liberal Protestant determination to get back to the real historical Jesus still persisted. Alongside it British Idealism also survived, dominant indeed among philosophers and suspicious of too much concern with history. Neither school of thought was as yet a spent force, though both were beginning to come under criticism, and it was not always perceived that they were almost diametrically opposed to each other. The pre-war generation was attracted by the optimism of the Idealists and the way in which they tended to emphasize one's obligation to be of service to society. William Temple, as an undergraduate, owed a great deal to Edward Caird, to whose genius he was 'drawn as by a magnet'.[1] Caird seemed to stand for idealism in both senses of the word and to be living proof that it was possible to be a person of outstanding intellect *and* believe in God. Yet there was a sense in which the Edwardian age in theology, as in so much else, was a silver age. Edwardian England seemed full of peace, certainty, and optimism, long hot summers, and the music of Elgar, but somehow it lacked the robust vigour of the nineteenth century. At least in matters of religion, the enthusiasms and the controversies—however real—seem shallower and, sometimes, almost trivial, like witticisms by Oscar Wilde.

Idealism made its most startling and controversial convert among theologians (Reginald John Campbell) in this very period. Campbell had been at Oxford a decade earlier than Temple, but had been far more vulnerable to the excitement generated by the Idealists. He was born in 1867[2] and came of much less sophisticated stock than

---

[1] F. A. Iremonger, *William Temple, Archbishop of Canterbury* (London, 1948), 39.

[2] It is sometimes very difficult to be precise about the facts of Campbell's life. His autobiographical work, *A Spiritual Pilgrimage* (London, 1916), and his entries in

Temple—'Ulster Protestant of Scottish extraction' was all he said of his parentage in *Who's Who*.

His father was actually a minister of one of the Methodist Churches and Campbell's connection with the north of Ireland seems to have been that he lived there with relations—probably because his health was poor, as a child—and he remained there until late adolescence.[3] These relatives brought him up as a Presbyterian but on his return to England he succumbed, not for the last time, to the attractions of High Anglicanism, and was confirmed in the Church of England. He worked for a few years as an apprentice teacher (*Who's Who* claimed a connection with University College in Nottingham), and then succeeded in obtaining a place at Christ Church, Oxford, in 1891. He was by that time 24, much older than the average undergraduate, and was already married, which must have marked him off from the other junior members of the college even more than his age would have done. He read modern history, taking his degree with a second class in the final honour school in 1895.

The Oxford of the 1890s was very different from the kind of place it had been earlier in the century. Pusey had died. *Lux Mundi* had been published. The examiners in the theology honour school were willing to recognize the existence of biblical criticism. Nonconformists had come to be accepted as a permanent feature of the university community. Fairbairn was established at Mansfield and was generally regarded as the unofficial leader of Free Churchmen in Oxford. The most vigorous manifestation of undergraduate religion was the Christian Social Union—a young French visitor to Oxford said that what his friends feared most was the growth of Christian Socialism.[4] This manifestation of socially concerned Christianity was derived from the teaching of the British Idealists, and Charles Gore (who moved from being principal of Pusey House to become vicar of Radley, just outside Oxford, in 1893) seems to have been the leading senior figure in the

works of reference, like *Who's Who* and *Crockford's Clerical Directory*, tend to omit crucial facts. His personal papers were destroyed on his death. The two most recent accounts, K. Robbins, 'The Spiritual Pilgrimage of the Rev. R. J. Campbell', *Journal of Ecclesiastical History*, 30 (Apr. 1979), 261 ff., and K. W. Clements, *Lovers of Discord: Twentieth Century Theological Controversies in England* (London, 1988), 19 ff., do not always agree in detail.

[3] Clements, *Lovers of Discord*, 25; Robbins, 'R. J. Campbell', 263.

[4] J. Bardoux, *Memories of Oxford* (trans. M. L. Woods, London, 1899), 23.

movement. Certainly Gore and Fairbairn were the two people who had most influence on the young Campbell, though he seems also to have venerated Francis Paget (the former contributor to *Lux Mundi*) who was the dean of Christ Church and therefore, presumably, a rather remote and awe-inspiring figure.

It is possible that there was something of a battle for Campbell's soul between Gore and Fairbairn, of which they may even have been completely oblivious. If there was such a battle, it was one that Fairbairn won. Campbell, while still an undergraduate, began preaching in the Nonconformist chapels in the surrounding countryside and discovered that he had a real gift for speaking eloquently, movingly, and with dramatic effect. As his graduation approached, Fairbairn advised him to enter the ministry of one of the Free Churches and Campbell became, in fact, a Congregationalist and the pastor of Union Street Church in Brighton in 1895.

In Brighton Campbell preached an 'evangelical and spiritual religion in terms consonant with what thinking people knew about the world of the time'.[5] His recently discovered talent for oratory drew a very large congregation to what had been an unfashionable chapel. Campbell's striking good looks (often described as 'angelic') and his abundant but prematurely grey, hair could not but add to his drawing power.[6] This period was, perhaps, the most successful and the most effective in the whole of his long life. It resulted in his being asked to become the minister of the City Temple in Westminster, the most prestigious position in all English Congregationalism, in 1903.

By this time Campbell had begun to put together his own particular amalgam of theological ideas, in which Idealism was one of the most powerful components. He began to read Caird, whose ideas he had heard about in Oxford. He continued, also, to be influenced by the kind of social concern propagated by Gore and the CSU in his undergraduate days, and he became interested in the writings of the French Protestant Auguste Sabatier, whose works were just being translated into English at this time. Sabatier was an exponent of the critical approach to the New Testament, but his

---

[5] Clements, *Lovers of Discord*, 27.

[6] Through the kindness of Mary Gilborson, I possess two photographs of Campbell which have been made into postcards. One of them was printed in Brighton and bears a message to a young lady from 'Jack', wishing her success in her examination and hoping that she 'will like this of Mr Campbell'. The style of the cards hint at something of a personality cult.

distinctive, and widely influential, contribution to theology was a revival of the central ideas of Schleiermacher, his concept of God-consciousness, the fundamental religious feeling of utter dependence upon God. He then interpreted Christian dogmas as symbols of these feelings, rather in the manner in which Ritschl interpreted the classical Christological formula as an expression of the Church's conviction that Christ was, in the most intense way possible, the revelation of God, rather than as an ontological statement about the being and nature of Christ himself.

Campbell interwove these ideas with others derived from Caird and the Idealists, and ultimately from Hegel. Evolutionary, dialectical, immanentist, social, and quasi-mystical, all this seemed richer and more intense, emotionally speaking, than the aridity of most Liberal Protestantism. At the same time it seemed as if it could be represented as respectable in terms of contemporary philosophy, science, and critical scholarship. It may seem an odd amalgam of ideas for someone who had read history as an undergraduate, but part of the motivation which drove Campbell to a voracious reading of all the latest theology seems to have been a desire to compensate for the fact that he had never had any formal training in theology at all. When his ideas began to attract public attention one of his leading critics, P. T. Forsyth, openly sneered, 'His is not the New Theology—it may be an amateur one.'[7]

The British Idealists' socio-political concern, which Campbell had encountered in a junior common room version in the Christian Social Union at Oxford, he began to translate into a more serious and practical involvement with left-wing politics. About 1906 he joined the Labour movement and was an associate of Keir Hardie, its leader. This was a period of sweeping Liberal party triumphs against a Conservative policy of tariff reform and the protection of trade with the colonies. In the immediate aftermath of the general election of January 1906, when fifty-one candidates supported by the Labour Representation Committee were returned to Parliament, the Labour Party came into existence. The educational policies adopted by the new government were actually policies that had been advocated for a long time by the Labour movement to make opportunities for advancement more open to working-class people.

In this exciting period in political history Campbell was actually

[7] Clements, *Lovers of Discord*, 32.

invited to become the Labour candidate for Cardiff.[8] If he had been
a clergyman of the established Church he would not have been
eligible for election to the House of Commons. Because he was a
Congregationalist there was no legal reason why he should not
have been an MP. But, although he declined the invitation, it was
very unusual for any Nonconformist minister to be so directly and
deeply involved in *party* politics. His involvement may, indeed,
have helped to make him unpopular among his colleagues in the
Congregational Union. It is possible, too, that simple jealousy of a
man who had come to occupy a fashionable pulpit and to receive a
good deal of attention from the press and from society in general at
a comparatively early age, also played its part. At all events by late
1906,[9] as his opinions became known and to be reported in the
press, he became the centre of a theological storm reminiscent of
the controversies of the mid-nineteenth century. *The British Weekly*
(and Robertson Nicoll, its editor), unofficial mouthpiece of
Nonconformity, mounted a campaign against him which included
scarcely credible threats of a possible heresy trial. Campbell's
supporters formed themselves into the 'New Theology League'.[10]

The New Theology was actually published in March 1907. It was
not a massive tome but ran to about 75,000 words. It was as much
a defence of Campbell's theological opinions against the attacks
already aimed at him as a positive statement of his beliefs. In spite
of the fact that Campbell asserted in the introduction that the book
was 'not the author's *Apologia pro Vita Sua*', and in spite of its
sometimes acerbic tone, it is manifestly an apologetic work, written
because his friends felt 'that recent criticisms of what has come to
be called the New Theology ought to be dealt with in some
comprehensive and systematic way'.[11]

Campbell claimed that he was motivated by a fear that 'the main
stream of modern life is passing organized religion by'.[12] What he
wanted was 'not to find a remedy which will save the Churches' but
'a driving force which will enable the Churches to fulfil their true
mission of saving the world';[13] and that combination of genuine
concern and sardonic phrasing was typical of his style. It was as

[8] Robbins, 'R. J. Campbell', 271.
[9] Campbell himself dated the outbreak of controversy to Jan. 1907: see R. J.
Campbell, *New Theology Sermons* (London, 1907), p. vii.
[10] Robbins, 'R. J. Campbell', 271.
[11] R. J. Campbell, *The New Theology* (London, 1907), p. v.
[12] Ibid. 11.   [13] Ibid.

though he was determined to demonstrate that he was the *enfant terrible* by making rude gestures at the denominational establishments while insisting, with apparent smugness, on the need for a *real* religion. He was scathing about 'pulpit and theological college religion', perhaps by way of revenge against P. T. Forsyth, who was principal of the theological college at Hackney at the time.[14] Not that Campbell claimed to stand alone: far from it. Part of the trouble was that he insisted that the new theology was, in a sense, the perennial theology, the *true* theology as it really always had been. 'The New Theology', he insisted, 'is an untrammelled return to the Christian sources in the light of modern thought. Its starting point is a re-emphasis of the Christian belief in the Divine immanence in the universe and in mankind.'[15] The divine immanence, he believed, had been too long forgotten and ignored.

But the allies whom Campbell claimed in the contemporary or near-contemporary world were all people whom authority would be inclined to regard as tiresome. In addition to Sabatier, he mentioned George Tyrrell, already in trouble but not yet forbidden to exercise his priesthood.[16] Tyrrell's work, *Through Scylla and Charybdis*, had been published with the subtitle 'The Old Theology and the New'. On the same sort of principle Campbell also cited Albert Wilberforce, Samuel's youngest son who had been born in 1841 and had been appointed archdeacon of Westminster in 1900—an office he was to hold until he was almost 80 years old. Wilberforce was to publish his own volume, called *New Theology*, in the year after Campbell's work appeared. Worse still, Campbell asserted that Ernst Haeckel, the English translation of whose *Welträtsel*, published in 1900, had been the cause of much scandal to the pious, should actually be regarded as one who believed in God. Haeckel, who would himself have been horrified by the assertion, had maintained that God, freedom, and immortality were the foundations upon which irrational superstition was built and which science must destroy. But Campbell thought that every scientist, willy nilly, proclaimed a 'vaster, grander conception of God, by giving us a vaster, grander conception of the universe'.[17]

The truth is that Campbell really believed that God and the universe are identical. The second chapter of his book began with the dramatic sentence 'All religion begins in cosmic emotion.' It

---

[14] Ibid. 9.   [15] Ibid. 4.   [16] Above, pp. 168.
[17] Campbell, *The New Theology*, 17.

then continued, 'It is the recognition of an essential relationship between the human soul and the great whole of things of which it is the outcome and expression.' And, by 'the great whole of things', Campbell meant both the universe and God. In a sense it might be argued that there was some justification for this. After all, if 'universe' means 'everything that exists', and God exists, God must be part of—or the whole of—the universe. As Campbell argued, 'There cannot be two infinities, nor can there be an infinite and also a finite beyond it.'[18] If infinite means that which has no limits, then the infinite *cannot* be limited by the finite; the finite must, so to speak, be comprehended within the infinite. Christian theology has, however, traditionally regarded the transcendence of God to be a matter of who, rather than where, God is. Campbell's understanding of the immanence of God seemed to be simple pantheism.

As one regards the opening chapters of *The New Theology* one begins to feel that one is in the grip of something like a Greek tragedy. Here is the beautiful, eloquent, intelligent hero who moves, as if bent relentlessly on his own destruction, from one disastrous statement to another, making enemies by his claim to be doing something novel *and* by his claim to be true to what is old; by his sarcasm aimed at the establishment *and* by his assertion that he has allies in high places; by his attempts to be true to theology *and* by his desire to identify with science. As he developed his ideas, it was as if he chose to embrace every nineteenth-century school of thought which had already proved to be unproductive. The new theology was almost a death wish on the grandest possible scale.

It is true that Campbell tried to defend himself against the charge of pantheism.

'Pantheism' is a technical term in philosophic parlance, and means something quite different from this. It stands for a Fate-God, a God imprisoned in His universe, a God who cannot help Himself, and does not even know what He is about, a blind force which here breaks out into a rock and there into Ruskin and is equally indifferent to either. But that is not my God. My God is my deeper Self, and yours too; He is the Self of the universe, and knows all about it. He is never baffled, and cannot be baffled; the whole cosmic process is one long incarnation and uprising of the being of God from itself to itself. With Tennyson you can call this doctrine the Higher Pantheism, if you like; but it is the very antithesis of the Pantheism which has played so large a part in the history of thought.[19]

---

[18] Campbell, *The New Theology*, 18.   [19] Ibid. 35.

Campbell's language here has obvious points of similarity with the kind of thing frequently said by the Idealists. T. H. Green had often spoken, half a century earlier, of God as the ideal self, but he had arrived at that concept by another route. He believed that Paul could provide one with a conception of the Christian faith which would not be vulnerable to historical criticism. Paul had not, after all, known the historical Jesus. His understanding of the person of Christ must, therefore, be independent of actual historical fact. What was known, or what might be discovered, about the historical Jesus could not affect the purely theologically conceived Pauline ideas. But Green also maintained that the ideas which he believed he had derived from Paul had to be presented in modern dress for the contemporary world. It was his duty, he thought, to reproduce 'with as much exactness as modern phraseology admits of, and without any conventional use of theological language, the essence of Paul's belief in Christ'.[20] Engaging in this process, for instance, in the matter of the significance of the death and resurrection of Christ, meant that one came to the conclusion that each person had to re-enact in himself the eternal act of God—a death to life and a life out of death—in order to be conformed to the being of God, to whom he is at every point related.

There is a very good instance of Campbell seeming to do precisely what Green advocated in a sermon on 'The Risen Christ', which was included in a volume published in the same year as *The New Theology*. The text is actually taken from Matthew 28: 6, and not from Paul, but Campbell's sermon very quickly became an exposition of 1 Corinthians 15 which showed 'beyond all possibility of doubt that primitive Christian belief centred on the conviction that Jesus was alive and reigning in the world unseen, and that presently He would return to establish his dominion over the kingdoms of the earth'.[21]

But the modern mind balks at the suggestion of an empty tomb, and this suggestion is with most intelligent people held to be the chief difficulty in considering the question today. . . . but I would point out that in my

[20] R. L. Nettleship (ed.), *Works of Thomas Hill Green*, 3 vols., (London, 1886–90), iii. 235. By 'without any conventional use' etc., Green meant that one should not use theological language which has no real significance but pays lip service to convention.

[21] Campbell, *New Theology Sermons*, 18. Internal evidence suggests that these sermons were published earlier than *The New Theology*.

judgement it is impossible to escape the conclusion that the primitive Christians did believe in the empty tomb *simply because they had no conception of an existence apart from the body.* . . . The modern Western mind tends to draw a hard and fast distinction between matter and spirit which did not exist in the minds of the writers of the New Testament.[22]

There follows a lengthy passage in which Campbell attempts to describe the way that people living in the Mediterranean world in the first century might have conceived the universe. It was the three-decker universe which Bultmann was also to ascribe to the New Testament writers.[23]

To them heaven was quite near, just above the sky; and they did not think of the sky as being much further away than an arrow could shoot. . . . They thought of heaven as a bright and glorious abode, a mile or two up above the surface of the earth, with everything in it just as real and concrete as things down here. To pass from one world to the other did not mean laying aside the body; it was simply a transition from one place to another.[24]

. . . such a view of the universe naturally made the primitive Christians attach great importance to the idea of a physical resurrection. They believed that when men died their souls went down into Hades . . . and that these souls were helpless until they got back into the body again . . . The kind of heaven to which they looked forward, therefore, was the restoration of the soul to the body. The body had then to become glorified—that is, made beautiful—and endowed with immortality, like the angels in heaven. . . . What the Galilean disciples of Jesus expected Him to do before he was crucified was to bring about an ideal existence on earth. Apparently they thought that when this ideal existence came no one would have to die any more. When He died Himself . . . they were thoroughly overwhelmed with despair . . . when they heard that He had risen again, those hopes not only returned with greater intensity, but became certainties. It is no use discussing whether they believed in the empty tomb or not . . . they had to believe in the empty tomb.[25]

In order to give a more or less complete picture of what he thought was the actual case, one needs to add that in a later section of the sermon Campbell explained that he was convinced that the belief in the empty tomb was not simply the consequence of this necessity.

---

[22] Campbell, *New Theology Sermons*, 19.
[23] e.g. in 'New Testament and Mythology', in H. W. Bartsch (ed.), *Kerrygma and Myth: A Theological Debate* (trans. R. H. Fuller, London, 1972), 1.
[24] Campbell, *New Theology Sermons*, 20. [25] Ibid. 21 f.

They really must have seen Jesus. I do not care in what way you try to account for their belief. You may hold that they saw a spirit, or that they were subject to hallucination, but it is hardly possible for any one to deny that these simple men and women were firmly convinced that they had seen Jesus.[26]

Leaving aside the question whether Campbell had confused Greek and Hebrew ideas or misrepresented what Paul was really saying about 'psychic' and spiritual bodies in 1 Corinthians 15, he does seem to have been *trying* to give an account of what the New Testament writers intended in other than conventional theological language. He was not willing to follow the Idealists in their attempt to protect Christian ideas from criticism by detaching them from history. And yet the conclusions to which his consideration of the resurrection led were not very different from those of Green. Another sermon in the same volume is actually called 'From Death to Life'. It works its way towards the final peroration in language which seems to be an elaboration of Green's idea that the Christian life was a re-enactment, in oneself, of the eternal act of God—a death to life and a life out of death—in order to be conformed to the being of God, to whom one is at every point related.

Here it is, this secret of eternal life—the hardest thing in the world, young men, and yet the easiest. Live for impersonal ends, and trust yourself to God. It is a glorious life! Let your life flow out to all mankind and, if need be, be prepared to suffer; but the suffering cannot kill your joy; it is the joy that no man taketh from you, the need of Him 'who for the joy that was set before Him endured the cross, despising the shame.' This joy is God's free gift to you and to all who try to live the ageless life. Just as selfishness leads to the death of all worth having, so love leads to more and ever more abundant life. . . . That young fellow on the threshold of manhood knows it as the vision flashes upon him that to live for pleasure or success is mean and ignoble, while to live for ideals, the full fruition of which he will never live to see, is alone worthy of one who walks the same earth as Jesus. As he lifts his face to the stars, his heart thrills with a new sense of gladness and power. It came from God, and it is God; it is the life eternal. Yes, this is the life that is life indeed, and the more closely it is lived to Jesus the greater our grasp upon eternity.[27]

In practice Campbell's combination of Liberal Protestantism with Idealism produced a curious effect. He handled all questions

[26] Ibid. 23.   [27] Ibid. 130 f.

of the relationship between theology and history in the same way. First of all, he would take the conventional orthodoxy apart, critically, explaining why he could not accept as historical most of the more spectacular events in the traditional story. Then he would assert that, in a sense, this did not matter. His beliefs, he would claim, preserved everything that was important in orthodoxy and were more effective than orthodoxy in inspiring a real and sincere Christian life. So, in Christology he maintained that 'I believe what the creeds say about the person of Jesus, but I believe it in a way that puts no gulf between Him and the rest of the human race.'[28] In hard concrete terms, this meant that he regarded the classical theological statement of the divinity of Christ as 'incredible'. He maintained, in fact, that deity, divinity, and humanity were fundamentally and essentially the same thing but could be arranged in a descending order—deity, divinity, humanity. In short, deity was the 'all-controlling consciousness of the universe'; divinity described its characteristics like love; humanity shared in those characteristics. In the new higher pantheism, of course, everything could be described as sharing in the divine but, as Campbell pointed out, 'it can hardly be seriously contended that a crocodile is as much an expression of God as General Booth'.[29] What distinguished General Booth from the crocodile was that he was divine in so far as the love of God was the governing principle of his life. Therefore, Campbell argued—explicitly denying any kind of two-natures Christology—in Jesus, who was never governed by any other principle, 'humanity was Divinity'.[30] The humanity of Jesus, however, was never radically different from the humanity of others; and that is why other human beings can imitate Christ, become conformed to his will, and participate in his life.

Campbell anticipated the rejoinder of the orthodox. 'But you make Him only a man! No, reader, I do not. I make Him the only Man—and there is a difference. We have only seen perfect manhood once, and that was the manhood of Jesus. The rest of us have got to get there.'[31]

The historical Jesus for whom Campbell was searching was, essentially, the historical Jesus of all Liberal Protestantism; but the reality which that historical Jesus represented was the Idealist's

[28] Campbell, *The New Theology*, 72.   [29] Ibid. 75.
[30] Ibid. 76.   [31] Ibid. 77.

universal mind, described in a way that restated orthodox theology in terms of an 'eternal truth', realizable in the life of every Christian. Edward Caird was fond of saying, at this period, that Idealism needed to be 'materialized and socialized' by being earthed in 'the round of duties that seem commonplace and secular,—these family ties, this college companionship, these professional occupations of law, or education, or commerce, these civic and political relations'. The ideal world, he maintained, was 'our own world given back again, item by item, with all the elements that constitute it multiplied a hundred-fold in value, raised to a spiritual power'.[32] Campbell seems to have been trying to do exactly the same sort of thing. It should come as no surprise, therefore, to find him saying that, if one wanted a concrete manifestation of the atonement, one should go to the House of Commons and listen to Keir Hardie's pleas for justice.[33]

In fact Campbell devoted a considerable part of his book to the atonement. No fewer than three chapters are given over to this one doctrinal issue. And inevitably, like all the liberals before him, Campbell launched an attack on the conventional understanding of the doctrine, the penal substitutionary theory. He characterized it as follows:

It was the dying of the death that was the all-important thing. It was in consideration of this death that God agreed to pardon sin. Jesus was put to death because God had arranged that He should be put to death, and because Jesus was willing to be put to death, in order that a satisfactory offering might be made to Divine justice for the sins of the world. God had to punish someone before He could be free to forgive his erring children, and therefore, with the consent of Jesus, He punished Him.[34]

This is a somewhat caricatured account of the conventional view, of course, and in a sense Campbell admitted it to be so; but he wished to demonstrate how unethical were the implications, as he saw them, of that understanding of the atonement.

His own view of the connection between the death of Jesus and the overcoming of human sinfulness went something as follows. Jesus's death was simply a judicial murder, a consequence of human wickedness. What made it different from other noble deaths was the complete innocence, the utter goodness of the murdered

[32] E. Caird, *Lay Sermons and Addresses delivered in the Hall of Balliol College, Oxford* (Glasgow, 1907), 70 f. and see above, p. 132.
[33] Campbell, *The New Theology*, 173.   [34] Ibid. 114 f.

person. The only sense in which it could be said to be the plan and work of God was that God did not intervene to save Jesus. On the cross the perfect love of Jesus fought the 'perfect hate' of his enemies, and overcame it by enduring it all, and remaining untainted by evil. Because of the completeness of the sacrificial self-offering of Calvary, the life and death of Jesus have become a moral force and a spiritual dynamic greater than any other. Far more, Campbell thought, came out of the tomb than went into it[35]— though not, presumably, Christ's body.

Between this account of what he believed the actual atoning work of Christ to be, and his claim that to see the atonement in operation in his own day one ought to listen to Keir Hardie in Parliament, was a chapter considering Semitic ideas of atonement, the essence of which, he thought, was the solidarity of humanity with God and of human beings with each other. A further chapter examined the history of the doctrine with a very brief survey of Patristic beliefs, Anselm's theory, and the ideas of the Reformers. Modern Evangelical theology, Campbell asserted, had demonstrated the impossibility of all these theories but had utterly failed to put anything more convincing in their place.[36] His own account of what he thought would be a more satisfactory explanation was muddied by the necessity he seems to have felt to go over again some aspects of the argument he had had with contributors to *The British Weekly* about the nature of sin.[37] When it finally emerged, it seemed to consist of a belief that 'Vicarious suffering willingly accepted becomes irresistible in the long run as a means of lifting a transgressor out of the mire of selfishness'. 'All that love can do is to share to the uttermost in the painful consequences of sin, and by doing so to break their power.'[38] He came, thus, to specific examples of situations 'where the spirit of self-sacrificing love is trying to do anything to supply a need or save a transgressor'. There, he believed, you see the atonement.[39]

There can be little doubt that Campbell's attempt to devise a 'contemporary' Christianity was an unsatisfactory one. All too often he was doing little more than fall back into a Liberal Protestant position, which had already been proved untenable. He frequently made the same error as Jowett, of ignoring the long

---

[35] Campbell, *The New Theology*, 126. [36] Ibid. 145.

[37] Campbell had said that even sin was, in a sense, 'a quest for God'.

[38] Campbell, *The New Theology*, 168 f. [39] Ibid. 172 f.

passage of tradition between the New Testament and his own time. In this he was typically Liberal Protestant, assuming that all that needed to be done was to ask oneself, 'if men who lived then expressed it like this, how should we have to express the same thing in our own day?' It is extraordinary that this simplistic view, so often exposed as inadequate, remained so tough and so tenacious. It is as if no amount of demonstration could prove to its exponents that it was fruitless until Schweizer's final destruction of the quest of the historical Jesus (the English translation of whose work was not published till 1910).[40]

In a sense, of course, Campbell was combining this Liberal Protestant methodology with that of the Idealists. His technique seems, on the face of it, much more historical than T. H. Green's, because his 'demythologizing' seems to be related to an understanding of the historical context in which the New Testament was written. When discussing the resurrection, Green ignored any possible link between Paul and the earliest Christian tradition so that he could assume that Paul's teaching about Christ was the product of pure theological thought, unaffected by historical event. Campbell, in undertaking his apparently careful and thorough reconstruction of the thought world of the New Testament writers, opened the history to critical examination and related Matthew's gospel to the Pauline tradition. But he was, in reality, every bit as cavalier with history as Green. If he is compared with Edward Caird, whose works he was reading at this time and under whose influence he was supposed to be, then it is quite clear that he had not learnt anything of Caird's later views, as expounded to the Oxford Society of Historical Theology.[41]

The publication of *The New Theology* did not, of course, end the controversy. If Campbell had ever hoped that clarifying precisely what he really believed would stifle the critics, then he was incredibly naïve. Whenever he claimed to be perfectly orthodox, though perhaps unusual, in the manner in which he interpreted the central tenets of Christianity, his formulations were more likely to enhance than to allay alarm. His sermon on the resurrection, which suggested that the appearances of the risen Christ recorded in the gospels might have been a ghost or a hallucination, would seem gratuitously blasphemous. The attacks on him continued and,

[40] Below, p. 231.   [41] Above, p. 143 ff.

indeed, grew sharper and more widespread. Later, in 1907, a group of Congregational ministers, Campbell's colleagues, contributed to a volume edited by C. H. Vine called *The Old Faith and the New Theology*. The contributors included the principals of the colleges at Bradford (Simon), Manchester (Adeney), and New College, London (Pryce), besides Forsyth of Hackney. All except four of them were doctors of divinity and they included R. F. Horton, who had been the most eminent of Free Church personalities in Oxford before the arrival of Fairbairn. In spite of the indubitably heavyweight nature of the contributors, the style of the essays was popular and appropriate to the pulpit, rather than technical and theological. They were probably aimed at ministers in local pastorates and were calculated to frighten them off Campbell's approach to Christianity.

Perhaps the most distinguished of the essayists was P. T. Forsyth, with whom Campbell had already exchanged sarcastic remarks.[42] His essay directly addressed the question of the differences between the presence of God in man, presupposed in the Idealists' concept of immanence, and that of the traditional doctrine of incarnation.[43] Both Forsyth himself and the editor of the volume were insistent that the criticisms contained in it were 'not at all in the nature of a personal attack on the Rev. R. J. Campbell'.[44] They were, rather, as Forsyth put it, criticisms of a whole school which was chiefly to be found in Germany.[45] Whether this was deliberately intended or not, the disclaimer allowed the contributors to deliver all manner of fairly vituperative attacks on the new theology while protecting themselves, at the same time, from any charge of unfairness. If it could be shown that Campbell did not deserve any particular criticism, his opponents could respond that, at that point, they had been attacking—not him but—some unspecified German. On the other hand, if no such complaint was made, then the Free Church public would certainly assume that the criticism applied to Campbell himself.

Forsyth's essay began with an attempt to devalue the whole immanentist approach. Immanence was, he insisted rather

---

[42] Above, p. 201 and 203.
[43] P. T. Forsyth, 'Immanence and Incarnation', in C. H. Vine (ed.), *The Old Faith and the New Theology: A Series of Sermons and Essays on some of the Truths held by Evangelical Christians, and the difficulties of accepting much of what is called the 'New Theology'* (London, 1907), 47–61.   [44] Ibid. p. v.
[45] Ibid. 41.

pompously, 'not even a theologoumen, but rather a philosopheme', in other words it was part of the preacher's mental furniture, contributed by his cultural context, rather than of his religion or his vocation. 'Its influence for thought has been great, for theology, but indirect, and for saving faith nothing.'[46] The heart of his attack on Campbell's theology was as follows:

The doctrine of immanence, taken alone, means, further, that in this process of spiritual evolution every religion has its place, and Christ's place is but on the summit, and on the summit only up till now. As we progress His place may be, probably will be, taken by another. For whereas the theology of the Gospel teaches us that the whole Trinity was involved in revelation and redemption, this theory teaches that the whole and final Godhead was not acting in Christ. You cannot expect the finality of what is merely an evolving series in its middle, but only at its close, which is still far away. God, it believes, has yet more light and truth to break out of our holy race than that contained in Christ. . . . So in Christ we have neither final revelation, absolute guilt, human dignity nor eternal salvation. All is flattened, diluted, and dispowered. And the cross is but in the nature of things. It is somewhere in the suburbs of Godhead, and not at its centre. Sin, therefore, does not go to God's heart. It does not sting Him mortally. It is not death to God, but a negative factor in his scheme. It does not challenge and kill what makes God God. It does not raise the last issue of humanity, and it does not elicit the last resource of God. It lives in the region of idyll and high-class melodrama. Guilt is not the tragedy of the universe. And indeed wise men do not take things tragically at all. And so they lived happy ever after.[47]

That Forsyth should be so bitterly opposed to the tendency of immanentist theology to make all the crucial (often literally crucial) facts and beliefs of Christianity into mere symbols of the way things are, is not surprising. He had himself, been an enthusiastic disciple of Hegelianism earlier in his career and his criticisms were an expression of the disillusionment of a disenchanted convert. It had come to seem to Forsyth that Hegelian immanentist thought had nothing to offer by way of an answer either to human sinfulness in general or to specific sins. Within the next three years he was to publish *The Cruciality of the Cross*, *The Person and Place of Jesus Christ* and *The Work of Christ*. These works were to set out his understanding of the incarnation and atonement, and what were later to be the central ideas of the books can be discovered in

---

[46] Ibid. 47 f.   [47] Ibid. 51 f.

embryo in his article. His was not a desperate, reactionary return to an older orthodoxy but an imaginative attempt to restate the doctrines of incarnation and atonement. And there was a kind of robustness about his rejection of Campbell's new theology which made it look pallid and temporizing. 'It was no theology of immanence', Forsyth declared, 'that uttered the bold, old cry, O *felix culpa!* O blessed sin, that brought thrice blessed God for its radical damnation.'[48]

Forsyth's attack on the new theology's version of the atonement is actually very unfair to Campbell, whose instances of atonement were really only illustrations of how suffering and caring were capable of lifting someone else out of a state of degradation.[49] He had, however, redefined the concept of satisfaction by saying that the only sense in which the death of Jesus could be a satisfaction to the Father was in the sense that it gives an artist satisfaction to express himself in his artistic creation. In that sense, Campbell asked rhetorically, 'surely the highest satisfaction that God can know must be His self-expression in the self-sacrifice of His children'.[50] That gave Forsyth the opportunity to attack:

It is very curious to note how the critics of an Atonement, as something offered to God (who, they say, needs no such thing) continue in principle that old fallacy. It only shows how little they work principles out. They translate Atonement simply as something offered for saving purposes by man to man. But it is still offered by man. What they do not seem to know is that in a theology of grace, *i.e.* in Christianity, Atonement has meaning and value only as offered by God to Himself.[51]

Forsyth was exaggerating, for polemical purposes, the point Campbell was making. He also exaggerated—and for the same reason, or so it seems in retrospect—the significance of the new theology itself. For he was prepared to go so far as to assert that the contemporary conflict in the Church made the central issues of the Reformation seem insignificant in comparison and was 'more critical for Christianity than any that has arisen since the second century'. The reference to the second century was quite deliberate, for Forsyth actually believed—or said that he believed—that the

---

[48] P. T. Forsyth, 'Immanence and Incarnation', 55.
[49] Campbell, *The New Theology*, 168 ff. [50] Ibid. 175.
[51] C. H. Vine (ed.), *The Old Faith and the New Theology*, 56. The last sentence of the passage quoted was, in fact, to be the theme of Forsyth's *The Work of Christ*, published in 1910.

new theology was Gnosticism revived. This conclusion was not really justifiable. The new theology was not dualist, as Gnosticism was, nor did it claim to offer a way of escape to spiritual beings imprisoned in an evil and material world. But Forsyth felt himself to be justified in taking this line because he believed that, like Gnosticism, the new theology sought to abandon the whole historical character of Christianity. In its place it offered a non-historical idealism. One was, he claimed, confronted by two quite different religions, not variants of the same religion. Whichever of them triumphed, it would mean the death of the other.

The eternal ideal Christ is a divine principle quite separable from its classic instance—the personality of the historic Jesus. The reproduction today of the second-century Gnosticism is extremely close, and often startling. There are the same vague speculations, often able, but often also of a pseudo-philosophic and dilettantist kind, welcome to connoisseurs of religion and amateurs of thought [a footnote says 'I mean among the laity.'] rather than to men of faith and due knowledge. There is the same etherealized conception of matter, the same amalgam of physics and dreams, the same animus against historic Christianity.[52]

For a while British theological circles seemed to share Forsyth's assessment of the significance of the controversy. The new theology was the subject of a very great many sermons, lectures, articles, and books. It was the dominant religious question in England in 1907, while the pope issued his encyclical *Pascendi Gregis* against modernism in the Roman Catholic Church, Edward VII set about fostering cordial relations with France, and Baden-Powell founded the Boy Scout movement. Among those who felt that it was an issue important enough to devote his attention to was Charles Gore, by this time Bishop of Birmingham. Before the year was out he had published a volume of lectures and sermons under the title *The New Theology and the Old Religion*. The new theology, he said, was important in that it 'fastened upon certain tendencies of thought which have been long at work amongst us, and brought them forward into the arena of common and popular discussion'.[53] Gore planned to demonstrate, in equally popular terms, the 'incongruity' between the new theology and the truth revealed in Christ.

[52] Ibid. 57 f.
[53] C. Gore, *The New Theology and the Old Religion* (London, 1907), p. vii.

One of the unusual features of the debate is that both Forsyth and Gore had themselves been influenced by the thought of the Idealists: Forsyth by Hegelianism and Gore by the ideas of T. H. Green.[54] They were both, therefore, in a peculiarly good position to judge how far it was possible to combine Idealism with traditional Christianity, and, in a sense, Gore's Anglo-Catholic criticisms of the new theology were not very different from those of the Congregationalist Forsyth. Gore, however, was able to take a more sympathetic line. He recognized the representative character of many of Campbell's ideas (and diverted some of the critical attention from Campbell himself by asserting that there was 'no manual which exhibits [the new theology] in so favourable a light' as *The Substance of Faith allied with Science* by the leading spiritualist Sir Oliver Lodge).[55] Gore's tribute to Lodge's 'favourable' treatment of the new theology need not be taken as ironic or even as an empty formality, and the respect was apparently returned. Lodge once said to Gore 'that the lives of many are better for the work and example of the first Bishop of Birmingham, that the services rendered to humanity will live long in the minds and hearts of the citizens, and that your friendship to the people will not readily be forgotten'.[56]

A subordinate theme of *The New Theology and the Old Religion* became prominent in the last of the sermons, 'The church and the poor', and there was an appendix to the book which consisted of the report of a joint committee of the upper and lower houses of the Convocation of Canterbury on 'The Moral Witness of the Church on Economic Subjects'. Gore's sympathy with those social and political concerns which were also so very important to Campbell occupied a surprisingly significant place in the volume.

Moreover Gore refused to act merely defensively in relation to many of the features of the new theology. He was able to recognize that there *were* a substantial number of people who were alienated by conventional Christianity and its divisions, by the worldliness of many of the supposedly orthodox, and by the

[54] Above, pp. 120 f.

[55] Gore, *The New Theology and the Old Religion*, 10. In the actual text of the lectures, Gore referred almost as often to Lodge as to Campbell.

[56] S. A. King, *Charles Gore, the Founder of the See and First Bishop of Birmingham, 1905–1911*, printed version of a public lecture given in Birmingham in 1945, p. 2. Gore had been consecrated bishop of Worcester in 1902, and chose to become bishop of Birmingham when the diocese was divided three years later.

Churches' failure to do anything about the moral and social degradation of the masses. 'A great many men, that is to say, disbelieve in current Christianity because they desire something more like Jesus Christ.'[57] In this, and in his admission that many of the fervently pious added to the prevailing scepticism by their frightened refusal to allow open discussion or free enquiry, he must have seemed to Campbell and his friends to be much more sympathetic than the typical exponents of 'theological college Christianity'. Gore was also, of course, terrifyingly well read, and in radical and modern works as well as in the Christian classics. A good deal of the first of his lectures reads almost as if he were showing off the breadth of his acquaintance with everyone from Oliver Lodge to Adolf von Harnack, from the French poet Verlaine to the English biologist Romanes.[58]

The essence of the 'old religion', which Gore believed to be so different from the new religion, seems to have consisted, in his view, of two things, humanity's need for God and God's corresponding revelation of himself. For Gore, the classic opponent of this true Christianity was not Gnosticism but Arianism.[59] Characteristically, he came to fasten upon Arianism not by looking, as Forsyth had done, for the most diametrically opposed enemy of Christianity—the challenger which was not a variant of the same religion but an entirely alien and contradictory religion. Gore believed Arianism was the great enemy because it was in opposition to Arianism that the creeds had been fashioned to summarize the revelation of God in Jesus Christ. 'These creeds', he said, 'I propose to take as the classical expression of the catholic religion, having supreme authority among Christian statements of our faith.'[60]

On the surface, Gore's particular veneration for the creeds seems somewhat illogical. He was prepared, it seemed, to permit a critical consideration of the Scriptures but would not countenance the slightest divergence from the strict letter of the creeds. And yet, if the creeds have any authority it must derive from the Scriptures which the creeds, as it were, summarize. The apparent paradox arose from Gore's belief that the Scriptures must be interpreted not

---

[57] Gore, *The New Theology and the Old Religion*, 3.
[58] For the links between Gore and Romanes see P. Hinchliff, *Benjamin Jowett and the Christian Religion* (London, 1987), 200 and 208.
[59] Gore, *The New Theology and the Old Religion*, 38 f.
[60] Ibid. 40.

as though they had been just 'dug out of the Syrian sand',[61] but within the tradition of the Church's continuing understanding of them. The creeds were sacrosanct because they enshrined the early Church's interpretation of the New Testament.[62] It is not surprising then, to find the creeds playing a central role in Gore's attempt to answer the new theology. He claimed that he was simply restating the 'old religion', the revelation of God in Jesus Christ, to which the New Testament is the ultimate witness. *This* religion needed no protection against Campbell's attack for he was really attacking something else.

The book consisted of a course of lectures delivered in Birmingham Cathedral during Lent 1907. They were delivered at midday, were fairly brief, and, like the collection edited by Vine, were popular rather than academic. To the lectures Gore added five sermons, the first two of which were 'The creed and the common life' and 'The permanent creed'. There is not a great deal in the book which is original or startling. Much of it consists of taking the traditional ideas which the new theology had attacked and explaining that they did not really mean what Campbell and his allies had thought that they meant. On the question of the immanence or transcendence of God, for instance, Gore said:

The Christian conception of God in fact holds a middle point between Deism, against which the New Theology is in somewhat violent reaction, and Pantheism, into which in its reaction it undoubtedly plunges. The New Theology is in reaction against what it describes as 'the old idea of God'— as if He were some great emperor who sits somewhere outside and above the world, who made it and set it going and occasionally intervenes to set it right again. This, which has been well called 'the carpenter idea' of God, is in fact not the old idea, if by that is meant the orthodox or scriptural idea. It is a gross distortion of it. . . . For the Christian God is in the world in all its parts and at every moment, revealing Himself in varying degrees in all its force, and order, and beauty, and truth, and goodness. But the universe does not exhaust Him or limit Him.[63]

One of the most interesting features of the volume was the lecture which dealt with 'The Atonement and the Inspiration of Scripture'. The very combination of the two subjects is interesting in view of the fact that so many of the liberals who first adopted a critical

---

[61] C. Gore, *Can We Then Believe* (London, 1926), 132.
[62] Above, p. 121.
[63] Gore, *The New Theology and the Old Religion*, 56 f.

approach to the Bible were equally determined to break free from
the prevailing penal substitutionary theology of the atonement.
Gore did not link the two themes in that sense. The common
feature which he detected in them was the fact that the tradition
had never given either of them 'a definite form in any authoritative
creed' which he thought to reflect 'a true instinct which caused the
catholic church to define its faith in terms of the doctrine of God
and the person of Christ, and to leave the belief in Christ's
atonement and the inspiration of Scripture undefined'.[64]

Gore believed, in fact, that it was possible, without defining the
undefined, to present a 'New Testament' idea of the atonement
which could be shown to follow inevitably from the fundamental
doctrines of God and Christ which *had* been defined. 'Christians,
from the very first,' he said, 'saw in Christ's death not only a crime
on the part of His murderers, but also on His part a voluntary
sacrifice, and a sacrifice by which their redemption had been
won.'[65]

... the Christian idea of atonement is bound up with the idea of Christ's
redemptive work as, first of all, a work done *for* us, without any co-
operation on our part; but that, on the other hand, the safeguarding of this
doctrine from moral abuse lies in the recognition that the work of Christ
for us is only the prelude to His work *in* us: that it is Christ in us, the
immanent Christ, which is 'the hope of glory'.[66]

The Christ *for* us and the Christ *in* us Gore called the 'two
complementary half-truths' which had to be held together by the
sacramental system. There was, he insisted, absolutely no evidence
at all in the New Testament for belief in vicarious punishment.

In the years since the publication of *Lux Mundi* Gore's views on
the inspiration of Scripture had evidently not changed.[67] He still
maintained the distinction between the spiritual truth guaranteed
by divine inspiration and the apparently fallible vehicle in which the
truth was contained. He thought that 'The Christian believer will
not hesitate to recognize in the early chapters of Genesis narratives
which are not historical, but gives us "doctrines in the form of a
story" '. Such a reader would not be shocked to find in the Old

---

[64] Ibid. 131 f.
[65] Ibid. 133. Campbell had maintained that the death of Christ was a judicial
murder rather than a divine act, above, p. 209.   [66] Ibid. 144.
[67] Above, pp. 116 f.

Testament legend, moral tales, or what Gore called 'poetical history', as well as history proper. 'For all these', he said, 'can be vehicles of the spiritual instruction of a nation.'[68]

He was far less radical with the New Testament, just as he had been in *Lux Mundi*, saying only:

[The Christian] will find the best reason for believing that the Holy Spirit did guide the apostolic writers 'into all the truth' about Christ. He need not believe that there are no mistakes or inaccuracies in the New Testament narratives; but he will recognize that we have there, when we judge the narratives simply as historical documents, trustworthy historical material; and in the spirit which animated the writers he will see the Spirit of truth.[69]

It was, he thought, a matter for thanksgiving that the Church was not tied to a doctrine of the infallibility of Scripture.

The most vulnerable point in Gore's position was, in fact, his oft-repeated assertion that there was a general historical trustworthiness about the New Testament records. The strength of his argument lay in the fact that he insisted that the Christian faith possesses its own history, which cannot be ignored and which is really a kind of witness to the truth of Christianity because it is a practical demonstration of the right way of believing. That insistence must have seemed attractive to anyone who became disenchanted with attempts to leapfrog over tradition, in order to come face to face with the historical Jesus.

It is tempting to believe that, if there had been a battle for Campbell's soul between Gore and Fairbairn in his undergraduate days, there was an even grander battle for his soul in the years after the publication of *The New Theology*. If there was, and if Forsyth was the protagonist replacing Fairbairn, then it was a battle Gore won. But perhaps the pressure upon Campbell was more diffuse than the image of a battle between Gore and Forsyth suggests. Attacks continued to come upon him from various quarters for some three years and they included threats to have him removed from the ministry. The pressure slowly became intolerable. By the outbreak of the First World War in August 1914 the controversy had virtually faded from the headlines anyway and Campbell had more or less made up his mind to become an Anglican. He quarrelled with the laymen who ran the affairs of the City Temple, resigned his ministry there, and recalled *The New Theology* in

[68] Gore, *The New Theology and the Old Religion*, 146.   [69] Ibid. 149.

1915. In the following year he was ordained to the ministry of the Church of England and became a curate of the cathedral in Birmingham.

It is very difficult to discover precisely how important a part Gore played in this 'conversion' of Campbell, though he received him into the Church of England on 15 October 1915.[70] Gore had, however, moved to become Bishop of Oxford in 1911, so Campbell's appointment to Birmingham Cathedral was not directly Gore's doing. But, in view of the moderately Anglo-Catholic theology Campbell was to hold in the future, it is difficult to believe that Gore's rejoinder to *The New Theology* played no part in the change of mind. Again, it must be pure speculation whether it was Gore's more temperate criticisms of the new theology, his sympathetic treatment of some of Campbell's ideas, their shared interest in politics, or the pull of their earlier association in Oxford, which was responsible for this.

An unusual feature of Campbell's 'conversion' to the Church of England is that it affected the apparent foundation upon which his faith was built, rather than the faith itself. He was not disillusioned with Christ, with Christianity, or with its application to the world. It was the particular underpinning in the New Theology, which he had created for it, which he abandoned, as if it no longer worked for him. But he did not cease to believe; he was as fully committed as ever; the underpinning was now provided by the classically traditional theology of the Anglo-Catholicism of men like Gore. That it was socially concerned, and that it was partly shaped by the Idealism of T. H. Green, may have made the transition easier. Campbell was still a passionate believer but he was no longer a zealot nor a disturber of the peace.

There is a something of an air of anticlimax about his long life as an Anglican priest. It would seem that those who shaped his career in the Church of England were hoping to re-create the magic of his early Congregational ministry. He seems deliberately to have been sent back over old ground, was vicar of Christchurch, Westminster from 1917 to 1921, and priest in charge of Holy Trinity, Brighton from 1924 to 1930. In neither parish did he display anything like the drawing power of his early days in Brighton and the City Temple. He never attempted any further essays in the restatement

---

[70] Robbins, 'R. J. Campbell', 275.

of Christian doctrine and he eliminated all mention of *The New Theology* from his entry in works of reference. This is not to say that he gave up academic things altogether. He took his DD at Oxford in 1919 and wrote popular biographies of Arnold and Livingstone during the years he spent in parish work. Some largely devotional books appeared a little later, when he was a canon of Chichester Cathedral between 1930 and 1946, and during that period he taught theology at both the training college and the theological college there. He died in 1956 at the age of 89, having spent forty unspectacular but useful years as an Anglican priest.

A MAN FOR ALL FASHIONS:
Pre-War Theology and B. H. Streeter

DISILLUSIONMENT is really the key theme of the Campbell story and not simply because Campbell reacted, in the end, against the optimism of both Liberal Protestantism and Idealism. P. T. Forsyth, Campbell's bitterest critic, was himself a convert from the Idealist camp. He had come to realize that the reductionism of much contemporary theology was powerless to cope with the human condition. Gore, too, had perceived that the superficial attractions of supposedly modern ideas needed the ballast that only traditional truth could supply. Campbell's disillusionment, though, was probably the most profound. He had been gripped by the splendour of the Idealists' assertion that the material was the mental, and that the mental was the spiritual, and by their belief that God and the universe were alike 'the great whole of things'.[1] When the vision failed; when it became clear that there were important aspects of the Christian tradition which could not be presented in an Idealist version of Christianity, he abandoned his 'new' theology. But his was not the only novelty in theological thinking in the early part of the twentieth century. Those years seemed to be the graveyard of many hopes for a redesigned and revitalized religion in tune with modern minds; they were also a time when new insights revolutionized the way in which scholars looked at the historical sources on which Christian faith was founded.

The generation that had been born as the last quarter of the nineteenth century began, the generation that was just a few years younger than Campbell's, produced a great many distinguished theologians in Britain. In the period between 1900 and the outbreak of the First World War they were therefore in their thirties and, for the most part, just beginning to make a reputation for themselves. Of them all, perhaps, Burnett Hillman Streeter searched most vigorously for the new and reinvigorating ideas. He also

[1] Above, p. 203 f.

perfectly exemplified the intellectual person, the principal events of whose biography take place in the mind and not in the external world.

Streeter was born in 1874. From the moment he began his undergraduate career, almost the whole of his adult life was lived in a single academic institution, The Queen's College, Oxford. He was an undergraduate there and then—after a brief period as a fellow of another college—fellow and tutor from 1905 to 1933. In that year, at a time when it was already unusual for a clergyman and theologian to be the head of an ordinary Oxford college, he became provost and remained in that post until he was killed in a flying accident in Switzerland in 1937. His ideas, and how they changed or failed to change, are what is interesting about his life. He managed to find the time to participate in almost every movement concerned with religion or theology—ecumenism, relations with other religions, the Modern Churchmen's Union, and, in his last years, the Oxford Group movement of Frank Buchman. No doubt he was caught up in the rivalries, the points-scoring, and the peripheral plottings of collegiate life, but the First World War was, so far as his writing and publishing were concerned, an interruption of a very productive period in his life.

Around the turn of the century the records of the Oxford Society of Historical Theology reveal just how many of what were to become new theological schools, trends, and fashions were being initiated at this period. A number of younger English scholars were beginning to lay the foundations of great reputations. On 26 May 1892 Hastings Rashdall, then 34, delivered a paper entitled 'A note on Medieval theology'. Three years later he was to publish his monumental history of medieval European universities and then, in 1915, deliver his Bampton Lectures on *The Idea of Atonement in Christian Theology*, a vigorous assertion of a subjective theology modelled on Abelardian ideas. On 26 November 1896 F. C. Conybeare, a man who made several revolutionary discoveries of Armenian manuscripts (and used them to make rationalist attacks upon Christianity), spoke on 'A newly found Paulician prayer book and catechism'. W. R. Inge, who was to become dean of St Paul's and an authority on mysticism, read a paper on 'Permanent influence of neo-Platonism on Christianity' on 2 December 1897. The 28-year-old Kirsopp Lake, who was to be a well-known, if controversial, figure in New Testament studies in the 1920s and an expert on Greek manuscripts, gave the society 'Notes on a recent visit to Mount Athos and some manuscripts there' on 26 October 1899. Another talk which threw similar long shadows, though its author was no longer a young man, was that of R. H. Charles on 5 November 1908, on 'History of the interpretation of the New Testament Apocalypse'. Charles was an Irishman who became archdeacon of Westminster in 1919, by which time he was already being recognized as the greatest living authority in Britain on Jewish apocalyptic writings. Streeter himself delivered a paper on 'Special characteristics of Q and the Synoptic Gospels' on 28 January 1909.[2]

Streeter's paper appeared, in a slightly extended form, as 'The Literary Evolution of the Gospels', in a volume edited by William Sanday and called *Oxford Studies in the Synoptic Problem*. Reading it now is to be made aware of the transitional nature of those years in the pre-World War twentieth century. In some ways Streeter's arguments clearly belong to the world of 'modern' New Testament scholarship compared with what Jowett, or even Westcott, Lightfoot, or Hort might have said. On the other hand, some of his assertions strike one as being curiously quaint or dated. In essence this paper argued that the gospels took shape in three distinct stages. The first was Q, which was intended to supplement a vigorous oral tradition, which—Streeter argued—accounted for the fact that it contained no passion narrative. Next came Mark's gospel which was, conversely, intended to supplement Q as the oral tradition began to fade, and therefore it contained little teaching. (At this date Streeter believed that Mark could be shown to have quoted from Q, but probably only from memory, not directly from a written text.) Finally there was a 'sub-apostolic' stage, the gospels of Matthew and Luke, which aimed at being complete and self-contained because they were intended to supersede both the oral tradition and the earlier written documents.[3]

Sanday himself seems to stand over the younger men of Streeter's generation like a protective colossus. Everyone seems to have been at one time or another Sanday's pupil and most of them claimed to have derived their own views from him, however much they differed among themselves.[4] Commenting on the way in which

---

[2] *Abstract of the Proceedings of the Oxford Society of Historical Theology, passim.*   [3] Ibid. 28 Jan. 1909, p. 37 f.   [4] Below, p. 243 f.

Sanday encouraged a whole generation of younger scholars, after a period when theology at Oxford had been rather in the doldrums as compared with the Cambridge of Westcott, Lightfoot, and Hort, L. E. Elliott-Binns once wrote:

Philosophy and dogmatics lay rather outside his interests, which may account for his being occasionally led away by new ideas whose implications he had not fully realized. Cautious by nature his advance in critical views, or perhaps in their proclamation, was very gradual; at one time, for example, he had accepted the truth of miracles which he would later deny.[5]

But, of course, that may simply be a way of saying that Sanday was a very careful scholar, ready to consider evidence and allow it to decide matters even where religious or dogmatic considerations made him hesitant. He seems to have felt, for instance, that the Cambridge triumvirate were full of ingenious ideas but insufficiently critical.[6]

Sanday had been born in 1843, which meant that when he was an undergraduate at Balliol, Jowett had not yet become master. In his thirties he went to be principal of Hatfield Hall, Durham, and then returned to Oxford in 1882 to hold two of the theology chairs there, in succession. He retired from the second of these in 1919 and died in the following year. Most of his life was given to preparing to write a 'Life' of Christ, a project which he never completed. The whole notion of writing such a life is very typical of the 1870s when Sanday was a young adult. Dean Farrar's famous attempt at one was published in 1874. Though Sanday intended a life which would be based upon a much more critical approach to the sources, the project itself was, by the turn of the century, outdated and impractical. As New Testament scholarship developed, it began to be realized that factors other than the historical had shaped the gospel accounts. The idea of composing a narrative biography from them began to seem fanciful or impossible. Yet, in spite of being himself in the forefront of English New Testament scholarship, Sanday never abandoned his original intention.

Another sense in which Sanday obviously straddled the generations is that he was himself an authority on a wide variety of theological disciplines. It was still respectable to be a polymath and

[5] L. E. Elliott-Binns, *English Thought, 1860–1900: The Theological Aspect* (London, 1956), 130.
[6] Ibid. 121 n.

specialization had not yet become the essential requirement of an academic reputation. By the time he returned to Oxford from Durham he had already published two works on the gospels in relation to history. A decade later he gave the Bampton Lectures, which were published under the title of *Inspiration*. In attempting to establish what it means to say that the Bible is inspired Sanday surveyed an enormous range of material, from the Old Testament to the Patristic age. He rejected the traditional view that 'the Bible as a whole and in all its parts was the Word of God, and as such that it was endowed with all the perfections of that Word' so that 'in history as well as in doctrine it was exempt from error'.[7] But he believed, nevertheless, that a proper understanding of the inspiration and authority of Scripture meant accepting not only that the consciousness of the biblical authors had been subject to the operation of the divine but also that a 'Higher Providence' had been at work in shaping the books of the Bible and the canon itself.[8]

After the publication of his Bampton Lectures most of Sanday's writings were intended to be preliminary studies for his projected life of Jesus. The notable exception was his commentary, with A. C. Headlam, on Romans, which was still being used in a serious academic context fifty years after it first appeared. First of all there was his immensely long article 'Jesus Christ' in Hastings's *Dictionary of the Bible*. Originally published in 1899, this article already admitted the supreme difficulty of the task as Sanday had begun to see it.

To write the Life of Christ ideally is impossible. And even to write such a *Life* as should justify itself either for popular use or for study, is a task of extreme difficulty. After all the learning, ability, and even genius devoted to the subject, it is a relief to turn back from the very best of modern *Lives* to the Gospels. And great as are the merits of many of these modern works, there is none (at least none known to the writer . . .) which possesses such a balance and combination of qualities as to rise quite to the level of a classic. What is wanted is a Newman, with science and adequate knowledge. No one has ever touched the Gospels with so much innate kinship of spirit as he. It should be needless to say that the Life of Christ can be written only by a believer. Renan had all the literary gifts—a *curiosa felicitas* of style, an aesthetic appreciation of his subject, and a saving common-sense which

---

[7] W. Sanday, *Inspiration*, 3rd edn. (London, 1896), 392.
[8] Ibid. 402 ff.

tempered his criticism; but even as literature his work is spoilt by self-consciousness and condescension, and his science was not of the best.[9]

The lives he was most prepared to recommend were those of Neander, Ewald, and Edersheim.

This article was reprinted with very little modification as a separate book and issued by the publishers of the *Dictionary* in 1905 (and was several times reissued in further editions).[10] In 1907 there appeared *The Life of Christ in Recent Research*, which was really a collection of lectures given at various times, and which either surveyed contemporary research and literature on the subject or dealt with specific topics—such as miracles or angels—which Sanday thought that anyone who was attempting to translate the gospels into a modern 'Life' would have to sort out for himself. His own approach can, perhaps, best be understood by his enormous enthusiasm for a picture of the temptations of Jesus in the wilderness, painted by William Dyce, the High Churchman and well-known religious artist whose style was influenced to some extent by the pre-Raphaelites. A photograph of the painting appeared twice in *The Life of Christ in Recent Research*, the detail of the figure of Jesus as the frontispiece, and the whole scene later in the volume. There were no other illustrations in the work at all. In Sanday's own words:

All that we see here [in contrast to the 'conventional fiend, with ram's horns and exaggerated bat's wings'] is a monotonous landscape and a Figure seated upon a stone, with the hands clasped and an expression of intense thought on the beautiful but by no means effeminate features.[11]

The landscape is, indeed, monotonous but is certainly not the wilderness of Judaea. The figure might well seem to some to be sentimental as well as pensive; but the message is clear. The temptation was something that happened inside Jesus's mind.

Almost everything Sanday did was incidental to his great enterprise. Even the volume of lectures published as *The Criticism of the Fourth Gospel* could, he said, 'be taken as justifying the use that is made of the Fourth Gospel' in his *Outlines*.[12] The most

---

[9] J. Hastings (ed.), *Dictionary of the Bible*, 7th impression (Edinburgh, 1906), 653.

[10] W. Sanday, *Outlines of the Life of Christ* (Edinburgh, 1905).

[11] W. Sanday, *The Life of Christ in Recent Research* (Oxford, 1907), 29.

[12] Sanday, *Outlines of the Life of Christ*, p. vii.

difficult issue of all he tackled in *Christologies Ancient and Modern* which was published in 1910. One could hardly write the kind of 'Life' which Sanday had described in the Hastings *Dictionary*, like a Newman with science or a believing Renan, without settling for oneself the question whether, and in what sense, the divine was present in Jesus of Nazareth. Sanday himself leant towards a kenotic Christology or, at least, he thought that the view he was putting forward was the same as that of the Anglo-Catholic Frank Weston, bishop of Zanzibar, whose *The One Christ* was a determined attempt to present the Christology of Cyril of Alexandria in kenotic dress as the only orthodox theology of the person of Christ tenable by modern minds. But Sanday thought Weston's view was the same as that of J. M. Thompson whose radical rejection of the whole of the miraculous element in the gospels Weston actually found grossly offensive and heretical.[13] One immediately, therefore, has cause to wonder whether Sanday had really understood the issues. He relied upon statements in Thompson's book like 'When he is most truly man, then he is most truly God', as if they were to be understood in a kenotic sense like Weston's.[14] In fact, Thompson meant something much more like Campbell's assertion that the human *is* divine. At all events Sanday's own summing up of what he regarded as the right account of the relationship between the human and the divine in Christ was:

It is true that the *surface* of our Lord's life is entirely human. Even the Deity in Him, on its way to expression, had to pass through, and is in this respect . . . limited by, the human medium. But there is no paradox in this. On the contrary, it is what was to be expected if there was to be any such thing as an Incarnation at all. The divine in man
> dwells in deep retreats
> Whose veil is unremoved.
And the same description applies even to the Godhead of the God-Man.[15]

For Sanday the 1911 volume, *Oxford Studies in the Synoptic Problem*, was one of the last publications of a distinguished career. For Streeter his contribution to the collection marked an early but

---

[13] See K. W. Clements, *Lovers of Discord: Twentieth Century Theological Controversies in England* (London, 1988), 51 ff., and cf. V. H. H. Green, *Religion at Oxford and Cambridge* (London, 1964), 331.

[14] W. Sanday, *Christologies Ancient and Modern* (Oxford, 1910), 213.

[15] Ibid. 213 f.

important step forward. It was then that he first began to attract attention as a scholar. But the three-layer hypothesis about the origins of the written gospels, which was perhaps for Streeter himself the most important part of the paper, was not what made the greatest impression when the essay appeared in print. Probably his immediate achievement was that it persuaded a great many people that the results of source criticism were both sensible and respectable. Streeter had—almost incidentally in the course of his argument—to produce the evidence for what were to be the two principal foundations of the 'four sources hypothesis': the priority of Mark and existence of Q. It is as the champion of this hypothesis that he is now chiefly remembered.

Streeter was, in fact, something of a polymath himself and did significant work in three distinct areas—critical New Testament scholarship; relating the Christian faith to modern thought; and the Christian attitude to other religions. The three works for which he is, perhaps, best remembered, all appeared in the 1920s and 1930s and were concerned with precisely these areas. They were *The Four Gospels* (published in 1924), a seminal work of New Testament scholarship, if already somewhat outdated in its approach; *Reality* (1926), an attempt to restate some aspects of Christian doctrine in the light of contemporary natural science and psychology; and his Bampton Lectures of 1932, *The Buddha and the Christ*, which attempted to set out more fully and more satisfactorily what he had already sketched, very briefly, in an appended note to the second chapter of *Reality*—'And in the Buddha we must salute him who, giving first place to love both in word and deed, might have reached the summit of inspiration, but for that "nay-saying" which deems life itself an evil.'[16]

In fact, Streeter was not merely a theological polymath. He may appear on the surface to be over-anxious to paddle in every fashionable pool, to express himself in terms of popular psychology not always fully understood; but his writings often exhibited a mixture of deep religious sensitivity with an enquiring rationalism. His involvement in every religious movement in turn was, no doubt, the result of a deep desire to find some way of giving expression to his personal sense of religion without denying what he thought to be important about modern 'scientific' knowledge.

[16] B. H. Streeter, *Reality* (London, 1926), 48.

Yet it is difficult not to suspect that his restless enlistment in one movement and another was symptomatic of a dissatisfaction or dismay.

His interest in the other great world religions could be described as fashionable in some quarters of the British theological world in the years before the war. It had been growing slowly over a long period and then suddenly gained pace rapidly after 1900. Max Müller had been a pioneer in the field. Twenty-five years after being made professor of Comparative Philology at Oxford he delivered a presidential address to the Society of Historical Theology on 3 November 1893 in which he argued that a properly *historical* theology would concern itself with the sacred writings of *every* religion. In 1908 the third International Congress of the History of Religions met in Oxford, organized by L. R. Farnell, fellow of Exeter College, for the exchange of ideas between anthropologists, archaeologists, philologists, and theologians. And in 1911 Farnell, who was to become head of his college two years later, delivered the Hibbert Lectures in Manchester College, a Unitarian institution, on the importance of a scientific and anthropological study of religion. Streeter's interest in Buddhism and Hinduism could be said to be in step with what was happening around him, and he seems to have held to the common belief that what was best in those religions was fulfilled in Christianity. His own approach to other religions was mystical rather than scientific, and one would have thought that a belief in a universal mysticism would sit very uneasily alongside some of the new historical insights of New Testament scholarship which he also embraced.

By the time Streeter's *The Four Gospels* appeared in 1924 his position had largely been overtaken by events. Schweitzer's *Quest of the Historical Jesus* had revolutionized New Testament studies by insisting that the historical Jesus was not to be understood apart from the apocalyptic fervour of some types of first-century Judaism. From the pages of Schweitzer's book emerged a picture of a Jesus who may have been mistaken, or even deluded, something of a fanatic, expecting his own death to bring in the cataclysmic, vindicating, eschatological judgement. He was certainly not the civilized and progressive Jesus of Liberal Protestantism nor was he, because Schweitzer's approach emphasized the historical particularism of the gospels, compatible with the eternal Christ-idea of the Idealists. While this new and revolutionary approach did not have any direct bearing on how one reconstructed the relationship between the literary sources of the gospels, it was bound to colour the context in which Streeter's work was being done. And he seems to have tried to come to grips with it.

More obviously and directly related to the kind of work Streeter was doing, and yet almost entirely disregarded by him, was the new form critical school which was just emerging in Germany. Scholars were beginning to look behind the written and literary sources of the Old Testament and their history, and to ask whether the traditions had a pre-history in an oral rather than written form. Inevitably, this also began to raise questions about the relationship between early Hebrew oral traditions and the traditions of other peoples of the Middle East. This meant, in turn, that the history of Hebrew religion could not be treated simply as if it were an account of how the divine revelation had been communicated to Israel, but must be looked at against the general history of religions as a whole. Again, the 'history of religions' school which now emerged was not quite the history of religions in which Caird had indulged with his Idealist's enthusiasm for treating the activities of the absolute Spirit 'scientifically'.[17] When it was transferred to the New Testament, the new historical understanding had a particularly profound effect.[18] The technique of form criticism was to break the text down into separate units. Each pericope, or unit, was then set in the *sitz-im-leben* or historical context that was believed to have given birth to it.

Something of this turmoil in ideas, and of Streeter's inability to come to terms with it completely, was revealed in a collection of essays which he edited called *Foundations: A Statement of Christian Belief in terms of Modern Thought*, published in 1912. This volume, satirized by Ronald Knox, in a parody of Dryden entitled 'Absolute and Abitofhell',[19] displayed the considerable variety of beliefs and opinions which had come to exist even among a relatively small group of younger and more liberal English theologians by this date. Streeter himself was 37 when the book appeared and was thought of as the elder of the group, which was in the habit of lunching together regularly to discuss the ways in which Christianity could be presented in terms which were

[17] Above, pp. 138 ff.
[18] R. Morgan (with J. Barton), *Biblical Interpretation* (Oxford, 1988), 124 ff.
[19] *The Oxford Magazine*, Nov. 1912.

compatible with contemporary thought. They were, therefore, more than just a chance collection of authors seeking a public.

There were, nevertheless, some ironies in the authorship of the essays. Inevitably *Foundations* would be seen as constituting one of a series of volumes of essays which, by dealing with critical issues, caused controversy and debate. In fact, of course, *Essays and Reviews*, *Lux Mundi*, and *Foundations* were so different in intention and purpose that they were not a *series* at all, except from the retrospective viewpoint of subsequent generations. In the introductory chapter to *Foundations* (written by Neville Talbot) the only reference to *Essays and Reviews* is a somewhat oblique one, in a footnote;[20] *Lux Mundi* is not mentioned at all. The truth is that each volume was really a manifesto of a particular group at a particular time. Nevertheless there was a sense in which *Foundations* could be said to mark a coming together of two very different traditions in liberal theology. Of the seven authors of *Foundations*, who were all Oxford men, one (William Temple) was the son of a contributor to *Essays and Reviews* and two others (Neville Talbot and W. H. Moberly) were sons of members of the *Lux Mundi* group.

Most of the contributors, however, belonged—if somewhat vaguely—in the *Lux Mundi*, rather than the *Essays and Reviews* tradition of liberalism. Even Temple, who did not, had begun by 1908 to rely on Gore for help and advice. His biographer does not explain how this close relationship came into being between two such very different men, but it is clear that Temple always consulted Gore when he had an important decision to make. He also regarded Gore as the person 'to whom more than any other (despite great differences) I owe my apprehension of the truth'.[21] Temple's particular connection with Streeter himself arose from the fact that they had been colleagues at Queen's, though Temple had become headmaster of Repton in 1910 before *Foundations* appeared.

Temple's essay reflects a good deal of his personal religious history up to that point. He had something of a tendency to Hegelianism, a consequence of the fact that he owed his first

[20] *Foundations: A Statement of Christian Belief in terms of Modern Thought: by Seven Oxford Men* (London, 1912).

[21] F. A. Iremonger, *William Temple, Archbishop of Canterbury* (London, 1948), 488, quoting Temple's dedication to Gore of *Studies in the Spirit and Truth of Christianity*.

introduction to formal philosophy to Edward Caird. All his later thought was coloured by it, though it is obvious that, as time passed, he moved away from the ideas derived from Kant and Hegel and returned more directly to Plato. He had been through a period when he had wrestled with the question whether his beliefs were sufficiently orthodox to enable him to be ordained. Bishop Paget of Oxford thought that he was not firmly enough committed to the virgin birth and the bodily resurrection of Christ but eventually Randall Davidson, Frederick Temple's successor as archbishop of Canterbury, had agreed to ordain him.

Some lectures of Temple's, which were to be published in 1910, *The Faith and Modern Thought*, seem to have been important evidence in convincing the archbishop that his theology was sound. Streeter, too, had played a significant part in convincing Temple himself that he could sign the undertaking required of ordination candidates. More surprisingly, perhaps, Henry Scott Holland (one of the contributors to *Lux Mundi* and a man whose social and political thought Temple had recently come to admire) persuaded him that if 'there were several articles of the Christian Creed which an enquirer knew by his own experience to be true, he might feel that the intervening ones also ... could be accepted'.[22]

Temple's lectures, reveal very clearly both his debt to Caird and how his thought had begun to move towards a more conventional orthodoxy, possibly because of the influence of people like Gore and Scott Holland. He hoped, he said, to bring together 'general principles, which have been reached as the result of past experience, and all the new facts bearing upon the subject which can be found'.[23] He remained enough of an Idealist to insist that 'the world shall be regarded as coherent, as all hanging together and making up one system'.[24] He seemed to reach this conclusion by one enormous leap from Kant's premiss. Temple said:

My knowledge of the existence of the table is quite as much a fact as anything else. My knowledge, then, is one of the facts that must be held together in this coherent scheme. Now that seems to involve, as far as I can understand the position we have reached, that there is some mentality (I know no better word for the purpose) in all the facts of our experience. I do not mean to say that the chairs and tables are thinking; I mean that

---

[22] Iremonger, *William Temple*, 108 ff. and NB p. 126.
[23] W. Temple, *The Faith and Modern Thought* (London, 1910), 2.
[24] Ibid. 3.

everything which exists must be the embodiment of rational principle. The Universe turns out to be a rational whole.[25]

The lectures, in fact, demonstrate what an eclectic thinker Temple was at this early stage in his career. He dealt with the authority of revelation, much as Gore had done in *Lux Mundi*, arguing that inspiration did not guarantee truth, nor provide solutions: it was a feature of the continuous development in man's knowledge of God. The influence of Streeter is obvious in the lecture on the historical basis of Christianity, with its examination of the synoptic problem. But in the lecture on the person of Christ, though his devotion to the Jesus of the gospels is very evident, his preference for the fourth gospel over the synoptics may be a hint that he still hankered after an Idealist's Christ, whom he described as pre-eminently the culminating point in all religion and ethics. When he came to deal with the atonement his critique of penal substitutionary theology was as sharp as Jowett's had been, though he recognized—as Jowett had not—that there was something to be said for it.[26] He insisted that the proper way of considering the atonement was, simply, as an expression of love. Love works by sacrifice, he said, that is always the mode of its operation. 'This we find, if we take St. John's great guiding principle, that in Christ we see the Father, so that in His attitude to His enemies we see God's attitude to us when we are at enmity with Him (for He is never at enmity with us).'[27] He continued:

I believe that if we work out that theory, thinking of the effect which love always has, when it is understood, upon any heart and remembering that the world has progressed a good deal since the earliest ages that we know, and progressed in love more perhaps than in any other quality, we shall find that it may be true that the whole world is moving onwards for ever under the impulse of the infinite love of God to a more and more adequate return of that love; we begin to think of the whole Universe as knit together in that love as its one controlling principle.

All these ideas, drawn from such a wide variety of sources, seem to have been boiling up together in Temple's mind. By the time he came to write the chapter for *Foundations*, he had come—without finally abandoning all vestiges of Idealist influence—to adopt a more Christocentric and incarnational emphasis in theology, very

---

[25] Ibid. 11.   [26] Ibid. 133 f., and cf. above, pp. 56 f. for Jowett's views.
[27] Ibid. 136.

reminiscent of *Lux Mundi*. His tone remained optimistically immanentist, like that of other essays in the volume. His contribution was on the divinity of Christ and very much more orthodox than Streeter's companion chapter on 'The Historic Christ'. His argument was similar to that of *The Faith and Modern Thought*, though it was aimed at a somewhat more academic audience. In it he maintained that it was wrong to start a consideration of the divinity of Christ from the question whether this historical, human person was also divine. Instead he argued that the correct approach was 'to take Jesus as the embodiment of the Supreme Principle, and to believe that its nature is the character of Jesus'.[28] The whole chapter was really a solid, learned, and well-constructed sermon, based on the fourth gospel: its text stood below the chapter heading—'Lord, shew us the Father, and it sufficeth us'. And it concluded with a triumphant rhetorical flourish in which there was a strong echo of an idea of Caird's about the Christ of the *eschaton*. That future Christ, Caird had thought, would be the Christ realized in the lives of his people. Temple, similarly, proclaimed that when all men have been drawn in to the purposes of God, and have come to constitute 'One Perfect Man', then 'for the first time will the Divinity of Christ be fully manifest; then for the first time will the God in Christ be fully known'.[29]

If Temple had moved somewhat away from his earlier Idealism, another contributor to the volume was still much influenced by it. The final essay, Moberly's chapter on 'God and the Absolute', is an agonized wrestling with the question whether an Idealist understanding of God is compatible with orthodox Christianity. He came to no final conclusion but it is clear that he believed that Idealism provided such a strong philosophical defence for theism that this outweighed many of the apparently unorthodox implications of its immanentism. On the other hand, the introductory chapter describing 'The Modern Situation', written by Neville Talbot, chaplain and fellow of Balliol, took a very different line. Not himself a Balliol man, Talbot had been appointed as chaplain in 1909 when Caird had already resigned the mastership. He was not, therefore, in any sense a product of the Jowett/Caird tradition, belonging to the theologically less liberal, and politically more

---

[28] W. Temple, *The Faith and Modern Thought*, 215.
[29] Ibid. 263.

'socialist', Anglo-Catholic school of thought influenced by Gore. After serving as a chaplain in the First World War, he was to become bishop of Pretoria and one of a group of 'Young Turk' Anglo-Catholic bishops in South Africa who were strongly affected by the English Life and Liberty movement in which Temple played a leading part.

Talbot's chapter located the volume in the context of 'modern' rather than 'Victorian' thought. He believed that the 'modern' age was marked off from its Victorian predecessor by three things. Darwin's writings had introduced a new scientific understanding of the universe, which made people feel that matter was more important than mind or spirit and that they lived in a world which was indifferent to their needs. Secondly, Victorian belief in the inevitable progress of man had been destroyed and there was a belief abroad that nothing was absolutely true or right at any given moment. And thirdly, the enormous confidence of the mid-nineteenth century in free trade ideology had evaporated. At that time the so-called Manchester School had opposed the idea of imperial expansion, in the belief that there was no limit, in principle, to the possible development of international commerce and finance. That had proved, Talbot thought, to be a false hope. He argued that 'the mind of society has become morbid with the sickness of an industrial order which has been built upon a philosophy of half-truths. The confident optimism of the era of the Great Exhibition and the Manchester School . . . has faltered in the face of the results of individualistic competition.'[30] This was, he said, a much wilder and more frightening world than that in which T. H. Green had been able to argue that the ideal was recognizable in the empirical. But, in spite of the pessimism of much of his chapter, it ended with an impassioned and emotional assertion that the very doubts and difficulties of the age were a sign of hope. 'A knowledge of darkness is needed to urge indolent man upon the quest after the light.'[31]

As if Temple, Moberly, and Talbot did not provide enough variety of approaches in a single volume, Streeter's own essay, from which *Foundations* derived some notoriety, was influenced by what Albert Schweitzer had written in *The Quest of the Historical Jesus* and adopted a sceptical attitude to the possibility of reconstructing

[30] Ibid. 8.   [31] Ibid. 24.

an accurate account of the Jesus of history. Streeter began by insisting that the historical particularity of Jesus of Nazareth was as essential for understanding him as a kenotic understanding had been for the contributors to *Lux Mundi*. Among the writers of the 'Eschatological School', whose insistence on this point had made so much impact, he classed Tyrrell as well as Schweitzer and others more usually reckoned as such.[32] Jesus was a man of his own time and place, a particular man in a particular nation, and not some sort of generalized, universal humanity. This had many advantages, Streeter thought, in enabling one to accept many of the sayings of Jesus reported in the synoptics which both liberals and conservatives had had to explain away. It also disposed once and for all of the older liberal supposition that much of historic Christianity had been foisted on to the figure of Christ by a Pauline theology.

> . . . the Christ whom this newer school reveals is a solitary, arresting figure, intensely human, yet convinced of His call to an office and a mission absolutely superhuman—a conviction which one will attribute to fanaticism, another to inspiration,—calling men to follow Him along a path which to some will appear the way of folly, to others the way of life. He came not to bring peace but division, and to 'separate them one from another as a shepherd divideth the sheep from the goats'.[33]

He thought it still perfectly possible to believe in the divinity of Christ provided that one began one's understanding of him from a study of the historic Jesus and not from the a priori, and possibly misleading, ideas of divinity which we may happen to possess.

This starting point—quite directly opposed to Temple's insistence that one cannot begin by asking whether the human Jesus of history can also be God[34]—led Streeter to consider the origin and historical value of the gospels, confining himself, for the purpose of the essay, to the synoptics. He then turned to examine what the apocalyptic eschatology and the messianic hope were, working his way through the prophets to the inter-testamental period, concentrating particularly on the Son of Man figure of Daniel 7 and of the Book of Enoch. He concluded this section by saying that, though Zealot leaders were not actually thought of as messiahs, 'It was believed . . . that if Israel had faith to draw the sword in their support, at the crisis of the war which must ensue, just at the

---

[32] *Foundations*, 76.   [33] Ibid. 78.   [34] Above, p. 236.

moment when a crushing defeat seemed inevitable, the supernatural Christ would appear.'[35]

Streeter believed that John the Baptist had converted this apocalyptic expectation from being a largely literary tradition into a direct prophetic message from God to the masses of the people.[36] Having established this point, at least to his own satisfaction, he then moved to a section devoted to 'The Call of our Lord and the Psychology of the Prophetic Mind'. What he had to say under that head is difficult to reconcile with the professed approach of the eschatological school; for Streeter asserted that what the Hebrew prophets described as visions and messages from God ought to be understood as really the 'voice of conscience or the conviction of vocation'. There is, of course, no evidence for this assumption at all. Streeter simply abandoned the strong case for the particularity of history and replaced it with generalizations about what happens at 'certain stages of culture', as if he had suddenly strayed into the world of Caird's lectures on the evolution of religion. At all events, he ended this section with the words, 'in all great minds and notably in all religious minds there is an element of deep humility, and without some such an experience of voice or vision as that attested by the earliest tradition it would be difficult to understand His absolute conviction that He was indeed Lord of Lords and King of Kings'.[37]

Streeter then considered the teaching of Christ. Since he rejected the conception of himself as warrior messiah, there remained for Jesus 'only the conception of the Christ to be Apocalyptically manifested'.[38] 'For a while, then, the Christ-to-be becomes, as it were, His own forerunner, and thus the last of the long succession of the Prophets.'[39] Most of the rest of the article was an explication of the teaching of Jesus as recorded in the gospels, understood as the teaching of one who looked forward to his own imminent return as the apocalyptic Christ, and whose concern, in the mean time, had been to prepare others for that return. The essay came to its climax with a consideration of the resurrection as the vindication of the messiah, for whom death was part of his vocation.

Streeter seemed to enjoy setting out what he thought were the possible alternative explanations of the resurrection, the traditional

[35] *Foundations*, 92. [36] Ibid. 93. [37] Ibid. 99.
[38] Ibid. 101. [39] Ibid. 103.

and the naturalistic (by which he meant 'subjective visions' resulting from acute psychological reaction). Both were, he thought, too obsessed with the material aspect of things. His own conclusion was that the post-resurrection appearances were indeed visions but in the sense that they were 'something directly caused by the Lord Himself veritably alive and personally in communion with' the disciples.[40]

Because of the way in which the essay swings between sensible, scholarly discussion of the New Testament text and its ideas and rather woolly attempts to devise 'psychological' explanations, it is easy to miss the potential significance of Streeter's suggestion that the historical Jesus should be understood as his own forerunner, that is to say as the forerunner of the eschatological Christ of faith. Schweitzer's work had, by emphasizing the historical particularity of Jesus, locked him into a specific time and place. As Streeter pointed out, this had the advantage of linking Jesus more firmly with the Judaism of his own time and with its Old Testament roots. Unfortunately, the deluded, fanatical Jesus, whom Schweitzer seemed to unveil, appeared to have little to do with the Christ of early Christian faith or even with the central figure of the gospels. Indeed, the combined effect of New Testament criticism, Liberal Protestant conceptions of the Jesus of history, and the Idealists' conviction that what really mattered was an eternal, unhistorical Christ, had been to separate entirely from one another the Old Testament and Jewish context, the actual person of Jesus of Nazareth, the theologically influenced gospel narratives, and the life and faith of the Church. Schweitzer's book seemed to force them even further apart: Streeter's essay hinted at a way in which those fragmented pieces might be drawn together again.

Between Streeter's essay and Temple's there was a third which also, in a sense, dealt with the relationship between Christ and history. This was written by A. E. J. Rawlinson and R. G. Parsons. Rawlinson (the future bishop of Derby) was a tutor at Keble College, and Parsons was the principal of the theological college at Wells. Their chapter is, perhaps, less exciting than the other two. They were, as they reminded their readers, not required to explain precisely what the resurrection—for instance—could possibly have been, but to say how the disciples had understood it.[41] Their

---

[40] *Foundations*, 136.   [41] Ibid. 154.

approach was closer to Streeter's than to Temple's, in the sense that they took as their starting point the eschatological concern of the first Christians. But they proceeded to argue that, though the earliest Christology had, for this reason, possessed a future form—it was a Christology about him who was to return in glory—the actual experience of the Church was experience of a living, *present* reality. And therefore, even within the time span of the New Testament canon, there had been a shift from a perception of a Christ who belonged to the past and the future to a Christ who was present *now*.

We have seen the clear-cut realistic expectation of the Lord's immediate Coming, which marks the earliest Christian writings, pass half a century later into the quiet mysticism of St. John—'Beloved, now are we sons of God, and it is not yet made manifest what we shall be. We know that if He shall be manifested, we shall be like Him; for we shall see Him even as He is.' It is probable that the language of St. Paul in Thessalonians is closer to the letter of our Lord's own words: shall we say that it is closer to their spirit or represents more truly that which essentially He meant.[42]

Rawlinson and Parsons were, in other words, concerned with the relationship between history and faith, in the sense that faith creates the history of the Church.

This variety of theological opinion within a single volume was symptomatic of the age. Theologians had become less certain that orthodox belief must be expressed in precise propositional formulations. Scholars with different ideas could seem to be allies against unbelief rather than traitors to the faith. Only two years before the publication of *Foundations* the first great international ecumenical gathering had taken place in Edinburgh—the world missionary conference of 1910. Ecumenism and agreement were in the air and Streeter was an ecumenist.

Yet this apparent amity among younger scholars from different schools of thought was not the whole picture. Within the Church of England the 1890s and the early years of the twentieth century were years of acute controversy in matters of Churchmanship. The Anglo-Catholic parishes and societies attracted most of the opprobrium, for they came under scrutiny from suspicious Protestants like the Church Association and Major Kensit's more extreme

---

[42] Ibid. 210.

Protestant Truth Society. Litigation, once again, became more frequent, but the Anglo-Catholics were also, themselves, conscious of their growing numbers and influence, and inclined to regard it as their proper function to rebuke those whom they believed to be betrayers of orthodoxy. Both sides seemed to possess a real zest for controversy, each asserting its claim to be the sole champion of Anglican truth. At the same time, matters of Churchmanship were becoming more directly political in a formal sense. Sir William Harcourt, a prominent Member of Parliament, was a leading protagonist in the Protestant and Erastian cause. How to discipline ritualists became once again an issue which concerned politicians and legislators.[43] Parliament and the established Church set out upon the process which was to lead, after the war, to the creation of the Church Assembly and the abortive attempt at the revision of the Prayer Book.

In this atmosphere *Foundations* aroused controversy just as *Essays and Reviews* had done, just as *Lux Mundi* had done. Frank Weston, self-appointed episcopal guardian of the Catholic faith within the Anglican Communion (which was not an easy vocation to follow in remotest Zanzibar), launched an attack upon the volume.[44] In a sense the bishop's position was straightforward. He was determined that Christian theology should not depart from certain orthodox propositional formulations of the faith. The whole purpose of his *The One Christ* (published in 1907) had been to insist that the Chalcedonian definition of the person of Christ was as important to contemporary believers as it had been to Christians of the fifth century. And yet Weston was alive to the necessity of indigenizing Christianity in Africa. He is famous for his vigorous objections to the proposals of the so-called 'Kikuyu conference' of 1913 which suggested a federation of Anglican and Protestant missionary agencies in East Africa. Weston's objections were not simply those of a High Churchman who feared pan-Protestantism, though it is this part of his criticism which is now

---

[43] For an account of a typical example of Churchmanship controversy, of the kind that beset the period, see M. Wellings, 'Anglo-Catholicism, the "Crisis in the Church" and the Cavalier Case of 1899', *Journal of Ecclesiastical History*, 42 (Apr. 1991), 239 ff.

[44] The story is told in G. K. A. Bell, *Randall Davidson, Archbishop of Canterbury*, 2nd edn. (London, 1938), 671 ff., and Clements, *Lovers of Discord*, 59 ff.

usually remembered. He also believed that it was totally absurd for the future of Christianity in East Africa to be decided by a group of expatriate missionaries without the participation of any Africans. When he was invited to attend a second, larger Kikuyu conference of 'a hundred delegates belonging to many sects . . . and not a single African was present', he was quite clear that this was a futile exercise.[45] Yet he does not seem to have perceived that there are cultural differences between one period of history and another, as there are between one continent and another. Nor would he admit that, if indigenization were allowed to affect externals like language, custom, and symbol, it would inevitably affect also the essential meaning of theological propositions expressed in them.

Weston received considerable support from other Anglo-Catholics, always inclined to believe that certain doctrinal propositions were sacrosanct, but he was deeply hurt by the fact that Sanday had been his own tutor as well as Streeter's. The bishop seems always to have believed that Sanday was essentially orthodox. In fact, Sanday's understanding of all religious history was a version of the theory of progressive revelation and it caused him to be sceptical about the possibility of there being an absolute truth which could be expressed in any eternally unchanging credal formula.

In the year after the outbreak of the war, Sanday was to read a paper to the Modern Churchmen's Union which finally made it clear beyond all doubt that he believed that the ways in which ideas were expressed, and even the ideas themselves, changed from one historical context to another. And he followed up that paper by saying:

In all that I have been saying the idea of Relative Truth, or of the relative expression of Truth, is an essential part. The scheme of Divine Providence is a progressive scheme. Truth has been implanted among us in the form of germs, which have gone on growing and developing. But the expression of truth at each successive stage from the very first has been strictly related and proportioned to the sum of the intellectual development attained at the time to which it belonged. It simply *is* so, and has been so, and no amount of theoretic manipulation on our part can make it otherwise.[46]

---

[45] H. Maynard Smith, *Frank Bishop of Zanzibar* (London, 1926), 169.

[46] W. Sanday and N. P. Williams, *Form and Content in the Christian Tradition, A Friendly Discussion* (London, 1916), 114.

There can really be little doubt that it was Streeter, rather than Weston, who was being faithful to their common master.

Gore, as bishop of Oxford, was drawn into the controversy which followed Weston's attack upon *Foundations* but he was not willing to be so outspokenly critical of the volume as Weston would have wished. The whole question of how much liberalism should be permitted in the Church of England came before convocation in April 1914. But a combination of the diplomatic skill of Archbishop Davidson and the outbreak of the war diverted the fury of the conservatives and the controversial volume was gradually forgotten. Temple, Rawlinson, and Talbot all became bishops and were not, as bishops, regarded as dangerous liberals; neither could Sir Walter Moberly really be regarded as anything other than a pillar of the establishment.

Perhaps the most significant section in the whole of *Foundations* had been Streeter's attempt to come to terms with Albert Schweitzer's *Quest of the Historical Jesus* and to make something positive of it. It is an immense pity that he never developed the embryonic ideas contained in his essay and remained content, instead, with the source critical theories which occupied most of *The Four Gospels*. Not everyone, however, thought that they need take account of Schweitzer's work, even when they were willing to express admiration for his scholarship. At Cambridge, F. C. Burkitt, a brilliant and in many ways unconventional scholar, remained convinced that Mark's gospel was not only the earliest of the gospels but a literal and accurate historical account of the life and ministry of Jesus. (Burkitt fell, chronologically speaking, between Sanday and Streeter. He was twenty years younger than Sanday; ten years older than Streeter.) In 1906 he gave a series of lectures in one of the London settlements which he subsequently repeated, virtually unchanged, as his inaugural course as Norrisian professor at Cambridge in the same year. The lectures were subsequently published later in 1906 as *The Gospel History and Its Transmission*. The book was obviously popular, and felt to have a lasting value, because it was reprinted in five editions, the last of which appeared in 1925.

The essence of the case presented by Burkitt was that Mark was the earliest literary source and that Matthew and Luke were both based on it. His arguments were designed to prove that there was no such document as an *Ur-Marcus* (an earlier version of Mark's gospel used as a common source by all three synoptic evangelists). Almost incidentally, they foreclosed on any possible case for some other source such as a hypothetical Q.[47]

> In S. Mark we are, I believe, appreciably nearer the actual scenes of our Lord's life, to the course of events, than in any other document which tells us of Him, and therefore if we want to begin at the beginning and reconstruct the Portrait of Christ for ourselves we must start from the Gospel of Mark. The other Gospels, even the Gospels according to Matthew and Luke, give us an interpretation of Jesus Christ's life. An interpretation may be helpful, illuminating, even inspired, but it remains an interpretation. The thing that actually occurred was the life which Jesus Christ lived, and our chief authority for the facts of that life is the Gospel according to Mark.[48]

No one would now suppose that 'uninterpreted factual history' of Christ's life was available, but Burkitt was willing to assume that that was what Mark's gospel was. He argued, for instance, that the curiously illogical journeyings of Jesus, described in chapters 5 and 8 of Mark, were accurately recounted and that the apparent oddness of Jesus's movements was a result of his need to avoid the territories of Herod Antipas.[49] He was also convinced that Mark's gospel was as complete as it was accurate, for he was able to argue that the raising of Lazarus could not have taken place—not because of any inherent improbability of miracles, but simply because Mark's 'narrative appears to leave no room to fit it in'.[50]

Burkitt remained certain of the correctness of his own conclusions. It may be wholly understandable that when von Harnack produced a new work on the Lucan writings while *The Gospel History and Its Transmission* was actually being printed, Burkitt should have made no more than minor adjustments to his argument.[51] But it seems incomprehensible that he reacted hardly more vigorously to the publication of Schweitzer's work when it appeared between the first and second editions of his own volume. This is particularly the case in that Burkitt recognized that, 'If there is one thing more than another that clearly issues from A. Schweitzer's admirable history of the attempts to write a life of Jesus . . . it is this, that the complete historical scepticism of Bruno

---

[47] F. C. Burkitt, *The Gospel History and its Transmission*, 5th impression (Edinburgh, 1925), 33 ff.　　　[48] Ibid. 102 f.
[49] Ibid. 89 ff.　　　[50] Ibid., p. viii and cf. 221 ff.　　　[51] Ibid., p. vi.

Bauer was not a mere individual eccentricity, but the expression of serious difficulties in an excessively complicated historical problem.'[52] Even in the third edition, when he had had plenty of time to react to Schweitzer, Burkitt declined to alter what he had said, offering no more than a few remarks in a new preface and then only to make a rather lame defence of his interpretation of the Marcan journeyings.[53] The main thrust of Schweitzer's thesis was not mentioned at all. Streeter had done very much better than that.

No doubt the optimism of Victorian England, which much of the theology of the period seems to reflect, was partly responsible for the refusal of the theologians to face up to the frightening questions posed by Schweitzer. It may also explain why their obsession with the historical Jesus persisted in spite of all the difficulties. They were simply refusing to accept that such an attractive alley could be a blind one. And there was very little in anything written at this time to suggest that theologians were equipped to understand the destructive war that was breaking about their heads. Their optimism was about to be dealt a heavy blow and they were simply not provided with the necessary tools to devise a theology of tragedy; so, when the war put an end to optimism, it also put an end to much that was fruitful in early twentieth-century British theology. Streeter's attempt to move beyond Schweitzer's apparently damaging thesis, for instance, was not pursued by him—or anyone else for that matter—and it is tempting to wonder why Streeter himself took up other, possibly less intellectually rigorous, religious causes. The innumerable calculations and arguments involved in sorting out the relationship between the synoptic gospels required the application of a good mind, but the demands made by a serious attempt to relate the Jesus of history to the Christ of faith, in the years after Schweitzer, would have been of an altogether higher order. But optimism, once shattered, does not encourage a new resilience.

It may be that optimism was not the only theological casualty of the Great War. British theologians were deeply shocked that their German counterparts were willing to express, publicly and vigorously, their conviction that right, justice, morality, and divine providence were on their side. In August 1914 von Harnack, together with other academics and pastors, signed an appeal, 'To

[52] F. C. Burkitt, *The Gospel History and its Transmission*, p. viii.
[53] Ibid., pp. xi ff.

the Evangelical Christians Abroad', which was outspoken in asserting the culpability of those whose enmity to Germany was, as they maintained, endangering Christian Europe's mission to the world. Two months later von Harnack was a signatory of the so-called 'manifesto of the intellectuals' which Barth was to describe as a perversion of Christian ethics, dogmatics, biblical interpretation, and understanding of history. At the same time, British theologians of every school of thought—Gore, Burkitt, Sanday, Selbie (Fairbairn's successor and biographer), P. T. Forsyth, *and* R. J. Campbell—were becoming more and more outspoken in their opposition to conscientious objection and in their support for the war.[54] It was even possible for one British academic to make the point that the German theologians were exhibiting the same stupidity in their interpretation of the international situation as they had shown, in his opinion, in their interpretation of history.[55] In circumstances such as these it must have been even easier than before for British theologians to insulate themselves from the work of German scholars and their disturbing ideas.

Yet the three central chapters of *Foundations*—Streeter's own, Temple's, and the essay by Rawlinson and Parsons—symbolize very well the position of British theology on the eve of the First World War. They indicate how wide was the variety of approach and understanding. They even suggest—correctly—that the *odium theologicum* was diminishing and that it was possible for different views of the truth to coexist more easily. More specifically, they represent the three most important and potentially fruitful developments within the whole question of the relationship between faith and history. Temple represents Idealism making its way back into closer touch with history and with the Christian tradition. Streeter represents the Liberal Protestant quest for the historical Jesus as it acquired a firmer earthing in the actual particularity of first-century Judaism. Rawlinson and Parsons represent the recognition that tradition is the *real* link between the historical Jesus of first-century Galilee and Judaea, and the Christ of twentieth-century Christian faith. Because there has actually been a continuous chain of shared experience across the intervening centuries, the history of faith is part of the truth about Christ.

---

[54] See S. Mews, 'Neo-Orthodoxy, Liberalism and War: Karl Barth, P. T. Forsyth and John Oman 1914–18', in D. Baker (ed.), *Studies in Church History*, 14 (Oxford, 1977), 361 ff.   [55] Ibid. 365.

Chronological Table

General	Theological	Biographical
		1772 Samuel Taylor Coleridge born
1789 French Revolution		
		1795 Thomas Arnold born
		1795 Thomas Carlyle born
		1880 Edward Bouverie Pusey born
		1801 John Henry Newman born
1815 Battle of Waterloo		
	1825 Coleridge's *Aids to Reflection*	1817 Benjamin Jowett born
		1825 Brooke Foss Westcott born
		1828 Thomas Arnold appointed Headmaster of Rugby
		1828 Newman made Vicar of the University Church in Oxford
		1828 Pusey appointed Professor of Hebrew at Oxford
		1828 Joseph Barber Lightfoot born
		1829 Edward White Benson born
	1829 Milman's *History of the Jews*	
	1833 John Keble's assize sermon on 'National Apostasy'	
	1833 Newman's *Arians of the Fourth Century*	

1834 Death of Coleridge		
1834 John Emerich Edward Dalberg-Acton born		
1835 Edward Caird born		
1836 Thomas Hill Green born		
1837 Accession of Queen Victoria		
1838 Andrew Martin Fairbairn born	1838 Gladstone's *The State in its Relation with the Church*	
	1840 Coleridge's posthumous *Confessions of an Inquiring Spirit*	
1841 Arnold made Professor of Modern History at Oxford		
1842 Death of Arnold		
1843 William Sanday born		1843 Great Disruption in Scotland
1845 Newman received into the Roman Catholic Church		
1845 R. C. Moberly born		
1845 Edmund Bishop born		
1846 Walter Lock born	1846 George Eliot's translation of Strauss's *Leben Jesu*	1846–78 Pontificate of Pius IX
1848 J. R. Illingworth born		1848–55 T. B. Macaulay's *History of England*
1852 Friedrich von Hügel born		
1853 Charles Gore born		1854–6 Crimean War

Chronological Table (continued)

General	Theological	Biographical
		1856 Stanley made Professor of Ecclesiastical History at Oxford
1857 Indian Mutiny		1857 Acton editor of *The Rambler* (*Home and Foreign Review*)
1858–70 Froude's *History of England from the Fall of Wolsey*		
1859 Darwin's *Origin of Species*		1859 Benson appointed first Master of Wellington
	1860 *Essays and Reviews*	1861 George Tyrrell born
	1862–72 Colenso's *Pentateuch and Joshua*	1862 John Caird appointed Professor of Theology at Glasgow
	1864 Papal encyclical *Quanta Cura* with *Syllabus Errorum*	
1865 Lecky's *History of the Rise and Influence of Rationalism*	1865 Seeley's *Ecce Homo*	
1866 *English Historical Review* founded		1866 Edward Caird made Professor of Moral Philosophy at Glasgow
1867–79 Freeman's *History of the Norman Conquest*	1867 Liddon's Bampton Lectures	1866 Stubbs appointed Professor of Modern History at Oxford
1868 Gladstone Prime Minister for the first time		1867 R. J. Campbell born
		1868 A. C. Tait appointed Archbishop of Canterbury
		1868 Friedrich Max Müller made Professor of Comparative Philology at Oxford

1869–70 First Vatican Council

1869 First volume of Lightfoot's *Apostolic Fathers*

1869 Peerage conferred on Acton
1869 Seeley made Professor of Modern History at Cambridge
1870 Jowett elected Master of Balliol
1870 Westcott appointed Regius Professor of Divinity at Cambridge
1873 John Caird made Principal of Glasgow University

1870 Appointment of committee to revise the Bible in English

1873–8 Stubbs's *Constitutional History of England*
1874 Disraeli Prime Minister
1874 Public Worship Regulation Act
1874 J. R. Green's *Short History of the English People*

1874 B. H. Streeter born

1875 Robertson Smith's articles in *Encyclopaedia Britannica*

1877 Golden Jubilee of Queen Victoria

1877 Benson appointed first Bishop of Truro

Chronological Table (*continued*)

General	Theological	Biographical
1878–1903 Pontificate of Leo XIII	1878 Newman's revised *Essay on Development*	1878 T. H. Green made Professor of Moral Philosophy at Oxford
		1879 Newman created Cardinal
		1879 Lightfoot appointed Bishop of Durham
		1879 Tyrrell received into the Roman Catholic Church
	1879 Jowett's sermon 'The Permanent Elements of Religion'	
	1880 E. Hatch's *Organization of the Early Christian Churches*	
	1881 Westcott & Hort's critical edition of the New Testament	1881 Death of Carlyle
		1881 Death of Stanley
	1881 Robertson Smith's *The Old Testament in the Jewish Church*	1881 Walter Moberly born
	1881–5 Publication of the Revised Version of the Bible in English	1881 William Temple born
		1882 Sanday appointed Lady Margaret Professor at Oxford
		1882 Death of Pusey
		1882 Death of Green
		1883–96 E. W. Benson Archbishop of Canterbury
		1884 Creighton elected first Dixie Professor at Cambridge

		1885 Edward King appointed Bishop of Lincoln
1884 F. Temple's Bampton Lectures		1885 Fairbairn appointed Principal of Mansfield College
1888–92 F. Max Müller's Gifford Lectures at Glasgow		1889 Dods appointed Professor at Free Church College in Edinburgh
		1889 Death of Lightfoot
1889 *Lux Mundi*		
1889 A. B. Bruce's *Kingdom of God*		1890 Westcott appointed Bishop of Durham
		1890 Death of Newman
		1890 Death of Liddon
1892 E. Caird's *Evolution of Religion*		1892 George Adam Smith appointed Professor at Aberdeen
		1892 R. C. Moberly made Professor of Pastoral Theology at Oxford
1893 T. H. Huxley's Romanes lecture on 'Evolution and Ethics'		1893 Death of Jowett
		1893 E. Caird elected Master of Balliol
1893 Fairbairn's *The Place of Christ in Modern Theology*		
1890 Lincoln Judgement delivered by Archbishop Benson		

Chronological Table (*continued*)

General	Theological	Biographical
		1895 Acton appointed Professor of Modern History at Cambridge
		1895 Lock appointed Dean Ireland Professor at Oxford
		1897–1902 F. Temple Archbishop of Canterbury
1897 Diamond Jubilee of Queen Victoria		
	1898 Maitland's *Roman Canon Law in the Church of England*	
	1899 Edmund Bishop's lecture 'Genius of the Roman Rite'	
1899–1902 Anglo-Boer War	1899 Tyrrell's 'A Perverted Devotion'	
		1901 Gore appointed Bishop of Worcester
1901 Accession of Edward VII		1901 Death of Westcott
		1902 Death of Acton
		1903 Campbell appointed Minister of the City Temple
		1903 Death of R. C. Moberly
1903–14 Pontificate of Pius X		1903–28 Randall Davidson Archbishop of Canterbury
		1905 Gore appointed Bishop of Birmingham
		1905 Streeter elected a fellow of The Queen's College

1906 Parliamentary Labour Party formed	1907 Decree *Lamentabili* and papal encyclical *Pascendi Gregis*	1908 Death of E. Caird
	1907 R. J. Campbell's *New Theology*	1909 George Adam Smith appointed Principal of Aberdeen University
	1907 Sanday's *Life of Christ in Recent Research*	1909 Death of Tyrrell
	1907 Tyrrell's *Through Scylla and Charybdis*	
	1907 Frank Weston's *The One Christ*	
1910 Accession of George V	1910 P. T. Forsyth's *The Work of Christ*	
1910 World Missionary Conference in Edinburgh	1910 Von Hügel on St John's gospel in *Encyclopaedia Britannica*	
	1910 Translation of Schweitzer's *Quest of the Historical Jesus*	
	1911 *Oxford Studies in the Synoptic Problem* edited by Sanday	1911 Gore appointed Bishop of Oxford
	1912 Wilfrid Ward's *Life of John Henry Newman*	1912 Death of Fairbairn
	1912 *Foundations*	

Chronological Table (*continued*)

General	Theological	Biographical
1913 Kikuyu Conference		1915 Death of Illingworth
1914–18 Great War		1916 R. J. Campbell ordained in the Church of England
		1917 Death of Bishop
		1920 Death of Sanday
		1925 Death of von Hügel
		1932 Death of Gore
		1933 Death of Lock
		1937 Death of Streeter
		1956 Death of Campbell

Suggestions for Further Reading

An older work on history and historiography in nineteenth-century Britain, but still useful in providing a straightforward, basic account, is: J. W. Thompson with B. J. Holm, *A History of Historical Writing*, 2 vols. (Gloucester, Mass., reprint of 1967). The second volume deals with the eighteenth and nineteenth centuries. More recent works are: J. W. Burrow, *A Liberal Descent: Victorian Historians and the English Past* (Cambridge, 1981); C. Parker, *The English Historical Tradition since 1850* (Edinburgh, 1990); and J. P. von Arx, *Progress and Pessimism: Religion, Politics and History in Late Nineteenth Century Britain* (Cambridge, Mass., 1985). It is also worth consulting: D. Forbes, *The Liberal Anglican Idea of History* (Cambridge, 1952). Books dealing with the impact of the new history on theology and biblical scholarship are: H. W. Frei, *The Eclipse of the Biblical Narrative: A Study in Eighteenth and Nineteenth Century Hermeneutics* (New Haven and London, 1974); V. A. Harvey, *The Historian and the Believer: The Morality of Historical Knowledge and Christian Belief* (London, 1967); R. Morgan with J. Barton, *Biblical Interpretation* (Oxford, 1988); D. L. Pals, *The Victorian Lives of Jesus* (San Antonio, 1982). There is a brief account in J. Rogerson, C. Rowland, and B. Lindars, *The Study and Use of the Bible* (Basingstoke and Grand Rapids, 1988). Books dealing with the impact of new ideas and discoveries on nineteenth-century British Christianity are: M. A. Crowther, *Church Embattled: Religious Controversy in Mid-Victorian England* (Newton Abbot, Devon, and Hamden, Connecticut, 1970); R. J. Helmstadter and B. Lightman (eds.), *Victorian Faith in Crisis: Essays on Continuity and Change in Nineteenth Century Religious Belief* (London, 1990); D. Jasper and T. R. Wright (eds.), *The Critical Spirit and the Will to Believe: Essays in Nineteenth Century Religion and Literature* (Basingstoke, 1989); E. Jay, *Faith and Doubt in Victorian Britain* (Basingstoke, 1986). I. Ellis, *Seven Against Christ* (Leiden, 1980), though specifically about *Essays and Reviews*, is a mine of reliable information about the state of affairs in the mid-nineteenth century. On the theology of the period: B. M. G. Reardon, *Religious Thought in the Victorian Age: A Survey from Coleridge to Gore* (revised edition, London, 1980); C. Welch, *Protestant Thought in the Nineteenth Century*, 2 vols. (New Haven and London, 1972 and 1985). A. M. Ramsey, *From Gore to Temple: The Development of Anglican Theology between Lux Mundi and the Second World War, 1889–1939* (London, 1960), is better on Anglican theology than on the historical context.

CHAPTER 2

A large number of books about Newman have been published, particularly at the time of the centenary of his death. They include two new biographies: S. Gilley, *Newman and his Age* (London, 1990); I. Ker, *John Henry Newman: A Biography* (Oxford, 1988). The second of these usually provides the fuller consideration of Newman's theological writings. Several volumes of essays were also published to mark the centenary: D. Brown (ed.), *Newman: A Man for Our Time* (London, 1990) (originally public lectures, these essays are somewhat uneven in quality); I. Ker and A. G. Hill (eds.), *Newman after a Hundred Years* (Oxford, 1990); D. Nicholls and F. Kerr (eds.), *Newman: Reason, Rhetoric and Romanticism* (Bristol, 1991). Works which deal in some detail with the *Essay on the Development of Doctrine* include: O. Chadwick, *From Bossuet to Newman* (2nd edn., Cambridge, 1987); N. Lash, *Newman on Development: The Search for an Explanation in History* (London, 1975).

CHAPTER 3

There are two biographies of Jowett, neither wholly satisfactory: E. Abbott and L. Campbell, *The Life and Letters of Benjamin Jowett*, 2 vols. (London, 1987); G. Faber, *Jowett, a Portrait with Background* (London, 1957). On Jowett's theology there is: P. Hinchliff, *Benjamin Jowett and the Christian Religion* (Oxford, 1987). It is also worth consulting: H. F. G. Swanston, *Ideas of Order: Anglicans and the Renewal of Theological Method in the Middle Years of the 19th Century* (Assen, 1974).

CHAPTER 4

The original official biographies of the main protagonists in this chapter are: A. C. Benson, *The Life of Edward White Benson, sometime Archbishop of Canterbury* 2 vols. (London, 1899); G. R. Eden and F. C. Macdonald (eds.), *Lightfoot of Durham: Memories and Appreciations* (Cambridge, 1932); A. Westcott, *Life and Letters of Brooke Foss Westcott, sometime Bishop of Durham*, 2 vols. (London, 1903); G. W. E. Russell, *Edward King, Sixtieth Bishop of Lincoln* (London, 1912); A. F. Hort, *Life and Letters of Fenton John Anthony Hort*, 2 vols. (London and New York, 1896). Much smaller and more modern books are: J. A. Newton, *Search for a Saint: Edward King* (London, 1977); G. A. Patrick, *F. J. A. Hort: Eminent Victorian* (Sheffield, 1987).

CHAPTER 5

There is a biography of Gore, G. L. Prestige, *Life of Charles Gore* (London, 1935), but the work lacks footnotes. Because Gore's own papers no longer exist, a new biography is unlikely to be written. Books on Gore's theology include: J. Carpenter, *Gore: A Study in Liberal Catholic Thought* (London, 1960); and a short, recent work, P. Avis, *Gore: Construction and Conflict* (Worthing, 1988). It is also worth consulting: A. L. Illingworth (ed.), *The Life and Work of John Richardson Illingworth edited by his wife* (London, 1917); S. Paget, *Henry Scott Holland: Memoir and Letters* (London, 1921). Essays by G. Rowell and P. Hinchliff, dealing with the history of *Lux Mundi*, are in R. Morgan (ed.), *The Religion of the Incarnation: Anglican Essays in Commemoration of Lux Mundi* (Bristol, 1989).

CHAPTER 6

The only biography of Edward Caird is H. Jones and J. H. Muirhead, *The Life and Philosophy of Edward Caird* (Glasgow, 1921). R. L. Nettleship (ed.), *Works of Thomas Hill Green*, 3 vols. (London, 1886–1890) contains a lengthy memoir of Green by the editor. There are a great many works which deal with the early British Idealists and their moral and political philosophy, such as: P. P. Nicholson, *The Political Philosophy of the British Idealists* (Cambridge, 1990); M. Richter, *The Politics of Conscience: T. H. Green and his Age* (London, 1964); G. Thomas, *The Moral Philosophy of T. H. Green* (Oxford, 1987); A. Vincent and R. Plant, *Philosophy, Politics and Citizenship: The Life and Thought of the British Idealists* (Oxford, 1984). There is, however, little about their religious thought other than a chapter by H. D. Lewis in N. Smart, J. Clayton, P. Sherry and S. T. Katz (eds.), *Nineteenth Century Religious Thought in the West*, vol. ii (Cambridge, 1985). Lewis's account of the relationship between Jowett, Green, and Caird is, however, inaccurate.

CHAPTER 7

On Acton the best work is: G. Himmelfarb, *Lord Acton: A Study in Conscience and Politics* (Chicago and London, 1952). Among the works having a particular interest in Modernism and Britain are: L. F. Barmann, *Baron Friedrich von Hügel and the Modernist Crisis in England* (Cambridge, 1972); B. M. G. Reardon, *Roman Catholic Modernism* (London, 1976); N. Sagovsky, *On God's Side, A Life of George Tyrrell* (Oxford, 1990); A. R. Vidler, *A Variety of Catholic Modernists*

(Cambridge, 1970); M. J. Weaver (ed.), *Newman and the Modernists* (Lanham and London, 1985).

CHAPTER 8

The only book about Fairbairn is W. B. Selbie, *The Life of Andrew Martin Fairbairn* (London, 1914).

CHAPTER 9

Campbell's autobiography is *A Spiritual Pilgrimage* (London, 1916). Since his papers were destroyed, it is unlikely that there will ever be a proper biography. The two most recent brief accounts are: K. Robbins, 'The Spiritual Pilgrimage of the Rev. R. J. Campbell', *Journal of Ecclesiastical History*, 30 (Apr. 1979); and a chapter in K. W. Clements, *Lovers of Discord: Twentieth Century Theological Controversies in England* (London, 1988).

CHAPTER 10

This chapter is rather different from the other chapters since it really surveys New Testament scholarship in England in the years immediately before the First World War. Further reading is best done in books mentioned in connection with Chapter 1, such as: D. L. Pals, *The Victorian Lives of Jesus* (San Antonio, 1982); R. Morgan with J. Barton, *Biblical Interpretation* (Oxford, 1988); J. Rogerson, C. Rowland, and B. Lindars, *The Study and Use of the Bible* (Basingstoke and Grand Rapids, 1988). Of the people chiefly mentioned, the only biographies are: G. L. Prestige, *Life of Charles Gore* (London, 1935); F. A. Iremonger, *William Temple, Archbishop of Canterbury* (London, 1948). Neither is much concerned with the issues of New Testament scholarship.

Index